AF593771

100 Years of Labor in the USA

100 Years of Labor in the USA

by Daniel Guérin

Translated by Alan Adler

Introduction by John Amsden

First published as *le Mouvement Ouvrier aux Etats-Unis de 1866 à Nos Jours,* François Maspero, Paris 1976.
©François Maspero 1976.

Chapter Four of present volume translated from *De L'Oncle Tom aux Panthères,* Editions 10:18, Paris and first published as *les Noirs et le mouvement ouvrier* in *Decolonisation du noir américain,* Editions de Minuit, Paris.
©Editions de Minuit

This edition first published 1979
©Ink Links 1979

Ink Links Ltd.
271 Kentish Town Road, London NW5 2JS

No part of this book may be reproduced without the permission of the publisher except for the quotation of brief passages for criticism.

ISBN 0906133 106 Cloth
ISBN 0906133 114 Paper

Typeset by the Russell Press, Nottingham
Printed by Biddles, Martyr Road, Guildford, Surrey

CONTENTS

I

Broad themes and important moments in the history of the American working class are too often ignored in the United States in favour of exhaustive studies of isolated events, or narrow institutional histories in the manner of the Webbs or that of the Wisconsin School of John R Commons, et al. *At least one historian has begun to chronicle the 1909-1919 period in which American labor reached a height of combativity and class consciousness which has not been equalled since.*[1] *But there has been a startling paucity of material documenting the massive political and physical repression unleashed on the American workers just after the First World War, when both the employers and their State were plunged into a murderous panic by the successful working-class revolution in Tsarist Russia. (William Z Foster's* The Great Steel Strike and its Lessons, *published in 1920, gives a worthy account of one of the key battles of that period – but then, of course, he was a trade-union organizer, not a historian.) Thanks to the folkways of academia we have numerous molecular, atomic, and even sub-atomic studies in the labour-history field — an iron moulders' local here, a strike there. And while such studies retain an interest and, indeed, importance which should not be dismissed, one cannot but comment on the extreme wariness with which American historians approach any broad description, syntheses and, most importantly, political analysis of the American workers' movement.*

In general, only outsiders dare to aspire to the breadth of vision necessary to comprehend the complicated and painful reality of labor struggles in the largest capitalist country in the world; a country built on genocide and slavery and maintained by an imperialism far vaster and more powerful than any that went before. The only exception to the general pattern is that of Philip

Foner, himself an outsider to academia by virtue of his long association with the CPUSA.[2] *(It is no doubt significant that Foner's massive work is as yet unfinished. It breaks off at roughly that point where the American CP began to be active in the labor movement.)*

Thus, in the present volume it is predictably not an American who will tell the story of labor in the United States. Daniel Guérin is French and a prolific writer of history, political commentary, and works of literature. He writes from within the Libertarian tradition but is far from hostile to Marxism. Like any scientific socialist since the time of Marx and Engels, Guérin considers the development of the class struggle in the United States as the key to changing the economic order on a global scale. Guérin wrote his first work on the United States over twenty years ago and has been a close follower of American affairs since that time. If the emergence of a permanent and, in many cases, corrupt bureaucracy in the trade unions is the number one problem in the American workers' movement in the recent period, and it undoubtedly is, then Guérin is one of the best persons to analyse this reality. Working in a tradition that is profoundly hostile to an entrenched 'leadership' of any sort, Guérin is not slow to point to the inertia and conservatism of the American labor bosses, or to the gangsterism and terror by which the labor barons have attempted to still the rumor of revolt which is once again beginning to issue from the ranks. Unlike middle-class editorialists, new leftists, and the followers of Herbert Marcuse, Guérin distinguishes clearly between the labor bureaucracy and the ordinary workers. He also shows the way in which the formerly unshakeable control exercised by the former may have represented little more than a temporary state of affairs resting on the intermittant successes enjoyed by American capitalism during the Fifties and Sixties.

The interrupted prosperity of the Fifties (there were two serious recessions in which both unemployment and inflation were relatively high) and the good days of the decade that followed are for many American workers below 30 too far ago to be even a memory, while for most of the rest they remain little more than that. As the American economy nears the end of the Seventies, it approaches the termination of nearly a decade of severe crisis with no end in sight. Like the crises of the Fifties, the hard times of the Seventies have been marked by a simultaneous unemployment and inflation which, as we shall see later, have thrown entire new strata of wage earners into the trade-union struggle. Under these conditions it has become clear that the official labor movement, like American capitalism itself, is in a state of permanent crisis.

To begin with, it should be pointed out that the official 'movement' is not a movement *at all since it has no independent political expression through which American workers can be represented within the state. On the contrary, the misleaders of American labor do everything possible to hand over the political allegiance of the workers to one or the other of the two capitalist parties, and have done so ever since the New Deal dispensation of the 1930s. At the level of industrial organization, too, the American movement is in crisis. Trade unions in the United States organize a smaller percentage of the workforce (around 20 percent) than in almost any other advanced industrial country. Large sections of the working class itself view the existing unions with suspicion and anger. To the racial and ethnic minorities and to women, existing unions often appear as, at worst, the main barrier between them and a good job, and, at best, as just another cynical and exploitative boss. To the workers in other countries the tirades of a George Meany and the cloak and dagger shenannigans of a Victor Reuther must make organized labor in the United States appear as little better than a cheering section for the adventures of American imperialism abroad. Guérin relates the story of how Peter Brennan of the New York City building trades organized street attacks on peace marchers in 1970 and then journeyed to Washington to present then President Nixon with an engraved hard-hat. Brennan was later elevated to the position of Secretary of Labor for his outstanding performance in the role of class clown. But Guérin is not misled by the incident. He shows us the high jinks of the 'labor lieutenants' in their halcyon days, but does not neglect to reveal the way in which the rank-and-file movements of a later period have begun to trouble the sleep of the trade-union mandarinate who luxuriate in six-figure salaries in the head offices of the various Internationals.*

Guérin finishes his book with accounts of emerging rank-and-file movements in the major unions which are nothing short of prophetic. Since the period in which he brings his account to a close there have been a number of events to confirm his suggestions concerning the nature of the creative forces beginning to unfold in the trade-union rank and file. To take only two examples: in the bitterly cold Winter of 1977-78 the American miners carried out the longest strike of their history and fought the coal bosses to a standstill despite the sanctimonious counsels of their union leadership; and in a less extensive but politically very significant action, the West coast dockers in the early summer of 1978 refused to load ships carrying armaments to the fascist regime in Chile. Evidently the American working class will not be constrained forever by the neo-corporativist system and ideology which has, for the last thirty years, allowed a time-serving bureaucracy to rest comfortably at the top of the labor movement.

The expression 'neo-corporativist system' requires a little explanation. It is used here in the sense of a system of class collaboration which gives a corrupt trade-union leadership a legal structure through which to negotiate and enforce its deals with the employers while at the same time insulating it from the anger of the rank and file. It is one of the merits of Guérin's approach that he is sensitive to the way in which the bureaucratic machine was created in the American movement, in particular the extent to which its creation was the outcome of a Faustian pact with the State. The permanence of a plutocratic officialdom in American trade unionism is due in no small degree to the fact that the labor 'skates' operate within the context of a national labor law which is very favourable to 'stability' and which is presided over by a Federal agency known as the National Labor Relations Board, thus permitting the State to influence agreements concerning employment right down to the local level.

An hypothetical example of this would be where the workers in a particular firm might wish to sack the trade union presently representing them and join a different one. In this case the workers would be required to petition for 'permission' to do so from the National Labor Relations Board which would then (after statutory delays and 'waiting periods') conduct the so-called 'de-certification' elections. In many cases the workers wishing to do this would discover that the 'bargaining unit' 'designed' by the NLRB would include workers in other work-places miles away. To interest these workers in a change of union could often prove so costly and time consuming that, in general, one can state that it is easier to get a divorce in the United States than it is to get different trade-union representation. The NLRBs also oversee union elections, intervene in certain aspects of grievance procedure, and play a role in arbitration. The net effect of their activities, or lack of same, is to guarantee that nothing changes. In this way the NRLBs provide an invisible support for existing trade-union leaderships who may or may not be truly serving the interests of their members. American laws concerning dues checkoff and the agency shop are also a boon to established trade-union officials. The Landrum-Griffin Act of 1959 was passed by a legislature profoundly hostile to organized labor and yet, as Guérin notes, it met with an opposition from the trade-union tops which was purely 'verbal and sterile'. The reason for this was that, in addition to allowing the federal government to vet trade-union elections, the act also permitted the national 'leadership' of any union to place any local into 'receivership' under certain conditions. This turned out to be a handy device by which the national bureaucracy could crack down on wildcat strikes initiated by the rank and file and, in addition, crush any political opposition within the union at the local level. It is a device that is frequently used within the International Brotherhood of Teamsters and was utilized at the very beginning when an opposition movement began to form within that union.

If Guérin's work has as one of its main concerns the explanation of the way in which a professional bureaucracy evolved in the American workers' movement, it has as one of its main advantages the author's ability to see back beyond the decade of the 1930s to the period in which the struggles for industrial unionism waged during the Depression were being prepared. Although he nowhere explicitly spells out an exact periodization for the development of the American workers' movement, Guérin's account is fully compatable with the following:

> *I 1877-1897: from the period of insurrections provoked by the growing power of the rail trusts to the end of the last great depression of the 19th Century. This is the period in which a largely English-speaking working class dominated by the ideas of 'producer consciousness' struggled for the control of the process in manufacturing industry as the first great waves of economic concentration and technological change swept over the organization of American capitalism.*
>
> *II 1897-1922: from the end of the depression to the national coal miners' strike, which was the last massive expression of working class belligerency before a decade of defeats. During these first two decades of the present*

century the American workers achieved extensive trade-union and revolutionary-political strength. This was also a period of sharp struggle within *the labor movement over the question of craft versus industrial organization. The strike actions of 1919 were fueled by this militancy and in proportional terms have been unequalled in size to the present day.*

III 1922-1929: a decade of disastrous defeats for the American working class. It is during this period that the first really important and completely centralized national bureaucracy was built (paradoxically in the miners' union) and in which the officials of a number of unions worked closely with their bosses to introduce the speed-up in certain industries (e.g., textiles) and to lubricate the insertion of 'welfare capitalism' into employment relations.

IV 1929-1948: from the beginning of the depression of the 1930s through the passage of the anti-labor Taft-Hartley Act. During this period the craft versus industrial struggle of an earlier day was ignored by the workers themselves who achieved the organization of basic mass-production industry after bloody and heroic struggles.

V 1948-1971: from the passage of Taft-Hartley to the prices and incomes policy decreed by the Nixon government. In the early years of this period the last of the Left were driven from the trade unions by a combination of witch-hunts and repressive legislation. The act itself denied trade-union organizers the use of tactics (the mass picket, hot-cargo clauses, secondary boycott) that had been crucial to the successful organization of the unions in the previous period. In the frenzied cold war atmosphere that followed the passage of the act the 'loyal' trade-union leaders joined with the State Department and the secret service to subvert anti-capitalist labor movements abroad. The result was the selection of a professionalized and anti-communist officialdom in almost all of the major American unions.

Whereas in the first of these five periods there was a titanic struggle over the question of whether or not trade-union organization would be permitted at all, in the last one there is open co-operation between a 'sanitized' trade-union leadership and the capitalist state. The question is, how did a professionalized, collaborationist trade-union officialdom emerge out of the magnificent history of struggle and achievement of the American workers in the late 19th and early 20th centuries?

To begin with, of course, there is Lenin's basic observation concerning the difference between trade-union and revolutionary consciousness. Trade unionism, Lenin argues (What Is To Be Done, *1902), produces among the workers a consciousness which is circumscribed by the logic of capitalist production. The growth of a permanent officialdom, one might add, is the natural result of trade-union consciousness once basic trade-union rights have been won. That such bureaucracies can exercise a heavy grip on the rank-and-file unionist in any period was noted by Michels long ago.*[3] *Some American trade unions of the 19th Century did indeed display certain of the characteristics of the 'iron law of oligarchy' described by Michels. Even so, the craft-dominated trade unions of the late 19th and early 20th centuries in the United States had a far more vibrant democratic air than is the case today. Convention floor fights were uproarious, leaders were removed, and the regional organizations maintained a stubborn independence. More than the phrase 'trade-union consciousness' or an appeal to the 'iron law of oligarchy' is required to explain the totalitarianism and scleroses of official trade unionism in the United States today.*

Firstly, one should be reminded that from the late 19th to the early 20th centuries American capitalism underwent a massive shift from the extraction of absolute *to the extraction of* relative *surplus value. The former, as explained in the first volume of Marx's* Capital, *relies upon two things: on the intensification of labor and on the lengthening of the working day. The extraction of* relative *surplus value, on the other hand, mainly involves the heightening of the organic composition of capital, that is, the replacement of workers by machines. While both of these strategies may be employed by capital in different industries at different times, there are historical periods in which one or the other strategy dominates with noticeable effect. The last quarter of the 19th Century was a period in which the extraction of absolute surplus value dominated industrial practice in the United States. In most industries during this period the principal conflicts between workers and employers centered upon the length and intensity of labor. In most cases the strategies adopted by industrial employers (the 'stretchout' in textiles, various forms of 'audacious robbery' in the coal mines) aimed at increasing the surplus in one of these two ways.*[4] *The spread of 'payment by results' systems throughout American industry in the 80s and 90s, for example, represented a massive exercise in the intensification of labor, of which the much vaunted system of F W Taylor was merely an inglorious tail end. As James Tobin of the Boot and Shoe Workers told the Commission on Industrial Relations in 1914, piece-rate systems in his industry had made the worker the willing accomplice of the employer in the destruction of his own standards long before Mr Taylor had appeared on the scene.*

When the employer was committed to a regime of lengthening the working day and to sweating the workers during the hours of labor, no sort of trade union was really acceptable to him, nor was one possible given capitalist competition among large numbers of relatively small employers. Under these circumstances the sort of trade union organization that survived was more often than not the one based on a monopoly of skill, in other words, the craft union. Insofar as this was the case, the main form of resistance by organized workers was that of a struggle over the nature of the industrial process. The craft unionist was wedded to his tools (as those who remain still are) and violently resisted any technological change that might have made his tools obsolete and thus destroyed his job monopoly based on skill. In some cases, of course, the craftsmen were swept aside by the relentless processes of competition and technological change (in boot and shoe, for example), but in others they managed to maintain positions of strength in factory industry. It was in the latter case that the employer had to try to smash the union. And here the craftsmen had left themselves relatively vulnerable to the bosses' offensive by their refusal to organize all the workers in their industry. Craft unionists were snobbish towards the unskilled worker to put it mildly. After all, the craft workers' organized strength depended on their willingness and ability to restrict entry to a particular labor market. Their exclusiveness, however, created a schism within the labor movement which allowed the bosses to prevail over the working class when, for one reason and another, the former were forced to change the ground rules of the daily contest between themselves and labor by undertaking fundamental technical transformations in the field of production.

To do this, of course, it was necessary to smash the hold of the craftsmen over production. Some writers such as Harry Braverman and David Montgomery have seen the role of 'Taylorism' as important in this regard, but the fact is that the time and motion studies and efficiency systems of F W Taylor were very little adopted.[5] *For the most part organized labor was strong enough to stop the stopwatch, and besides the employers themselves found more effective ways to sweat their labor. Briefly, they utilised the payment by results systems (that had been in existence long before Taylor's time) when economic conditions permitted them to drive their workers and when such conditions were wanting they launched into basic technological change. To achieve the latter, however, it was first necessary to break the craft unions. This was a political (and at times military) problem, but not one that could be settled on the shop floor. The clearest example of a long term and well co-ordinated employer's offensive with this aim in mind is the one described by David Brody in the case of the American steel industry.*[6] *the battle of Homestead, which the workers won, and the ensuing legal and political struggles which they unfailingly lost, were the curtain-raisers for the massive conflict between labor and capital which occurred in the second period mentioned above. This period of struggle resulted in harsh defeats for the American workers: partly because of their disunity both amongst the different crafts and between the craft workers and the unskilled, and partly because the capitalist class had been galvanized into unanimity by the spectre of social revolution rising in the East. Liberal historiography in the United States has almost entirely occluded the episodes of political and physical repression suffered by American workers in the period just after the First World War. The numerous lynchings and mob attacks that occurred between 1919 and 1923 are commonly disguised as 'nativist' and 'racist' in character, but the fact is that the self-described* 'fascisti' *of the American legion and the hooded boobies of the Ku Klux Klan directed much of their violence towards the individuals and institutions of the organized labor movement. It was only* after *the complete defeat of the American workers by these means that the strategy of relative surplus value extraction could be employed on an extensive scale. Then began the era of assembly-line mass production industry, or what Antonio Gramsci called 'Fordism'.*

The shift from absolute to relative surplus value extraction was accompanied by a number of other fundamental transformations in the nature of the class struggle in the United States. Within the restricted compass of this introduction it is only possible to list these, but doing so seems worthwhile since the qualitative change in the character of American trade unionism is part of the same process as the other transformations listed below:

from the late 19th through the early 20th century	**from approximately 1920 until today**
absolute surplus value	*relative surplus value*
competitive capitalism	*monopoly capitalism*
laissez faire economics	*the Keynsian managed economy*
'democratic' forms	*bureaucracy*
'producer consciousness'	*consumerism*
craft unions	*industrial unionism*
isolationism	*imperialism*

To sum up the hypotheses implied by this dual list of social and economic transformations, one might say that monopoly capitalism has replaced 'democratic' forms with bureaucratic rule, and that the bureaucratization of the trade unions represents an important aspect of this process.

This is correct as far as it goes, and as far as it goes it resembles the so-called 'corporate liberal' hypothesis put forward by American radicals in recent years.[7] *What has been left out of the 'corporate liberal' formulation is the most important thing of all: the militant self-organization of the working class. We should be clear from the start that the industrial unions created by the American workers in the 1930s were won only through extensive and bloody battles, and were not merely put in place by an infinitely crafty and far-sighted ruling class. That was not the way it happened as the history described by Guérin will show. In Guérin's chapters on the Thirties we see former 'Wobblies', displaced coal miners, and politically motivated labor organizers move into the mass production industries to revive the tactics of the sit-down strike, the mass picket, and the wildcat tactics that had been used in the earlier period of mass struggles. After almost a decade of bitter conflict and at the cost of incredible sacrifices by ordinary workers, industrial unions in auto, rubber, textiles, and steel were won at last. The capitalist ruling class, having been* forced *to accept trade-union organization in basic industry then set out to de-fang their new and powerful enemy, and to turn the new system to work in their own interest. In this task they had as their unexpected allies the Communist Party of the United States of America.*

It is one of the great virtues of Guérin's approach that he carefully follows the evolution of the CPUSA policy as it affected Communist practice in the labor movement. And that policy takes some careful following. In the so-called 'third period' (roughly 1928-34), the CP adopted an 'ultra-left' line and advocated dual unions. This moved sharply against powerful prejudices among American workers and the party made almost no headway. Then with the announcement of the 'popular front' (after Hitler's rise to power in Germany) the American CP became one of the staunchest allies of the first great bureaucratic dictator of American labor, John L Lewis, and of his fast friend Franklin D Roosevelt. At this time rank-and-file party members made great personal sacrifices while helping to organize the unions, but their individual heroism was not sufficient to affect party policy; or at lease we can assume not, for in the next period, during which the Soviet Union was allied with Nazi Germany (and shared with the Nazis in a carve-up of Eastern Europe), popular front friendships had to be put under wraps in the United States. When the Nazis invaded the Soviet Union (1941) the CPUSA emerged again, and the period of 'social patriotism' was inaugurated as the cadre of the party gave their all to introduce Stakhanovism into the American factory. This was all to the delight of the war profiteers who were growing fat on 'cost-plus' economics and who, as Guérin notes, welcomed CP organizers in their plants over almost any other kind. The CPUSA supported the notorious 'no-strike pledge' to the hilt — a policy which may have cost them considerable support among ordinary rank-and-file workers.

Regular negotiations over wages and working conditions, and contracts binding on both parties for given lengths of time were far less convenient for employers when the principal means of squeezing the workers amounted to lengthening the workday or stepping up the pace of labor. Competitive capitalists did not wish to be bound by contractual obligations for lengthy periods, but rather wanted to be free to alter the terms of the bargain the very moment changes in economic conditions made this possible. The monopoly capitalist, on the other hand, can afford greater 'stability' in employment relations and, furthermore, wants to be free to increase relative surplus value by regular changes in the technical basis of production. Whatever this may 'cost' in higher wages can now be paid out of monopoly profits and, of course, there are fewer workers employed proportional to total capital each time this technical cycle is completed. What this has meant in the years since World War II is, to put things bluntly, that the trade-union bureaucrats have developed the policy of selling jobs in return for higher wages. In coal mining, for example, Guérin points out that between 1959 and 1964 the miners' salaries were increased by 73 per cent, but at the same time 28 per cent of the miners lost their jobs. The miners were not unique in making such deals. Harry Bridges concluded a similar agreement in West coast longshore in 1960.

Bridges himself was unique by 1960, however, for he was one of the few individuals associated with the CPUSA who remained at the top of a major trade union. The others had been rewarded for their wartime loyalty by witch-hunts and repressive legislation after the beginning of the 'cold war' (1948). From that time until approximately the year which saw the judicial murder of the Rosenbergs (1953), long-standing alliances between ordinary trade-union officials and the Left broke down as the politically motivated trade unionists were either chased from the movement or driven under ground. At the same time right wing forces within the labor movement joined in a 'social pact' with the Department of State and the secret service to subvert anti-capitalist labor movements abroad. In this way a 'responsible' trade-union bureaucracy selected itself politically just as the new structure within which they would operate was being fashioned legislatively.

That legislation was forthcoming in the anti-labor Taft-Hartley law of 1948. It was the rank-and-file organiser and the wildcat striker who were the victims of Taft-Hartley restrictions (picketing limitations, no secondary boycott, an obligatory 'cooling off' period in some cases where strike action was imminent) and not the new trade-union leadership. Despite promises to fight the 'slave labor act' to the death, the untion tops preferred to remain comfortably in their national headquarters rather than to lead working class opposition to the act. In fact one aspect of the act even made the bureaucrats' life easier in that the employers were required to swallow the bitter pill of the closed shop although smuggled into the legislation under another name. The closed shop is, of course, an important defensive institution, but on the other hand it only defends positions that have already been taken. A living trade-union movement needs constantly to expand, and if American trade union officialdom have shown anything in the 1948-71 period, it is that bureaucrats don't organise. On the contrary, the movement has actually shrunk as recalcitrant employers have fled to safe 'right to work' states in the south, and as a massive shift from basic manufacturing industry to services has begun to modify the shape of the American workforce. Rather than organize the non-union regions and occupations, the existing bureaucracy have, for the most part, simply become an administrative agency for dealing with the numerous aspects of the employment relationship. In the 1920s the capitalists themselves attempted to create powerful controls over the workforce through the strategy of 'welfare capitalism'. Now health, welfare, and pension schemes are administered not by the employer but by the union; their administration, it goes without saying, represents a powerful reinforcement of the political positin of the bureaucracy within the trade-union structure. The nature of American labor struggle in the Seventies has been one of rank-and-file workers trying to overcome the conservative resistance of an inert bureaucracy in the face of the many economic, political, and structural factors that are transforming the American working class. It is to a consideration of this struggle by the American workers that we now turn.

II

The basic conundrum of the American working class movement remains what it has been in the past: politics. Alone among almost all workers in the advanced industrial countries, the American wage earners seem to get along without any. What explains the perennial failure of working class politics in the United States? Is it about to be repeated in the present crisis? What will be the role of the existing unions, heavily bureaucratized and proportionally unrepresentative of the working class though they may be? These are difficult questions, and while few would hazard definite answers to any of them at the present time, it is possible to point to a number of trends that will affect the course of class struggle in the '80s. In almost every case what present conditions suggest are greater possibilities for the politicization of the class struggle in the United States than have existed in the immediate past.

To begin with, the growth in real earnings of American wage earners has shrunk almost to nothing during most of the Seventies and for one or two years during the decade has actually been negative. In the 1947-62 period American workers enjoyed annual real wage improvements in the region of 2.5 per cent.[8] *Since 1962 real earnings have increased at a rate of only 1.2 percent, and, during the 1973-75 crisis, real wages actually declined (2.5 per cent) for the first time since the 'Great Depression'. The high standard of living of the American working class is slowly being eroded away. This is the fuel that is stoking up the flames of rebellion in the rank and file of certain AFL-CIO unions and throughout the public sector.*

One way in which American workers have attempted to maintain their living standards is through the employment of married women, who used to remain at home. In 1920 only nine per cent of all married women worked for wages. The labor force participation of married women shot up during the Second World War and by 1950 23 per cent of all wives worked. By 1970 this figure was up to 41 per cent and as the end of the decade approaches it is closer to 50 per cent.[9] *Not surprisingly, new female entrants to the labor force did not replace men in the basic manufacturing (and heavily unionized) sector. Instead they flowed into the rapidly growing service and public sectors after the war and remain 'crowded' into these sectors today. In a number of cases, but particularly in hospital and teaching strikes, women workers have recently shown a toughness and militancy (including the willingness to go behind bars in defense of the right to strike) that has surprised many a judge, administrator, and policeman. It is to the existing trade unions, however, that the flood of women workers into regular employment presents the real challenge, for most working women are still unorganized.*

The second great challenge that faces the AFL-CIO bureaucracy is the so-called 'runaway firm'. While the growing multinational firms exported a little over one million jobs between 1966 and 1973 (with 735,000 of these in manufacturing), there was also an internal domestic flight of location from the heavily industrialized states of the Northeast and Midwest to the South and West. Firms relocating in the 'sun-belt' are fleeing the unions to states where 'right to work' laws (outlawing the closed shop) have been passed. Between 1960 and 1975 manufacturing employment increased 67.3 per cent in the Southwest, only 9 per cent in the Great Lakes Region, and actually declined 13.7 per cent in the Midwest and 9 per cent in New England.[10] *The main reason for the shift, of course, is lower wage costs. GM, for example, pays $2 an hour less in its Monroe Louisiana plant than it did in the plant in Indiana where the same work was originally done before the transfer. Most of the AFL-CIO unions have not been exactly fearless about taking on the employers in their Southern strongholds. Where union organizing is not pushed through largely by the workers themselves as part of a mass movement, all of the expenses of a campaign come directly out of the international treasury. Few trade union officials in top positions have wished to release organizing funds where there is not a sure chance of winning. Even in cases where the workers in a particular firm, such as at J P Stevens (textiles), vote to join the union, success is not assured by election alone. Employees in seven of Stevens's Southern factories voted to join the Amalgamated Clothing Workers three years ago. The employer has stalled the case in the courts while continuing to carry on an anti-union campaign and blithely handing over more than one million dollars in fines while continuing to operate the plants on a non-union basis. The official labor movement, apart from placing Stevens goods on a long list of products to be boycotted, has not rallied massively to support the Stevens workers, and for the most part the South continues to be unorganized.*

In addition to the geographical shift southward by major manufacturing firms there has been and continues to be a massive occupational shift in the United States workforce from 'blue collar' (manual) to 'white collar' (technical, sales, and services). Between 1960 and 1970 the white collar workforce grew 34 per cent while the number of blue collar jobs increased only 9 per cent (agricultural jobs actually dropped as a proportion of the total labour force).[11] *This trend is expected to continue throughout the Seventies and into the mid-eighties so that by 1985 it is anticipated that white collar workers will make up half of the workforce while the blue collar proportion will drop to 32 per cent. If these trends hold, the AFL-CIO unions (which have been concentrated in blue collar employment) will be forced either to organize in entirely new sectors or to see their already shrinking numbers diminish still further.*

There are one or two unions which are making the effort to move into new territories, notably in the public sector, where the federal, state, or local government is the employer. The numbers of workers paid out of the public revenue has grown extensively in recent years. From 1965 to 1977 public employees have gone from about 16 per cent to 19 per cent of the workforce with the largest area of growth being at the State and local levels.[12] *In absolute figures this means an increase from a little over ten to almost fifteen million workers with employment in the Federal service accounting for almost none of this increase.*

Public Employment and Payrolls: October 1966 to October 1976

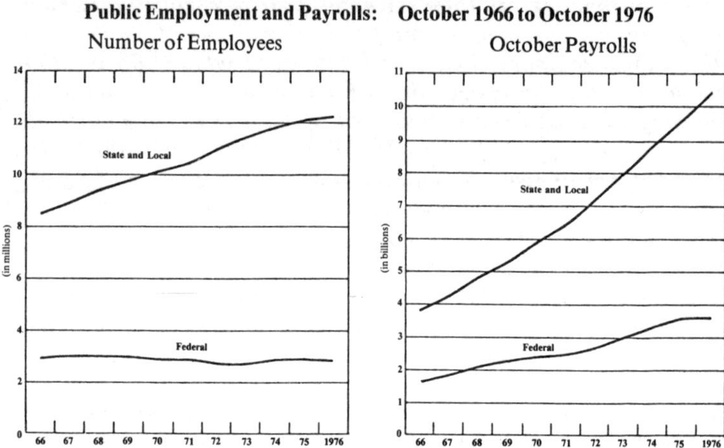

Source ★See 1972 Census of Governments, Vol. 6, No. 4: **Historical Statistics on Governmental Finances and Employment,** which provides summary nationwide data by level of government for the period 1940 through 1972, and also State-by-State figures, by function, for selected years.

This growth partially explains the phenomenal expansion of the American Federation of State, County and Municipal Employees (AFSCME). This union organizes workers in all categories except teachers, who are members of the American Federation of Teachers (AFT). AFSCME has made incredible advances in membership in the recent period having increased by about a factor of six since 1960. There are now just over a million and a half members making AFSCME the second largest union in the United States. The Service Employees International Union competes with both AFSCME and the AFT and organizes certain workers, particularly in hospitals, in both private and public employment. There have been a number of strikes in both teaching and hospital work in recent years, and despite the fact that these workers are relatively new to this sort of industrial action, they have shown an admirable ability to withstand both legal and media harrassment in the course of their strikes. In many of these cases striking workers were quick to feel the full weight of Governmental intervention, especially where there are legal prohibitions against striking public employees. It is likely that workers in such circumstances will come to see their struggles in a political light relatively quickly. Recently, school teachers in both New York state and New Jersey spent time in jail for strike activity. It is difficult to imagine them continuing to cherish cast-iron illusions concerning the class-neutral State.

The development of a political response to trade-union struggles in the private sector is perhaps more noticeable at this time, but has come about in an unusual way. Basically, the only rank-and-file opposition movements in key industrial unions that have survived opportunism on the part of their leaders and repression by the incumbent bureaucrats are those related in some way to class struggle politics. The following three examples from coal, steel, and trucking are arranged on an increasing scale of political consciousness.

As Guérin's account of the origins of rank-and-file opposition movement in the United Mine Workers (UMW) shows, strains began to develop inside the miner leadership not long after Lewis's retirement in 1963. Joseph Yablonski, formerly a UMW official himself, attempted to contest for power with President Tony Boyle, a corrupt hack who had inherited the levers of power that worked the Lewis machine. Yablonski and his wife and child were murdered by gunmen on Boyle's payroll on Christmas Eve 1969. In the wave of indignation and disgust that followed, the Miners for Democracy Movement of Arnold Miller led an assault on the citadels of bureaucratic power and put a rank-and-file team in the UMW national headquarters for the first time in approximately sixty years. Constitutional changes were instituted to preserve the rank-and-file victory and one of particular importance required rank-and-file approval of collective bargaining contracts on a local-by-local basis. Old-line bureaucrats (left over in great numbers from the Lewis-Boyle apparatus) feared that such democratic changes would 'weaken' the union's position. What had really weakened the UMW, however, had been the bureaucracy's practice of selling jobs for higher wages without at the same time organizing the new areas being exploited for coal production. Not only had the UMW officialdom failed to organize the strip mines being opened up in the Western states, but they had also neglected traditional areas of coal production such as in Eastern Kentucky. By the Autumn of 1977, when a new contract was due to be negotiated, nearly half of the yearly coal output in the United States was being produced by non-union workers. The coal employers (now themselves part of vastly larger steel and energy monopolies) talked gleefully of 'restructuring industrial relations' in the coalfields. Arnold Miller had by this time already been faced with challenges to his power from some of the old-line officials and like any other trade union leader had responded with purges and reorganizations. Just before contract talks were to begin Miller was assisted in the task of rebuilding his organization by friends at the highest level of the American government: White House trouble shooters on loan from Jimmy Carter!

None of this prevented the longest strike in UMW history from unfolding that Winter. The scenes of scab-herding, gunfights, and picket line confrontations witnessed during that conflict recalled to many the bloody battles of the 1930s. Many of the same individuals were there as well as the older people counselled their sons and daughters on strategy, tactics, and endurance. The older generation also walked the lines at the pits while the younger men formed flying pickets whose task was to stop convoys of scabs crossing state lines. Throughout the Winter and into early Spring the miners unwillingness to buckle under heavy police pressure, economic hardship, and media harrassment was an inspiration to workers in other industries throughout the country.

What the role of the Miller administration during these events seemed to show was that a former rank-and-file leader will act just like any other top official when subjected to the sort of pressures that the government and employers can bring to bear at the national level. The Miller team did not 'lead' during the strike. The miners themselves carried on the struggle against the employers, the courts, and the armed forces of the state. The UMW officialdom followed along complaining about the intransigence of the rank-and-file and apologizing to the 'public' every step of the way. In a re-enactment of the great Truman-John L Lewis showdown of 1948 the Carter government threatened the miners with the anti-strike sanctions of the Taft-Hartley Act. As their fathers had done before them the miners defied the law with total unanimity. Of the 160,000 miners on strike, not one showed up to work on the day Carter said they must.

Interestingly enough, it was the question of pension provisions which helped to delay the settlement of the strike until late March. The employers proposals concerning the pension plans would have seriously penalised retirees and those about to retire. The younger miners declared their solidarity with the 'men who built the union' and refused to go back until a better deal on retirement pay was offered. The leadership did everything it could to 'sell' the contract to the membership, including the payment of vast sums out of the union treasury to a public relations and advertising firm for televised messages urging the miners to accept the latest contract offer and go back to work. This and a whole range of other matters raised by the strike gave rise to a storm of hostile criticism directed at the Miller leadership. Much of this criticism issued from socialist organizations active in the rank-and-file. There is at the moment no national rank-and-file movement in opposition to Miller, but since the strike the basis for one exists.[13]

The situation is somewhat different in the United Steel Workers' Union (USW). Here a national rank-and-file opposition to the bureaucracy exists and has contested the election for the presidency of the international. The campaign was headed by a man who calls himself a socialist, but who carefully avoided socialist rhetoric during his election bid. As Guérin relates, the replacement of D McDonald by an oppositionist candidate, I W Able in 1965 was nothing more than a palace revolution; a split between rival sections of the bureaucracy. Abel won and soon enough proved what great distances separated him from the ranks by signing the notorious Experimental Negotiating Agreement of 1973 which experimentally negotiated away the steelworkers' right to strike until 1980. The puny (3.3 per cent) wage increases delivered by the Able team in the contract of the following year caused a number of steelworkers to put two and two together and many of them began to listen more carefully to Ed Sadlowski. Sadlowski is a Chicago steelworker who had defeated a machine candidate for the Directorship of District 31 only after the voting had had to be held twice — the second time under federal government supervision. Sadlowski's low-level social radicalism and shop-floor image made him attractive to some sections of the American left and also to some prominent liberals such as John Kenneth Galbraith who contributed money to Sadlowski's election campaign which was aimed at defeating Abel's hand-picked successor, Lloyd McBride. Other voices on the left, however, criticized Sadlowski for soft-pedalling the ENA no-strike-clause issue. The election was hotly contested but the Sadlowski forces were insufficiently large to vet activity at the preponderance of the polling stations. There is some possibility that McBride 'stole' the election, but the fact remains that the pro-Sadlowski forces were not large enough to oust the incumbents in an American trade-union election. What is commonly required is a landslide. Sadlowski only won 47 per cent.

The steelworkers who had remained loyal to the Abel-McBride machine (however many they were) soon received their reward when the team they had (probably) put in office accepted the massive layoffs and plant closures decreed by the steel bosses in the Autumn of 1977. The steel monopoly shut down several entire plants and laid off thousands in others for reasons of their own convenience which included favourable tax writeoffs on obsolete plant and equipment as well as the hope of influencing the government to erect barriers to the importation of cheaper Japanese steel. Fifteen thousand or more steelworkers lost their jobs for this, some of them their pensions as well, but McBride and his assistants took the whole thing with an air of philosophical calm. But McBride went further than a sublime inactivity in his response; he made an appeal to what he supposed was the average steelworker's xenophobia as well. His only real act in the situation was to join with the employers in a call for tariff protection against 'unfair competition' and 'dumping'. Nevertheless, jingoism did not pacify all of the steelworkers, for when McBride appeared in a televized confrontation with workers from the shut down Youngstown Ohio plant one of them, a shop steward, told him:

'In the last two weeks, 14,000 jobs have been eliminated at Johnstown, at Lackawanna, and here at Youngstown Sheet and Tube. And instead...instead of saying that we're not going to be thrown out in the street like a bunch of dogs to starve...they're parroting the company line. the companies say that "it's too bad we have to do this to you...we feel terrible." We're saying we don't care how the companies feel; we don't care if they pay it or the government pays it, we want our jobs.

'Lloyd McBride goes around and says it's too bad, it's a cry of despair. It should be a battle cry, it should be a battle cry of all steelworkers that we're going to stand up and fight for our jobs, that we're not going to go back and starve. The people that own this company are not going back to shacks and eat Wheaties,

they're going back to mansions and eat caviar...

'Youngstown Sheet and Tube...cry about imports; yet they buy roll-making equipment from Japan. Republic Steel cries about the imports, yet they bought slab steel from France last year...They have been eliminating our jobs for years, combining jobs, speeding us up, shutting down plants, and they want to focus our attention...on the Japanese.'

McBride's response to this was more straightforward than clever:

'...it's the kind of rhetoric that really, on close analysis, makes no sense. I'm sure that Youngstown did not close the Youngstown plant in order to prove any kind of point. They have decided to...take out of operation a multi-million dollar operation. If there was a market for the steel...I think they would much prefer to sell that steel at a price that would give them a profit.

'...Im interested in preserving jobs. The wild rhetoric that you just heard won't save jobs. We're in a free economy; there's no law that can force a company to operate a plant against its will, and all of the anger and the frustration that was demonstrated by that steelworker is understandable, but it doesn't answer anything. The answer is how are we going to have our members make steel that can be sold in this country against unfair competition. And the only way I know that's going to happen is to remedy the unfair competition.'[14]

The most notable thing about the above exchange is that the problems involved so easily escape the usual framework of a discussion of trade-union strategy and tactics. It seems obvious that only an analysis based on a fundamental critique of the development (and decline) of capitalist production as well as of the historic development of the workers' movement (e.g. the need for international solidarity, etc.) could provide a program of struggle for American steelworkers at this point. The shop floor official's angry remarks quoted here show that basic class instincts still survive in the American proletariat. This includes the instinct of international solidarity. It remains to be seen, however, if the sort of opposition movement that has been active in the USW will be capable of transforming these instincts into an effective mobilization of the rank and file.

The most effective and the most political mobilization of rank-and-file workers in the American trade unions so far has been, paradoxically, in the most bureaucratic and gangster-ridden union, the International Brotherhood of Teamsters (IBT). At almost two million, the IBT is the largest union in the United States. It organizes lorry drivers, freight dock workers, and, in a lesser degree, other occupations. The goings on in the IBT, its leadership's links with the Mafia, the Nixon White House and so forth are described by Guérin and he also outlines the standing attraction for syndicated crime represented by the union's vast pension funds. These funds have been 'lent' to underworld figures who presumably do not have the sort of credit facilities offered to other businessmen by the banks, and who often need large sums on short notice. This constant danger to retirement monies in addition to the inferior contracts that the Fitzsimmons bureaucracy has delivered in recent years has electrified the Teamster rank-and-file. Rank-and-file movements have developed in different ways in different parts of the country but they have in common these two concerns.

In Los Angeles a 1970 wildcat strike in the notoriously rebellious local 208 just happened to coincide with a strike of university students to protest the Nixon bombing of Cambodia. At the suggestion of striking teamsters some of the students joined the truckdrivers on the picket line thus freeing other drivers to attend to strike activities in other locations. This incident gave rise to an association of left-wing intellectuals and rank-and-file IBT members which, to some extent, continues in the rank-and-file movement of today. A revolutionary Marxist group called the International Socialists worked to maintain these contacts in the early Seventies through an opposition movement called Teamster Union Rank and File (TURF). This organization foundered, in part because of the defection of some of its members to the forces of the Fitzsimmons bureaucracy. It was superceded in 1975 by another organization of rank and filers called Teamsters for a Decent Contract. The contract in question was the 1976 Master Freight Agreement and TDC agitation aimed at putting pressure for more ambitious demands on the Teamster officialdom. After the contract ratification (which did not take place in the absence of wildcat strikes protesting its terms) the TDC reformed itself as a permanent group called Teamsters for a Democratic Union (TDU). TDU publishes a paper called Convoy with a claimed circulation of 40,000 and may have as many as 2000 members in some forty cities across the US. One of TDU's nationally prominent members, Pete Camarata of local 299 in Detroit, stood against and nearly defeated *a machine candidate for the presidency of Hoffa's home local. Recently, he rose to challenge the IBT leadership at a national convention in Las Vegas. Here in the measured tones of a US Labor Department observer is what happened: 'Delegate Peter Camarata (Local 299 Detroit) responded to a proposed 25-percent increase in officers' salaries by offering an amendment setting absolute limits on officers' remuneration. The salary limits proposed are not a matter of record since he was not able to complete the presentation of his amendment. The convention went on to unanimously adopt the proposed increase, raising the salaries of the president and general secretary treasurer to $156,250 and $125,000 respectively.'*

CONCLUSION

Thus, in the end, the administrative neo-corporativist style of trade unionism which has developed in the United States since the Second World War, may in the event, have produced its dialectical counterpart in the trade-union rank and file. The interesting fact is that, under a competitive capitalist regime of the extraction of absolute surplus value in the 19th century, the principal conflict in the employment relationship was that between workers and their employers over union recognition, wages and hours, conditions of labor, and rules governing the workplace. Now, under a regime of monopoly capitalism and the extraction of relative surplus value (through more or less constant innovation of the production process), the struggle pits the rank-and-file worker first and foremost not against the company or state institution he or she works for, but against those who carry out its dirty work and behind whom it hides: the bureaucratic clique which rules his union under the protective mantle of state power. The bureaucracy protects its power by fair means or foul and rarely meets with objection to its rule by the governmental bodies which were put in place allegedly to oversee the trade-union movement but in reality to restrict further organization and to 'stabilize industrial relations'. The bureaucracy bases its modus vivendi *with the employers on a transaction which consists in selling jobs (allowing technological change) and of paying for wage gains out of the monopoly price for the product. This is a foolproof mechanism as far as the threat from the rank and file is concerned because, obviously, those workers who have been thrown out of their positions won't be around to cause the trade-union leader problems any more while those who remain will enjoy higher wages. On the other hand, there is a curious sense in which the bureaucrats preside over the dismantlement of their own power base. Like absolutist rulers in earlier times, they may simply be thinking, 'after me the flood'. The only lasting opposition to bureaucrats of this type has been shown to be that based on class struggle principles. In cases where this has not been so, the new 'leadership' thrown up by the rank and file has very quickly come to resemble the old. In the last analysis what is required is not a series of rank-and-file 'leaders' of the Abel, Miller, or even Sadlowski type, but a rank and file* movement *which is the only possible counterweight to bureaucratic power given the American system of 'industrial relations'. (This in turn would bring in its wake a break with the two party system as it is practiced in America today.)*

Things operate somewhat differently in the public sector, where in many areas workers are being brought into the unions for the first time, and where the relationship between the trade-union bureaucrat and the 'employer' obviously cannot have the same characteristics as in private industry. Both the numbers of public employees and their salaries have skyrocketed in the last ten years; and this has taken place at precisely the moment when a whole complex of factors (including the movement of industry to the South and overseas) has reduced public income in a number of American cities where unionization has been high. The result of all of these developments taken together has been a head on clash between newly organized workers and the powers of the state. Thus, the workers in the public sector have been introduced to the politics of class struggle immediately upon being organized into a trade union.

In both the private and public sectors of the economy then, possibilities for the politicization of the class struggle in the United States have begun to become visible in a way that was unthinkable to most Americans even ten years ago. It is one of the great virtues of the book that follows that its author has been able to discern the beginning of a rank-and-file revolt as it has evolved through time.

Los Angeles, California
Labor Day, 1978

Foreword of 1968

The American labor movement is little known but much disparaged. To a certain degree, of course, that is its own fault. It has been gradually degenerating over a number of years. Its fighting spirit is becoming atrophied and shows itself only in intermittent bursts of anger. The bureaucratic apparatus that runs it is repellent. The havoc wrought by corruption in some unions (and only in some), which the distant observer tends to generalize and magnify, is nauseating. Labor's attitude toward the race problem, aside from that of a few big progressive unions, is disappointing and sickening. Last but not least, the labor movement has allowed itself to be integrated into the formidable apparatus of the world's most powerful empire, which it serves faithfully. In particular, it has shown itself incapable, in its overwhelming majority, of reacting to the genocide in Vietnam.

However valid they may be, all these facts are nevertheless likely to give us a distorted image of Labor. The history of its birth and growth is one of the most dynamic and exciting in the world. The relatively recent development of *industrial* trade-unionism in the United States can be described, without exaggeration, as epic. The workers in the basic branches of industry (autos, steel, rubber, etc.), who were, for the most part, newly arrived immigrants, in contrast to the highly skilled, native-born Americans in the craft unions, had never been organized, for reasons which will be analyzed in this little book. They are today. Despite the shortcomings of its leadership, despite its prejudices, despite its political shortsightedness, the American working class constitutes a tremendous force. When it reveals its strength in social conflicts, its power immediately assumes gigantic dimensions. Moreover, the present pause in union recruitment as the top leadership marks time does not alter the fact that Labor's forces remain intact. It has never suffered a major defeat.

Today there is, in a sense, a phenomenon of 'dual power' in the United States: Big Business vs. Labor. Both of them are too powerful, and one of them has got to go. This can be seen, for example, in the case of the coal mines, where the mine owners and John Lewis confronted each other on an equal footing. The tragedy is that the labor hacks are afraid of having to make use of the power conferred on them by their membership and the remarkable degree of organization of their forces. Given free rein, the millions of militants would be capable, as Walter Reuther said, of moving mountains. At the 'summit', American trade-unionism resembles an overdeveloped athlete from whom a single blow could be fatal and who therefore makes sure never to lose self-control.

But the rank and file does not always show the same restraint and now and then it is barely, if at all, kept in check by union discipline. Even today it is chafing at the bit. Might there not be unforeseeable circumstances in which it would be led to challenge the other power? Will it not be on American soil that expansionist, warmongering Big Business, before which the world trembles, encounters its negation; and will the immense blue-collar cohort not finally be its gravedigger?

There was a man 80 years ago who bent over infant Labor in its cradle and had a presentiment of its revolutionary potential: Friedrich Engels. In 1886-87, he kept up a correspondence with F A Sorge, a German socialist who had emigrated to the United States, in which he closely followed the evolution of the American workers' movement. Furthermore, at around the same time he wrote a preface to an American edition of his classical work, *The Condition of the English Working Class*, devoted solely to the American workers' movement.

In his writings of the period, Engels immediately sensed the enormous significance of the great strike wave which had reached its peak in 1886 and marked the entry of the American working masses, onto the stage of history. At last 'the spell was broken' and the American workers had 'sprouted wings':

> 'No one could then foresee that in such a short time the movement would burst out with such irresistible force, would spread with the rapidity of a prairie-fire, would shake American society to its very foundations.'
>
> 'The spontaneous, instinctive movements of these vast masses of working people, over a vast extent of country, the simultaneous outburst of their common discontent with a miserable social condition, the same everywhere and due to the same causes, made them conscious of the fact that they formed a new and distinct class of American society; a class of – practically speaking – more or less hereditary wage workers, proletarians.'

Engels was delighted that the movement had begun in America 'with such gigantic and imposing strength'. He greeted the Knights of Labor as 'the first national organization created by the American working class as a whole;' 'an immense mass of potential energy evolving slowly and surely into actual force'. Their weaknesses and inconsistencies were of little importance: 'to an outsider it appears evident that here is the raw material out of which the future of the American working-class movement and, along with it, the future of American society at large, has to be shaped.' This is a remarkable prediction if one bears in mind the way in which the CIO was to be formed half a century later.

Engels grasped very well the essentially pragmatic character of the American workers' movement, so disconcerting for a European: 'It is much more important that the movement broadens out, that it advances regularly, that it takes root and embraces as much as it can of the entire American workers' movement than to see it set forth and progress right from the start along a perfectly correct theoretical blueprint.' 'I know my Americans less well than I imagined if they were not to astonish us all by the size of their movement . . . . In practical matters ahead of the whole world and in theoretical matters still in diapers . . . . A people full of energy like none other.'

Engels thought that the lightning development of industry in the United States was likely to compensate, to a certain degree, for the theoretical inadequacy and the low level of class consciousness of the American workers:

> 'It is precisely the revolution carried out in all the traditional areas by the development of industry which also carries out a revolution in people's heads. Capitalist centralization strides ahead with you in the USA in seven-league boots . . . . As for what is lacking still, the bourgeoisie will see to it: nowhere else in the whole world do they operate in such an impudent and tyrannical way as over there. . . . Wherever the bourgeoisie prosecutes the struggle in such a fashion, it quickly comes to a sticky end. . . . I would swear blind that from now on the movement will make good headway, perhaps quicker than with us. . . . When the moment comes, things will move with colossal speed and energy over there. . . . Once the Americans get down to it, but with an energy and virulence unique to them, we in Europe will be children by comparison.'

This little book aims to show that, in the course of its magnificent and tumultuous history, Labor has not belied

Friedrich Engels' predictions as much as might be thought today. Its present paralysis is perhaps only temporary. If it occurs, its awakening might well, to cite Engels once again, 'plunge the whole world into astonishment'.

Not wishing to act the false prophet, we have refrained from predicting what form this awakening might take – *economic:* revolutionary unionism, factory occupations, general strike – or *political:* a break with the Democratic Party and the formation of a Labor Party. Neither did we want to debate the pros and cons of one or another of these means. Our purpose is neither to theorize nor to predict what will be but, more modestly, to describe what is.

In the present conjuncture, the world is overawed by the crushing technical and nuclear superiority of the American Empire (the expression of the super-capitalist monopolies), by its inordinate pride, its cruelty and its boundless audacity. The world stands in need of a combination of struggles if it is to free itself: those waged on the fringe of the metropolitan heartlands by revolutionary peoples relying on their own efforts and a gigantic clean sweep by the labor movement from within. Though the American trade-union movement may appear today, at first glance, to be the accomplice of the worst enemy of humanity, will it not someday be its adversary? Though the Black leader Stokely Carmichael could, quite rightly, accuse it of confining itself to picking up the crumbs from the capitalist banquet instead of struggling for the redistribution of American wealth, who can be so sure that the advanced wing of Labor will not join the Black Power movement in a common challenge to American capitalism?

At a meeting of socialist intellectuals in New York in September 1966, Professor Herbert Marcuse claimed that, contrary to the traditional teachings of Marxism, the working class in the advanced capitalist societies had become nonrevolutionary and hostile to socialism, and that it could no longer be considered the motor force of progress.

The late-lamented Isaac Deutscher reproached the detractors of Labor for not showing any interest in the American working class. He said he was convinced that the proletariat remained the decisive instrument of socialism in the United States. He was not at all sure that the workers were so corrupted by the meretricious privileges conceded to them by a capitalist system which owed its prosperity to war. He thought that, though the older American workers had certainly been more or less touched by this corruption, the same was not true of the younger generations of workers, whose numbers were constantly increasing. He was convinced that, beneath their apparent political apathy, they were basically dissatisfied with the existing order. He urged American intellectuals to find the way through to them, so as to contribute to rousing the sleeping giant of Labor, without which it would assuredly not be possible to storm the bastions of capitalism.

Foreword to the 1976 edition

In this bicentennial year of the American Declaration of Independence, a new edition of this little book may prove useful. Its concerns are quite unrelated to the bombastic official celebrations which our ruling class here in France, ever on its knees before the most powerful and ever keen to dish up history in its own sauce and for its own benefit, is revelling in. Like Monsieur Perrichon in the play by Eugène Labiche, it feels more at ease in the role of lifesaver than in that of recipient of relief. This anniversary has provided it with the opportunity to celebrate with great self-satisfaction the little helping hand (magnified out of all proportion for the good of the cause) provided long ago by Lafayette to aid the birth of the American Federation. Almost no-one cares to remember that the settlers across the Atlantic liberated *themselves*; almost no-one cares to recognize that the French intervention in the 18th century was far from disinterested.

This little book is concerned with another history and another America: not that of the capitalist bourgeoisie still in its infancy in 1776, which was to triumph and achieve adulthood in next to no time, but that of the epic of the exploited working class, its century-old struggle, its handicaps, its setbacks and its victories.

Such a reminder is all the more necessary as today the young generations of internationalist militants seem to know almost nothing of a past which should surely not leave them indifferent. Their underestimation of the American Labor movement and the silent and contemptuous indifference which they show toward it are doubtless accounted for by several factors. First of all, young people prefer the America of jazz, rock 'n' roll, pop singers, westerns and movie stars. Then there is the question of distance as well as lack of information: most of the numerous books and documentaries on the United States dodge this particular subject or avoid giving it sufficient emphasis. There is also anti-American prejudice, absolutely legitimate when its object is the tyrannical hold of the big Yankee monopolies over their own country and over the rest of the world, but relatively unjustified in relation to the behavior, past and present, of Big Business's slaves. Finally, there is the declared hostility of post-May 68 youth, whether in France, the United States or elsewhere, to a degenerated, bureaucratized trade-unionism, integrated into the established order.

But it would be a grave misjudgment of America to point out only its repugnant aspects; and it would likewise create a partially false picture of the American workers' movement if we were to single out only its negative features, namely its complete adherence to the capitalist system, the absence and rejection of any perspective of social transformation, its apathy or compliance toward employers, its selfish corporatism and bureaucracy, the irremovability of its leaders, its gerontocracy and its corruption, which, aping the surrounding capitalist society and political system, rots some organizations to the core, ending up with a workers' Mafia linked to the big Mafia, business unionism engaging in fraudulent and even criminal practices.

The fact nevertheless remains that the American labor movement, in spite of its handicaps and defects, its stagnation and decline, retains a certain dynamic, a sense of solidarity in struggle, and an explosive violence when it loses patience and kicks over the traces none of which is easily matched by the working class in Europe. To be sure, in recent years, its fighting spirit has been blunted and its integration increased, while the bureaucracy has grown stronger. But it is not clear that this period of low tide can be seen as eternal; and care must be taken to avoid overly simplistic generalizations: American Labor with, in 1976, its 20 million or so paid-up members, is far from being a homogeneous colossus. It contains the best and the worst, the most obtuse reaction and the most progressive aspirations, the opposition between more combative young workers and the older ones, racial diversity and antagonism, profound differences in working conditions and modes of exploitation. American Labor is not one but many. It is not doomed to a single, indivisible future, but doubtless to diverse futures. Labor is undeniably integrated into the American Way of Life, but that integration could prove redressable or otherwise, permanent or temporary, as the case may be, including all the shades of variation in between.

That said, today's young reader is entitled to smile at the

really very optimistic predictions of Friedrich Engels, cited by me perhaps too complacently in the preceding foreword, written eight years ago. These Marxian prophecies have the excuse of being nearly a century old and it has to be admitted that they are far from being confirmed by the present situation. But who knows? Maybe Marx's companion was more far-sighted than we are . . .

Our youthful skeptic may also be staggered at the more recent confidence placed in the American workers' movement by a contemporary, the late Isaac Deutscher. But the opinions expressed by him, also cited in my foreword, were not entirely mistaken. Certainly the American workers as a whole are more 'corrupted' than he realized by the privileges which the system lavishes on them. But he may not have been wrong to distinguish the mentality of the younger generations of American workers from the much more sedate mentality of their elders. Neither did he err in encouraging the intelligentsia across the Atlantic to rouse the sleeping giant of Labor. Finally, he was right in his conviction that the working class remains the decisive instrument for the future passage to socialism in the United States and that, without it, without its gigantic battering ram, capitalism's walls of Jericho would be impregnable.

My foreword of 1968 also, and above all, requires clarification as far as the views I attributed to Herbert Marcuse are concerned. Did I not, involuntarily, somewhat distort the illustrious philosopher's thinking by accrediting him with the assumption that the working class could no longer be viewed as the motor force of progress? Then maybe I was misinformed; maybe, too, the philosopher has subsequently nuanced or deepened his thought.

In his little book published in 1969 (which is, in my view, the most readable of his writings) – *An Essay on Liberation* – Marcuse in no way underrates the working masses and their revolutionary potential. He emphasizes that the radical transformation of today's society still depends, at least potentially, on the class which constitutes the human basis of the productive process. This class (however uncommon and unpopular the word may be in America) has not lost its historic role. It remains the source and reservoir of capitalist exploitation:[1] 'By virtue of its basic position in the production process, by virtue of its numerical weight and the weight of exploitation, the working class is still the historical agent of revolution.' And Marcuse adds, as a warning against errors of interpretation which have become standard currency for some today, that it would be 'aberrant' to claim that other social layers, such as intellectuals, those on the fringe of society, petty bourgeois, etc., have become a radical political force capable of supplanting the proletariat in its revolutionary class function. Thus, in the eyes of the philosopher, a student movement like the one in France in May 68, rich as it may have been, 'is not a revolutionary force, nor even perhaps a vanguard, as long as there are not masses capable and desirous of following it'.

Alas! reckons Marcuse, it is only in an *objective* sense that the working class retains its ultimate vocation, that the workers still constitute the revolutionary class. But, *subjectively,* 'it is no longer true'. How remote are the days when the proletariat was endowed with socialist consciousness, when it waged the class struggle to the point of challenging the very existence of the system, and when it defined as its goal the abolition of capitalism! Today, in the advanced capitalist countries, the working class is, to a greater or lesser extent, integrated into the existing system. It contributes to its stabilization. In its majority, it has become a conservative force (and here Marcuse uses a very strong epithet which his followers make excessive use of). He adds: 'indeed counter-revolutionary'.

What has happened? Why this decisive change?

First of all, there have been big changes in the organic composition of the working class, an observation which has become commonplace today: while the proportion of 'blue-collar' workers is constantly diminishing, the wage-earners with clean hands, the 'white-collar' workers, are growing in numbers as well as in importance all the time. What the philosopher does not hesitate to call the 'working-class intelligentsia', which is, he specifies, an 'instrumentalist' intelligentsia, but an intelligentsia all the same, plays a more and more decisive role in the productive process. This 'new working class', as he chooses to call it, is quite incapable of contemplating using its preponderant position to overturn the mode and relations of production, because it has no interest in doing so. It does not feel it to be necessary, it is fairly well-paid, and it feels quite comfortably off in a system of high productivity, constantly expanding markets, neo-colonialism and technocratic democracy.

Advanced capitalism, far from having pulled out the plug, has kept afloat. It has managed to integrate the majority of the working class into its system and, what is more, it has had the same success with the workers' organizations, that is to say the reformist bureaucracies which keep the workers in line with a strong and vigilant arm. Monopoly capitalism and the multinationals have found ways of nipping in the bud any inclination toward socialist consciousness. Thanks to the powerful mass media which they have at their disposal, and the relative narrowing of the gap between the level of consumption of the masses and that of the privileged, they have encouraged the vast majority of workers to share the specifically petty-bourgeois desire for social stability.

There is, however, one point which is omitted from Marcuse's analysis. He fails to indicate one of the additional reasons why the integration of American Labor has gone much further in recent years than it had ever gone before – much further, too, than the integration which has befallen the working class in Western Europe. It is important never to lose sight of the fact that the American working class bears little resemblance in the way it was formed to the proletariats on the other side of the Atlantic. It came into existence in the same way as geological formations, by successive layers brought in from outside, originating from all parts of the world. This immigration continued for nearly two centuries. Using the language of prehistory, it could be suggested that the stratifications and alluvial deposits that formed Labor by stages accumulated from the 'primary' to the 'quaternary'.

The memorable periods of American working-class struggle have in fact coincided with the entry into the field of production of successive arrivals of recently-landed foreigners. Some of the Anglo-Saxon immigrants had brought with them forms of social struggle traditional to the countries of their origin. Subsequent immigrants had not succeeded straightaway in entirely assimilating the American way of life; they had not acquired all the material advantages of their precursors' full Americanization. They had had to make do with the lowest, the worst-paid, the most manual, the dirtiest and the least regarded jobs.*

During their first years in the New World, they had been paralyzed with timid docility. When they began to chafe at the bit, when they dared to go on strike, when they showed themselves aggressive and violent it was not so much, if at all, a result of the awakening, or reawakening, of a socialist consciousness; their purpose was much more to accede in their turn to the relatively privileged status which had earlier been won through sheer hard work by previous immigrants, particularly the first arrivals, those of Anglo-Saxon stock. The 'primary' and 'secondary' layers had hoisted themselves to the top of the labor aristocracy. They had solidly and egotistically entrenched themselves in so-called 'craft' unionism, in the most narrow and reactionary corporatism; and they had thereby been the first workers to be integrated into the 'free enterprise' system, a disguised pseudonym for the capitalist system. They had been followed by successive generations of immigrants who supplied large-scale modern industry with a work-force as abundant as it was heterogeneous, liable to forced labor at pleasure. Initially unorganized, rejected or scorned by the craft unions, this swarming throng, a proletarian Tower of Babel, eventually gained access to organization and Americanization through the Homeric battles begun just after World War I and victoriously resumed during the 1930s, which saw the birth of industrial unionism and the founding of the CIO (Committee for Industrial Organization).

But now the days of that amazing leap forward, that radical

---

*This explanation does not deal with the fate of the Black contingent of the American working class. This history is sensitively described by Guérin in his book *De L'Oncle Tom aux Panthères*, from which chapter seven only has been extracted (chapter four below). For, while every national component of the American working class has suffered racial discrimination from those who preceded it to the shores of America, they have all (with the exception of the colonial and semi-colonial immigrants or indigenous peoples from Puerto Rico and Mexico, as well as the Native Americans themselves) overcome this to a greater or lesser extent, and have succeeded in becoming more or less accepted as American. But the American Blacks, the first immigrants of non-Anglo-Saxon stock, remain, as they were before, at the bottom of the ladder for the most part or, to use Guérin's image, the deepest alluvial deposit over which the other layers have been laid. This singular constant of American 'socio-political geology' may allow us to continue Guérin's metaphor: in order that this the deepest deposit in American society's sub-soil may find its place in the sun an earthquake would be required. But such an event would so change the topology of the country that the political atmosphere itself would become profoundly altered [Ed.].

mass struggle, are long gone. The workers in heavy industry have in turn extracted their share of material and moral advantages from the system. They have secured relatively high levels of pay, purchasing power and comfort and, finally, some degree of job security (in spite of the increase in unemployment during the most recent recession, which in any case is hitting young people, women and Blacks much more than the white, adult, male workers). They attribute the credit for what is after all a considerable improvement in their condition to the free enterprise system, the big capitalism dominated by the monopolies which has diabolically succeeded in integrating them, buying them, corrupting them and having a sort of contagious effect upon them, just as it had previously managed to incorporate the first waves of immigrants. This is one of the reasons for the more and more pronounced integration of Labor into the system and, in consequence, for the setback and decline in its fighting capacity.

This also accounts, in the field of organization, for the compromise arrived at between craft unionism and industrial unionism, with the old American Federation of Labor and the CIO now coexisting in one and the same trade-union federation, the name of which – the AFL-CIO – is sufficient to indicate that what occurred was not a fusion but a superposition. This trade-union reunification worked out for the benefit of the older and more conservative of the two union federations. The unified federation is still presided over today by a fanatically reactionary octogenarian, George Meany, while ex-CIO leader, Walter Reuther, before his accidental death, saw the failure of his hope of injecting a minimum of dynamism into the reunified federation.

The main pillars of industrial unionism – autos, iron and steel, rubber, coal mining, the teamsters (whose powerful union recruits in the most incongruous industries) – now practice a contract policy which ties them to the big employers. This pattern of social relationships is seen as quite satisfactory by the rank and file, because, as Marcuse sharply observes, the individual adapts 'to an atrocious but profitable society' and, on the employers' side, this system is appreciated, since it avoids major upheavals in their relations with labor. But Marcuse neglects to mention that these relationships are neither idyllic nor free from all tension, that from time to time they involve some fairly tough bargaining, and that, far from eliminating all clashes, both 'wildcat' and official work stoppages still occur frequently. Integration, yes, for sure, but dead calm on the social front, no.

Furthermore, and here Marcuse is fully in agreement, there are still layers of the working class which remain cruelly underprivileged. But those minorities still subject to the brutality of exploitation are precisely those which have ceased to play a preponderant role in the productive process. Likewise, the black population does not occupy a central position in production either, in spite of the violent episodic outbursts of Afro-American revolt. And its living standards, together with the racial prejudice which it faces, maintain an 'immense distance', as Marcuse says, between it and the young white intelligentsia, for all that the latter is radicalized and emancipated.

Having got thus far in his analysis, Marcuse presents those of his views which have found the widest echo and the expression of which has led many readers and militants to forget the preceding remarks.

It is a patent fact that the internal development of society has transferred the mission of challenging the capitalist system to a new type of militant intelligentsia: the integration of the majority of the working class into the system has resulted in the emergence of a new political consciousness spurred by the need for radical change. This phenomenon has arisen among social groups which, for various objective reasons, are relatively free from the conservative aspirations and interests which have brought about the integration of the bulk of the working class. It is certainly true that these groups are still limited and that their level of organization is either weak or non-existent. But in the present transitional period they are playing a decisive role. They are acting as catalysts of revolt. And it happens that their total opposition to the system makes them the objective representatives of 'the common interest of all the oppressed', even though the latter are usually unaware of it.

The appearance of these minorities is therefore not a superficial phenomenon, but expresses fundamental trends toward change, of a breadth and depth which exceed by far the forecasts of traditional socialist theory, on which the integrated working class has in any case turned its back. As this latter has ceased to be, or wished to be, the 'grave-digger' of capitalism, its mission is now being assumed by others. But – and Marcuse insists on this point – these youthful detonators of transformation can have no other valid and realistic objective than to bring their influence to bear on the working class 'from the outside'.

Their political agitation is only a first step towards liberation. Thus, Marcuse suggests, stimulated by the novel forms of action of these new political formations, the exploited may free themselves from capitalist exploitation.

The protest of this 'New Left' concentrates on extra-parliamentary struggle. So great is its audacity that it does not hesitate to question both the democratic, Parliamentary conception inherited from 1776 and 1789 and the now-outmoded revolutionary schema of 19th-century Marxism. It is neither liberal nor communist. It contains 'a strong element of spontaneity, even anarchism'. 'The anarchist element is an essential factor' in this new sensibility, hostile to all repression and all domination. This completely new outlook is expressed in the form of boycotts, sabotage, attitudes of 'dysfunctioning', such as resistance to work, feeling fed-up, generalized civil disobedience, the rejection of accepted values, negligence, indifference and insubordination in all its forms. Aside from a fringe element of young workers, the working masses are likely to regard this behavior as somewhat extravagant, and it is by no means sure that it can be of such great help to them in finding the road to their emancipation as Marcuse would like to hope.

But what then, according to Marcuse, are those social groups which are resistant to integration and therefore give us grounds not to despair of the future? Here the philospher's analysis is neither very clear nor always convincing. There is no doubt that he seeks to put too many eggs in the same basket. Those 'relatively free' minorities he enumerates are very varied in character. In first place he puts the students, together with those adult intellectuals who support them in their revolt; then come the most harshly exploited workers, those most disadvantaged by the system. Then there are the ethnic minorities, the ghetto and slum populations and, finally, the *Lumpenproletariat.* Marcuse does not deny that these social groups are heterogeneous, unstable and more or less unorganized. So how can they be brought together in common action? On this point his thinking is evasive. He admits that some of these groups are ambivalent and unpredictable. Thus the ghetto and slum youth can just as easily become a purely negative factor of violence for its own sake, as militant aggressiveness fighting against the repressive forces better than the students and acting as the pioneers, 'if not of a revolution, at least of a revolt'. As for the underprivileged layers of the working class, who suffer exploitation in its most brutal form, their subjection might indeed 'lead to their radicalization', but could equally well make them 'the mass support of the counter-revolution'.

As far as the Afro-Americans are concerned, they do not form a homogeneous community; the class struggle creates a divide in their ranks between the bourgeoisie and the proletariat. And then racial conflict comes between the black ghettoes and their white allies. In the eyes of the victims of racism, the whole white population, even the workers who are exploited, is regarded as an accomplice in and a beneficiary of the global crime perpetrated by its race.

We encounter the same difficulties in judging the university milieu. Marcuse holds that a considerable proportion of students belong, 'potentially' anyway, to the working class. Hence the brutality with which their revolt is put down. But this assertion is rather vague and, besides, it hardly accords with what the philosopher otherwise admits, namely that the student movement 'is not a revolutionary force, nor even perhaps a vanguard'. In addition, the idea that students are not integrated is too simplistic a notion. When they leave university, they run the risk of being recuperated by the system, of being brought back into the bosom of the middle class from which they came.

Moreover, Marcuse does not have too many illusions about the development of the student movements. He agrees that the student opposition is 'weaker and more diffuse than any opposition in history'. Just after May 68, he noted that militancy, which at one time was heightened to the point of recklessness, had become bogged down in apparent or temporary failures and had given way to neurasthenia, a lapse into purely negative and apolitical forms of behavior, evasion of reality, couldn't-care-less attitudes, all manner of mysticism and manifestations of nonconformism which were apt to be merely artificial and contrived.

In his analysis of the student movements, the philosopher gropes in the dark and sometimes seems to contradict himself. Thus, on the one hand, he grants that the young intelligentsia has awakened the historical memory of the labor movement which, in France, had been totally chloroformed by its bureaucratic and reformist misleaders; he is grateful to the students of Paris for having, albeit for only a short time, 'revived the power of the general strike and factory occupations, of the red flag and the *Internationale*'; and he congratulates the student opposition for having, for the first time in France, 'challenged a regime which deployed all its power against it, rediscovering for a brief period the libertarian power of red and black flags'. But, on the other hand, he takes pleasure in emphasizing that the students of May 68 did not so much link up again with the revolutionary tradition as *innovate*, that they went beyond out-of-date 19th-century Marxism, proclaiming the permanence of rebellion – the Great Refusal – criticizing even the most spectacular achievements of technical progress, raising the specter of a revolution for which the development of the productive forces and the growth in living standards are secondary considerations, and wanting to make their lives as human beings at last worth living.

But is that really a contradiction? And, if so, is it not inherent in the phenomenon of the so-called 'ultra-Left' rather than in Marcuse's analysis? Has the philosopher not simply observed and reflected it? It is a fact that the radical movement which, to take France as an example, emerged from May 68 is oscillating between a return to the classical sources of the socialist class struggle and a longing to put into practice new, higher and more ambitious (some will say more chimeric) forms of refusal, since it sets itself the goal, no more nor less, of 'changing existence'.

The first attitude, which flows from the traditional revolutionary heritage, is capable, to some degree, of facilitating a future reconciliation of 'ultra-Leftism' with the working class and giving the former the hope of being accepted and listened to by the latter. In France that is the risky bet made by the supporters of Alain Krivine and the daily paper *Rouge*. The second attitude, boldly innovative and less tainted with opportunism, runs the risk, on the other hand, of perpetuating, if not actually increasing, the incomprehension of the workers, who are put off by what is presented to them as the eccentricity of bearded, long-haired kids in dirty jeans. That is the impression conveyed by some of the articles in the daily *Libération* or other publications of the same ilk.

But, over and above these difficulties, contradictions, failures and differences, what counts more than anything is whether or not it is possible to infuse the radical consciousness attained by the rebellious minorities into the working masses. Marcuse has the merit of being a materialist and not an idealist. And, for this transfer to be able to take place, 'the capitalist economy would have to come to be critically weakened'.

The subjective wish of marginal vanguards to transform the world and change the pattern of existence 'may assume material force in conjunction with the objective economic and political strains to which the system will be exposed on a global scale. Then, and only then, that political climate would prevail which could provide a mass basis for the new forms of organization required for directing the struggle.'

Therefore, in countries such as France, the philosopher strongly reproaches the Communist Party for helping to *inhibit* rather than *promote* the growth of a radical political consciousness among its working-class following.

But, even if we had use of a telescope, where nowadays could we see, apart from a recession which is tending to be resolved, those miraculous upheavals which would endanger world capitalism?

The same negative observation can be made as regards the United States in particular, for, despite ever present inflation and unemployment, the system, stimulated by arms expenditure, remains fairly stable and coherent. Far from dying, it has lately been trumpeting news of a 'recovery'. There are hardly any signs on the horizon (not yet anyway) of the economic tensions and the political climate which – 'then, and only then' – would enable the radical minorities to draw the working class into anti-capitalist struggle.

Furthermore, those American minority groups in whom the philosopher saw, in 1969, the harbingers of a new 'humanism', and the bearers of the 'enlightenment' which precedes historical change, happen to have been in sharp retreat in recent years. Their practice of demonstrations, confrontations and rebellions, which had a great impact for a time, already belongs to a bygone past. It had been stimulated and pushed to its height by the massive protests against the Vietnam war which mobilized the student youth as well as the boys in uniform and the vanguard of the labor movement. Then again, the Black revolt, after starting from dramatic urban riots and developing into armed struggle against the police, has now been demobilized. The effective end of the Panthers, brought about by savage repression and the elimination or cooption of their leaders, has created a big vacuum. Renouncing frontal attack, black and white militants are now challenging the system only indirectly and surreptitiously, through social welfare activities or attempts at self-management on the reduced scale of the neighborhood and the small community.

The increase in urban delinquency, particularly in the big cities is not at the moment leading to political radicalization. Neither can it be said that the few violent struggles of the Indian survivors of the genocide, such as the one at Wounded Knee, South Dakota (winter 1974), or even the localized struggles of the Chicanos, mark the entry of the 'ghetto population' into the pre-revolutionary arena.

While the integration of the working masses into the system continues, the catalysts and detonators which, according to the philosopher, were to promote the growth of a radical political consciousness among the workers have not shown up in the present period. One of Marcuse's mistaken prognoses was doubtless his over-estimation, in the dizziness of the radical turbulence which punctuated the Sixties, of the spearhead role of the marginal groups. In the end it is to Labor, that enormous numerical mass on which, as the philosopher moreover acknowledges, the world's most powerful productive apparatus is based, that we must turn our attention today. Social observation must be refocused on Labor after losing sight of it too much for a period.

Because it is very clear that socialism – a libertarian form of socialism, as envisaged by Eldridge Cleaver in his revolutionary years – could never ever triumph in the United States without the consent and the active will of at least the advanced wing of the working class. At no time does Marcuse distinguish the traditionally most reactionary sections of Labor from those which, in the relatively recent past, have shown themselves to be the most progressive and combative. For, on the one hand, as noted, we have the craft unionism of the ex-AFL, the heir to Gompersist corporatism, whose egoism, lack of solidarity and inveterate conservatism, so characteristic of labor aristocracies, is well known; and, on the other hand, we have industrial unionism, brought into existence by the ex-CIO, which, by virtue of its very structures and the key industrial sectors in which it has succeeded in taking root, is led to practice workers' solidarity and a certain degree of racial tolerance, and has even today not lost all its fighting spirit. And that is despite two serious handicaps: firstly, it, too, is bureaucratized and integrated, though less so than the craft unions; secondly, as already pointed out, since trade-union unification the conservatism of the craft unions has somewhat taken the sting out of the industrial unions' combativity.

By way of conclusion, may the reader excuse the author for a vestige of optimism, which a fresh reading of his own book and a re-examination of the present, however bleak it may be in immediate terms, have not completely shaken. The outlook for American Labor is perhaps not as overcast as one might fear. How can one refrain from hoping, along with old Engels, that the day the awakened giant stirs, as a result of suddenly losing confidence in the capitalist system, it will be 'with an energy and virulence' in comparison with which 'we in Europe will be children'? Because capitalism on the other side of the Atlantic is the keystone of world capitalism, the American revolution, still invisible today, could well be, when its hour strikes, the most violent, extensive and formidable revolution of all time.

CHAPTER 1

From the Knights of Labor to the IWW

The First Union Federation (1866-1873)

There have been two clearly distinct periods in the history of the American Labor movement: the first stretches from the foundation of the United States to the industrial revolution which followed the victory of the North in the Civil War; the second, which alone concerns us here, opens with the arrival of the great industrial Barons upon the scene and the mass influx of immigrants. Working-class revolt against the monopolies really takes off with the latter.

As a preamble, mention should be made of an attempt to establish a national trade-union movement in the United States. This organization, the National Labor Union, was formed in 1886, and a year later it adopted statutes and affiliated to the First International. On account of its poverty, however, the young organization was unable to send any delegates to the Lausanne Congress of the First International Working Men's Association.* The moving force behind it was William H. Sylvis (1828-1869), the first great American trade-union leader. He had come out of a casters' union in Philadelphia and had taken the initiative in organizing an International Union among the workers of that trade. As there was not yet a federation which could unite the different International Unions and the existing local unions, Sylvis was one of those who understood the necessity of such a body. He died prematurely, at the age of 41, and the National Labor Union survived him by only a few years: it collapsed in 1873 in the upheaval caused by a severe economic crisis.

The First Rising (1877)

Big capital had sunk its first roots in the railroad industry. Between 1870 and 1880, Jay Cooke, Jay Gould, Cornelius

*This body was set up in 1864 on the initiative of the London Trades Council and French workers, mainly followers of Proudhon. Throughout its existence Karl Marx played a crucial role. The defeat of the Paris Commune in 1871 and the faction fight with the supporters of Bakunin led to the Internationale's virtual demise, aided by Marx, and its official winding up in 1876 [Ed.].

Vanderbilt and James Hill had built up vast railroad empires. At that time the railroad companies were the largest employers in the country – the largest and also the most universally loathed, not only by those they exploited, but also by those who used their services.

And so the first significant revolt against Big Business was a revolt of railroad employees, supported by the mass of the population. And it took place at a time when the yoke of the big monopolies was pressing particularly heavily on the wage-earners – during a long period of economic stagnation opened up by the 1873 panic. The wages of the railroad workers, already cut by ten per cent in 1873, were reduced by the same percentage again in 1877. The workers responded with a wave of insurrectionary strikes in New York, Baltimore, Saint Louis and a number of other cities. The movement spread to the West Coast. In Pittsburgh, the Pennsylvania State militia, which had fired on the crowds, killing twenty people, was besieged by the rioters and had to evacuate the city under heavy fire. For two days the insurgents were in control of the situation. Bourgeois 'public opinion' was struck with dismay and spoke of a new 'Paris Commune'.

In Chicago, a strike by railroad employees at the freight station developed into a general strike. The same thing happened in Saint Louis where, for a few days, the workers, black and white, were masters of the city. One local paper wrote that what was occurring was not a mere strike, but a workers' revolution. P Foner, the American labor historian, has observed,[1] '. . . in St Louis (the strike) developed into a systematically organized shutdown of all industry – *the first truly general strike in history*'.

The movement was elemental and spontaneous, but the masses linked up with the conscious vanguard, the socialist party, which at that point was called the Working Men's Party. In Chicago, the party, led by Albert R Parsons, the future 'Chicago martyr', was instrumental in the success of the general strike. The repression hit the party leaders. But it was in Saint Louis that the leadership of the movement passed most clearly into the hands of the socialists. They were responsible both for initiating the strike and for extending it into a general stoppage. The strike committee, which ran the city for several days, was under their control.

For the first time since the Presidency of Andrew Jackson,

not only the State militias but also Federal troops were used for the repression of strikes. The 1877 revolt advanced the spirit of solidarity and the class consciousness of the working masses. The railroad workers were organized into craft 'Brotherhoods', which maintained a jealous independence from each other: there was the mechanics' Brotherhood, the firemen's, the engineers', etc. But in Pittsburgh a railroad workers' union was set up on the eve of the strike, incorporating all crafts into a single organization.

Even more significantly, the revolt heralded an unprecedented unity between skilled and unskilled workers as the factory proletariat, still unorganized, fought side by side with the trainmen.

The Knights of Labor

In 1878, a number of socialists formed an International Labor Union, with the intention of organizing the unskilled workers on an industry-wide rather than a craft-wide basis. They succeeded in unionizing a few thousand textile workers, notably in Hoboken, Paterson and Fall River, New Jersey, but the results of their efforts were short-lived. The fight was resumed a few years later, this time with great success, by another organization: the Order of the Knights of Labor.

Created in 1878,* the Knights of Labor had been engaged for a long time in mole-like work, which was conducted in strict and ritualistic secrecy due to repression by the employers and the Government. Their organizers had played an important but still concealed role in the great strike of 1877. From 1880 onwards, they emerged publicly and became a mass movement. They were able to adapt to the lightning development of heavy mechanized industry, which was reducing the mechanic to the level of a day laborer, absorbing workers of all races and ethnic backgrounds, and breaking down the boundaries between different jobs. Hence the need to create a new type of organization. They opened their doors to all workers, extolling human brotherhood and the solidarity of the exploited. 'An injury to one is an injury to all' was their

*In fact the first local assembly bearing this name was secretly organized in Philadelphia as far back as 1869. The first General Assembly of the Order was, however, in 1878 [Ed.].

motto. They were able to win the hearts of the humble, the crushed, the frustrated. They brought them not only material improvements, but an ideal.

The Great Rising (1884-1886)

Circumstances favored the Knights of Labor well beyond their expectations. A new economic crisis generating unemployment and poverty provoked a wave of rebellion, beginning with a series of rail strikes between 1884 and 1886, in which the combativity of the railroad workers was high. The movement spread to industries employing unskilled labor and recent immigrants. The success of most of these movements led to an influx of unskilled workers into the Knights of Labor. About 700,000 workers, most of them unskilled, joined up.

This great spontaneous movement was impregnated with socialist and revolutionary ideas. The elemental upsurge of the masses was guided by a conscious vanguard. Joseph R Buchanan, the Knights' organizer in the West, was linked to revolutionary internationalist socialism.

The great rising reached its climax in the battle for the Eight Hour Day, which began on 1 May 1886, and which was the first attempt to stage a general strike at a national level in the United States. The initiative did not come from the Knights of Labor, but from the trade unions, which were prodded into action by the competition they were facing from the Knights. However, having left the means for carrying out their decision undefined, the trade unions applied it rather half-heartedly, since they had neither sufficient numbers nor adequate financial resources to carry it into effect. It was the Knights of Labor, their members and their local organizers (in the absence of their national leadership, which came out against the movement) who, to a considerable degree, ensured its success.

The agitation for the Eight Hour Day found its most conscious expression in the city which at that time was in the vanguard of the American Labor movement: Chicago. In that metropolis there was an active nucleus of revolutionary socialists with libertarian leanings. They had broken away from the socialist party (Socialist Labor Party) because they no longer believed in the efficacy of the ballot box and placed the emphasis on direct action and armed struggle. Under the influence of the International Anarchist Congress,* which was held in London in 1881, and of Johann Most, a German revolutionary socialist-turned-anarchist, who arrived in the United States in 1882, they created a revolutionary party, the International Working People's Association in 1883. Attitudes within the organization towards the trade-union movement varied quite a bit. The most sectarian of them (among whom was Most) had a tendency to underestimate wage struggles, while the others (the Chicago group) argued the need to link up with movements of the masses. At first they turned a deaf ear to the Eight Hour Day campaign, which they characterized as a 'compromise with wage labor'. But the Chicago group, which had strong connections in the local unions, finally threw in its lot with the movement and assumed the leadership of it. Without its energetic intervention, the movement would doubtless have ended in a fiasco. But it succeeded beyond all expectations.

1 May 1886 had been designated as the date on which the eight hours were to come into effect. Out of 350,000 workers who struck throughout the country during the first two weeks of May, 40,000 were from Chicago. On 1 May and the following days there were imposing mass demonstrations in the city. The bourgeoisie, frightened by the wave of rebellion, was panic-stricken and decided to decapitate the movement by means of a bloody provocation if necessary. On 4 May 1886 a bomb mysteriously thrown at police officers' legs during a street meeting in Haymarket Square provided the desired pretext. The leaders of the revolutionary socialist movement were arrested, condemned to death and finally hanged. Here our story moves beyond the confines of the American labor movement. For since that time, the Chicago martyrs – Parsons, Fischer, Engel, Spies and Lingg – belong to the international proletariat, and the universal celebration of May Day commemorates the atrocious crime perpetrated by the knights-errant of 'free enterprise' in the United States.

*This regrouped Bakunin's forces after Marx had successfully moved at the Hague Congress of the First International in 1872 that its headquarters be transferred to New York. However, the Anarchist International did not last long, never developed a coherent unity and the 1881 Congress was its last [Ed.].

The Decline of The Knights of Labor

The great popular torrent which, for a moment, had aroused deep fears among the propertied classes soon spent itself. The savage repression and anti-working-class terror which followed the Haymarket bomb contributed to the movement's defeat. The Chicago group were not the only ones to be hounded by the bourgeoisie; the Knights of Labor were persecuted, driven out of their jobs and placed on black-lists, while Pinkerton detectives (named after Allan Pinkerton, who had formed a private police agency specialized, in particular, in the art of strikebreaking) were unleashed against them.

The Order could have resisted if it had been built on solid foundations. But such was not the case. The organization had grown too quickly. It had recruited workers who, because they were for the most part unskilled, were ignorant and who were heterogeneous by virtue of ethnic and linguistic differences; besides, the organization had not held them for very long. And, further, it had not wholly freed itself from a Utopianism which had been, at least initially, the characteristic feature of the workers, in the United States as much as in Europe: the hope of escaping wage labor, becoming their own masters and liberating themselves through the creation of producer co-operatives, through cheap credit, etc.

The Knights' petty-bourgeois mentality led them – especially after the decline of the great workers' rising of 1886 – to admit non-wage-earners, shopkeepers, small producers, members of the professions and even farmers into membership. By a curious paradox, the Knights of Labor were at once progressive and retrogressive. They were in tune with their time – and even ahead of it – when they grasped the necessity of organizing the unskilled workers, responding to the concentration of the employers with workers' solidarity and exploding the old craft boundaries, which were being daily dislocated in any case by technological advance. But they were pitting themselves against time when they persistently dreamed of escaping the wage-earning condition and signed up non-wage-earners, while the industrial revolution was more and more dividing society into two camps: the bosses and the workers. In addition, they were led by an old reformist of limited intelligence, Terence V Powderly, who displayed combativity only when he was pushed forward by the mass movement, but who was fundamentally hostile to strikes.

Finally, the Knights of Labor failed on a decisive point: they did not succeed in finding a solution to the problem of the relationship between skilled and unskilled workers. The representatives of the skilled workers accused the Knights of seeking less to serve them than to make use of them in order to strengthen the position of the unskilled. As it happens, this accusation was ill-founded: in more than one case the Knights placed their organization, which drew its numerical strength from the unskilled, at the service of the specific demands of the skilled workers.

However, the Knights did not give much importance in the structure of their organization to trades. Certainly they organized them, not only on a local, but also on a national basis; but although the statutes provided for the admission of national unions organized along trade lines, few such bodies were affiliated to the Knights, and those that were were not looked upon with great favor. The preference of the Knights of Labor went to mixed local assemblies, which were like union coalitions; these constituted the essential basis of the Order.

Nevertheless, there was no real incompatibility structure-wise between the Knights of Labor and the skilled workers' Internationals. It was simply that they were in competition for the affiliation of local trade-union sections. In fact, at the height of their success, the Knights were such a strong force of attraction that local craft unions passed over to them lock, stock and barrel. Those Internationals not affiliated to the Knights, and having a total membership of 140,000 in 1886 (as opposed to 700,000 Knights), very much disapproved of this nibbling. In particular, relations deteriorated when the Knights of Labor brought into their Order a New York cigar-makers' union which had rebelled against its national leader, one Samuel Gompers. In 1881, in a self-defensive reflex, Gompers united the craft Internationals into a federation which, to begin with, involved nothing more than an annual meeting. In 1886 he formed a real trade-union federation – the American Federation of Labor (AFL) – and declared open war on the Knights of Labor.

This split cut off the skilled from the unskilled for several generations. In the conflict between the principles of workers' solidarity and corporate egoism, the latter triumphed. The Knights disintegrated as much from the blows directed at them by their rivals and the bosses as from their own failings. Meanwhile, Gompers was setting up solid and lasting organizations of privileged workers, realistically, if cynically, based on the narrow layer of a labor aristocracy. This layer of workers, exclusively preoccupied with their own caste interests, turned a blind eye to people in other trades, even fighting them on occasion. Worse still, they deliberately abandoned and refused to organize the mass of those exploited by American big business: the unskilled workers.

Gompersism

Gompers, in his Memoirs,[2] claimed kinship with Karl Marx. 'He (Marx) grasped the principle that the trade-union was the immediate and practical agency which could bring wage-earners a better life . . . he urged the formation of trade-unions and the use of them to deal with the problems of the labor movement.'

But it was tendentious of him to invoke such patronage. Gompers' trade-unionism had very little in common with trade-unionism as it was conceived and propagated by Marx and the First International. It lacked the fundamental principle on which the latter was based: class solidarity. The reformist leader also tried to create the impression that he took as his model the British trade unions. He did, it is true, borrow a few organizational concepts from the British, particularly the idea of high dues and benefits (and even then only some British unions were benefit societies), but his conception was a good deal more exclusive and rigid than that of the British Trade Union Congress.

What Gompers took from Britain had indeed existed there, but forty years earlier. British trade-unionism had since that time shown remarkable flexibility in adapting to the development of industry, opening its doors wide to the unskilled, creating organizations with lower dues for them, amalgamating craft unions, and avoiding a rigid separation by not granting any of its national unions privileges of 'jurisdiction'. Finally, British trade-unionism, unlike Gompers' version of it, was permeated with the spirit of class solidarity.

Gompersism was based on the idea that the skilled worker, being a scarce and sought-after commodity must make himself still more so by organizing into a craft union which would jealously guard its gates against newcomers. Thus protected, he would sell his skills at the highest possible price, worrying neither about other skilled workers, who also enjoyed a monopoly guaranteed by constitutive charter, nor about unskilled workers, who were abandoned to their sad fate. This conception was harmful to the skilled workers themselves, since it isolated them from and pitted them against each other. Since each craft union was linked to the employers by agreements expiring on different dates, no trade wanted to risk breaking a current agreement in order to rush to the help of another trade which was on strike. Thus while one group was fighting, the others would stand aside, refusing to give any assistance; in this way each group would be defeated separately.

The trade-union federation, as it was conceived by Gompers, had scarcely any degree of centralization nor the right to impose any united action on the different craft Internationals which were affiliated to it. As for local trade-union coalitions, which formed the essential basis of the Knights of Labor, they had no power in the AFL compared to the craft Internationals. In such conditions, a sympathetic general strike, whether local or national, becomes very difficult to organize; even more so that kind of strike whose objectives go further than an immediate question of daily bread, a struggle for a demand of a higher order, which concerns the entire working class. Furthermore, the refusal to organize the unskilled has boomeranged on the skilled; for the bosses, the mass of unorganized workers have made up a reserve army of strikebreakers who have been thrown into the fray whenever the skilled workers have downed tools. Lastly, the very notion of a monopoly has provoked friction and fratricidal conflict between different trades. They have each laid claim to such and such a group of workers and have gone so far as to engage in long, costly, and often bloody strikes in order to impose their 'jurisdiction' on rival trades.

In addition, Gompersism has unfailingly led to class collaboration, corruption, and even gangsterism. First of all, the craft monopoly and the very large number of craft unions rapidly gave rise to a bureaucracy of trade-union 'high-priests'. The official term for these full-timers, borrowed from the vocabulary of capitalism, is *business agents*. That, in fact, is what they are. Their only function is to sell their membership's labor power to the employers as expensively as possible, maintain their monopoly by any means necessary, including the use of physical violence, and live exorbitantly thanks to high membership dues and bribes taken both from the employers and from their own members. This bureaucracy has become a formidable vehicle for preventing social change, tied as it is to the established order and committed to its maintenance.

Moreover the privileges enjoyed by the very skilled workers, their petty-bourgeois lifestyle, their financial investments, mortgages, life-insurance policies, and so forth have inclined them to favor the capitalist system. Actually, Gompersism described its own practice as trade-unionism 'pure and simple'. Although it acknowledged the existence of a struggle between capital and labor, its objective was never the abolition of wage labor and its intentions did not include the transformation of society.

For their part, the employers went along quite happily with Gompers' brand of trade-unionism. A strong craft union working hand in hand with the employers' organization helped to stabilize the corporation and eliminate competition. Besides, anything which divides the working class works to the bosses' advantage. They feared nothing so much as the organization of the mass of the unskilled; they saw craft unions as a safeguard against mass trade-unionism, business unionism as a bulwark against social revolution. In exchange for the services rendered by Gompers, who ignored the pariahs of manufacturing industry and fought socialism, they were ready to toss the highly skilled workers a few crumbs from their banquet.

But the biggest indictment of Gompersism, without any doubt at all, is the fact that, through its neglectful selfishness, the organization of the workers in manufacturing industry exploited by the big corporations was delayed by fifty years. Gompers and his friends tried to make out that the entry of the unskilled workers into the trade unions was impossible. The AFL hypocritically advanced the theory that each group was responsible for organizing itself. If, it was argued, a group could not display sufficient energy and spirit of sacrifice to organize itself successfully with a minimal degree of outside help, its admission into the family of organized labor would be of dubious value.

This ideological excuse, which was advanced as a justification for indifference towards the unorganized, was prettified by a word borrowed from philosophical jargon: 'voluntarism'. The theory, which at first sight seems to pride itself on its lofty morality, and which even has a libertarian ring about it, does not stand up to examination if one considers the example of the mass production industries. What initiative could be expected from workers left to themselves in the face of powerful monopolies with millions of dollars at their disposal to smash any attempt to organize? Only an outside intervention, a centralized recruitment campaign, backed up by large sums of money, provided by those labor unions which were already established, could enable trade-unionism to take root in those industries (albeit with a risk of bureaucratization in cases where organization takes place from above and from the outside, as will be seen).

As for the argument that the unskilled were hostile to unionization, later events were to demonstrate its falsity; doubtless the unstable and precarious conditions of these workers, their ethnic and linguistic heterogeneity, and the boss and police terror which they experienced in the industrial prisons of Big Business and the company towns made them more difficult to recruit than the skilled workers. But it was not impossible for the trade-union movement to assimilate them. In fact their very exploitation meant that their class consciousness often proved more advanced than that of the skilled workers. It was Gompers and his cronies in the AFL who were the main obstacle to organizing the unskilled workers, not the latter themselves. The high admission fees, and the doors kept jealously closed to them, prevented them from joining the craft unions. And no attempt was made to recruit them in any other way.

The AFL bureaucracy, eager to perpetuate itself, feared being swamped by a sudden invasion of workers from heavy industry. Moreover, to organize them would have required costly campaigns and the craft unions, blinded by their selfishness and their stinginess, were loath to invest their money in 'philanthropic' ventures. Finally, the very structure of craft unionism made it extremely difficult to organize the workers in heavy industry: having permitted them to sign up as members, the AFL bureaucrats split them up and allocated them to several dozen craft unions. That, after a fashion, is what happened from 1919 onwards, as will be seen.

However, Gompersism was not accepted passively and without resistance by the American working class. A number of attempts were made to promote a trade-unionism based on the opposite principle: organization on the basis of industry, and not craft egoism and collaboration with the bosses. Sometimes these attempts succeeded, sometimes they ended in failure. But the energy spent on these occasions was never spent in vain; the class consciousness of the American proletariat was raised each time; Gompersism was obliged to do violence to its principles and make a few concessions (quite inadequate, to be sure) to those conceptions which it had sought to deny and banish.

Debs and the American Railway Union

The first such attempt was made on the railroads. The trade-unionism of the railroad workers was a combination of Gompersism and something still worse. Of the twenty or so different craft organizations among which the railroaders were divided, the majority were in fact affiliated to the AFL. But the most important unions, in terms of the crafts they covered, remained jealously outside the federation. Known as Brotherhoods, they were more mutual insurance societies than trade unions organized for economic struggle; their outlook was so exclusive and reactionary that Gompers' federation appeared relatively militant by comparison. In addition, the Brotherhoods waged fratricidal war on each other. And even when, laying aside for a moment their blind egoism, they managed to reach agreement on some point, one Brotherhood, the organization of the most skilled workers, the locomotive engineers, persistently clung to a haughty and contemptuous isolation.

This situation rapidly appeared intolerable and disastrous to a man who had been one of the founders of the Locomotive Firemen's Brotherhood and had devoted all the ardor of his youth to the organization: Eugene V Debs. As early as 1885 he had been delegated by his Brotherhood to the Brotherhood of Locomotive Engineers' convention, so as to try and cooperate with the latter; but 'his proposal of friendship never reached the convention floor'. As a result of this experience, he wrote a seethingly restrained article against the arrogant chief of the engineers, P M Arthur, under the title: 'The Aristocracy of Labor', and began to campaign in favor of unity of action among the railroad workers' organizations.[3]

In 1889, Debs succeeded in setting up a Supreme Council of the united orders of railroad employees. But the new organization was from the start seriously handicapped by the engineers' refusal to join it. Furthermore, it was not long before it was torn apart by a quarrel about 'jurisdiction' between the workers who actually worked on the rolling stock and the other participating organizations. The Supreme Council had to be dissolved in 1892.

During that same summer, another class battle took place, which made a profound impression on Debs as indeed it did on the whole of the American working class. The steel magnate, Andrew Carnegie, had entrusted the management of his enterprises to a pugnacious employer and a fierce adversary of workers' trade-unionism, Henry Clay Frick. The iron and steel workers were covered by a craft International, the Amalgamated Association of Iron and Steel Workers, which, with 25,000 members, was then the most powerful organization in the American labor movement. Frick deliberately provoked it, with the clear intention of destroying it. He suddenly cut the wages of the 4,000 workers at his steel mills in Pittsburgh, Pennsylvania. The workers went on strike on 29 June. Frick then hired 300 Pinkerton detectives and transported them by boat to the Homestead factories, which lay along a river. The workers, forewarned of their arrival and hurriedly armed, supported by the whole population, prevented them from reaching the river-bank. The detectives were beaten and driven back. Blood flowed on both sides. Other Pittsburgh steel mills struck in solidarity. The State militia occupied the town. After several months of struggle the workers had to go back to work. Their union was eliminated from most of the steel mills in the Pittsburgh area.

It was both a defeat and a victory. The heroic resistance of the workers, and the guts with which the armed workers had thrown the Pinkerton detectives into the river, 'sound(ed)', as the American anarchist Emma Goldman noted,[4] 'the awakening of the American worker, the long-awaited day of his resurrection'. Emma's companion, the young anarchist Alexander Berkman, succeeded in breaking into Frick's office and fired a revolver at him. He did not manage to kill him, and received a fifteen-year jail sentence for his action.

The Homestead tragedy threw Eugene Debs into a state of 'intense excitement'. He wrote that 'it would serve to link the workers' organizations into closer union and that it would awaken all American workers to the meaning of the dangers with which they were threatened'.

The economic panic of 1893 followed soon after, giving rise to unemployment and poverty, radicalizing the masses, and making the workers more combative. Debs 'seized the time' and drew the lesson from the previous struggles. He resigned from the Brotherhood which had been his life-work and which gave him a comfortable wage in order to create a new organization, with an industrial rather than a craft basis: the American Railway Union (ARU). The leaders of the craft Internationals felt their fiefs and privileges to be threatened. Gompers was, in his own words, 'genuinely shocked'. He denounced the new organization as divisive.

The new organization was welcomed by the workers, particularly by the unskilled and the unorganized, with such eagerness that even its founders were surprised. Never had the railroad workers shown so much enthusiasm. The new organization developed so quickly that it suffered from a shortage of experienced organizers. Yet it was barely on its feet when it won the laurels of victory: in April 1894 it felt strong enough to take on the powerful railroad magnate, James J Hill, and launched strike action on his network, the Great Northern. The leaders of the craft Brotherhoods naturally opposed the action or adopted an attitude of hostile neutrality. But the 9,000 company employees fought as one man and James Hill was forced to capitulate to Eugene Debs.

In one year Debs signed up 150,000 members, whereas all the Brotherhoods combined had no more than 90,000 members and the railroad unions affiliated to the AFL had trouble holding on to their membership of 175,000.

The Pullman Strike (1894)

But Debs was hardly in the saddle when he was thrown off by a powerful coalition of the employers, the forces of Government repression, the leaders of the Brotherhoods and, to cap it all, Samuel Gompers.

In May 1894 the workers in the George M Pullman workshops (Pullman pioneered and also monopolized the production of the American sleeping car) rebelled against a series of wage cuts which had been imposed as a consequence of the economic crisis. They lived in a company town just outside Chicago named after and entirely dominated by their employer. The majority of them had just joined the American Railway Union. Although they had begun their strike without consulting the organization, the latter considered it its duty to support them. Debs, who knew all the shortcomings of his young industrial union – its inexperience, its lack of organizers and shortage of funds – desperately tried to reach an amicable settlement. Pullman's intransigence forced Debs to take the path of struggle. He appealed to the railroad workers for solidarity and ordered a boycott of sleeping-cars, which meant a strike on all lines not agreeing to take the Pullman cars off their trains. Most of the Brotherhoods opposed the boycott and tried to smash the action. If they had supported it, the strike would undoubtedly have been won. Many members of the Brotherhoods did, however, make common cause with the strikers, even though their leaders had forbidden them to do so. More than 100,000 men stopped work and the boycott was spreading all the time.

The prospects were favorable. The sympathy of the population sustained the strikers, who were the masters of the situation, and the movement seemed certain to succeed. It was then that the Federal Government rushed to the help of the employers. Using the Sherman Antitrust Act of 1890, a law which had been passed for use against the trusts and not against the labor movement, the Government issued an injunction against the strike leaders instructing them to call off the boycott. At the same time masses of strikebreakers were recruited by the companies, and the President of the United States, Grover Cleveland, in spite of the protests of Governor Altgeld of Illinois, sent Federal troops into Chicago. These provocations enraged the strikers. Violence and destruction ensued. Blood flowed.

Debs and his associates were served with an injunction. The entire Chicago labor movement felt the affront. The city's trade-union coalition (AFL) called for a general strike, a call which was heeded to some extent, and urged the federation to convene a meeting of its Executive Council in Chicago right away. Gompers, who had been conspicuous from the outset by his neutrality, obliged and came personally to deliver the *coup de grâce* to the great movement. He had the Executive Council condemn the idea of a general strike and order all those who had struck in solidarity to return to work. The Chicago trade-union coalition had to call off the general strike. The movement collapsed. Debs and the leaders of the ARU were thrown into jail. The American Railway Union did not survive the defeat and the persecutions which its members suffered on the various networks. Debs, meditating in his cell on the causes of its defeat, became a socialist.

John Mitchell and the Anthracite Miners

After laying its foundations on the railroads, American big business extended its power by gaining a monopoly over the anthracite mines. There were several reasons for this: firstly, unlike pit-coal, which can be found in nearly 30 States, anthracite is concentrated in five fairly small counties in Pennsylvania. Furthermore, since the deposits lay deep down, mining them required the investment of very large sums of capital. Finally, the Eastern railroad companies, which commanded considerable funds, were interested in anthracite because this fuel was the main commodity they transported.

So seven or eight railroad companies between them acquired ownership of the mining basins of Pennsylvania. The king of American finance, J Pierpont Morgan, after getting rid of the smallest owners, amalgamated the mines into one powerful monopoly around the Philadelphia and Reading Coal and Iron Company, and was thus able, by eliminating competition, to increase the selling price of anthracite.

If the dictatorship of Big Business was to be defeated, it was necessary, after organizing the railroad workers, to go on to unionize the anthracite miners – a difficult task. The miners were as divided as the bosses were united. Economic divisions between the skilled and the unskilled, and ethnic and religious divisions, reinforced each other. The skilled workers were the long-settled, English-speaking workers (English, Welsh, Scots and Irish). The unskilled workers were the recent immigrants, who had arrived *en masse* since 1880 from Southern and Eastern Europe. Mostly Slavs or Italians, they were themselves subdivided into some twenty ethnic groups, each with its own language and church.

In addition, these still largely unassimilated 'foreigners'

had been imported in thousands as strike-breakers during the defeated strikes of 1875 and 1887. They had a reputation for being content with an extremely low standard of living and accepting the worst working conditions without complaint.

The young President of the American miners' International Union, John Mitchell, undertook to organize the 150,000 anthracite miners. He was not yet 30 and had just proven himself by leading a strike of pit-miners in 1897, the first nation-wide victory won by the American miners.

When he made contact with the anthracite basins, the skilled workers tried to convince him of the inanity of his venture. They told him that the unskilled, the 'foreigners', could not be organized, that they were ignorant and coarse, and that they lived like animals, with five families crammed into one decrepit hovel which would not have been considered suitable accommodation for even one 'American' family. But this pessimism concealed self-interest (or rather what, in their blindness, they took to be self-interest): they were determined to use any and every means to prevent the 'foreigners' becoming skilled miners; in a world of poverty and frustration they were trying to preserve for themselves as much social prestige as possible.

John Mitchell was formed not in the school of Gompersism, but in that of the Knights of Labor. His union had largely come out of the Knights and had inherited from them the notion of class solidarity. He had wielded the miner's pick since the age of nine. Although he had recently been elected President of his organization, he still belonged, in his mentality and behavior, to the rank and file. Moreover, he was an organizational genius. He understood how to go about organizing workers in mass-production industry. He could have staked everything on the skilled workers, the English-speaking miners. Such an attitude would not only have won him their support, but also the enthusiastic approval of Gompers and the leaders of the craft unions. He rejected this easy solution.

Mitchell understood that, in order to succeed in organizing those exploited by the anthracite monopoly, he had to gain the support of the recent immigrants. He first turned to the few local leaders he could find among the English-speaking miners. But he not only asked them to work within their own group; he also entrusted them with the task of discovering and training leaders among the 'foreigners'. He took to the field himself, interviewing every possible candidate, checking the man's references with the local foreign-language associations, the various lodges and the clergy. When he found capable organizers he placed them on an equal footing with those whose language was English.

Indefatigable, he went up and down the mining districts, haranguing the miners in halls or in the open air, addressing them from church pulpits, finding his way into their homes. Everywhere he urged them to lay aside their ethnic antagonisms and everything which divided them. The 'foreigner' was to be looked down upon no more. He too was a miner and a brother-in-suffering: 'The coal which you extract,' he would say to them, 'is not Slav, Polish, or Irish, it's simply coal'. Turning to the English-speaking miners, 'who lacked consideration for those who did not speak English', he asked them 'to cease these practices and to give these foreigners as much consideration as they claimed for themselves'.

But that was not all. Mitchell understood the influence which their church ministers and foreign-language journalists had over these men. He visited each priest or minister, pleading the union cause. As might have been expected, he found the greatest response among the lower ranks of the Catholic clergy, who were in close contact with these immigrants from Europe and were dependent on their support.

Mitchell succeeded so well in his venture that, by the following year, he was able to take on the anthracite employers in a big strike, which lasted a month, and ended in a clear victory. The International Union, which had some 8,000 members before the battle, came out of it with over 100,000.

Thus, on the basis of industrial trade-unionism and the systematic organization of the immigrants, was established once and for all the powerful International Union which has remained to this day the backbone of the American labor movement, and which served as a model for all future efforts to organize the workers in manufacturing industry.

But Mitchell's very success, and the fact that he had managed to unite into one organization the most highly skilled workers – engineers, pumpmen, drivers, carpenters and blacksmiths – as well as the immigrant unskilled workers, made him enemies. The craft Internationals, which claimed 'jurisdiction' over each of these groups and, behind them, the

American Federation of Labor raised their voices in protest.

After long negotiations a compromise was reached. The AFL could not risk losing such an important organization as that of the miners. At the Scranton Congress, in 1901, Mitchell received permission to include the disputed crafts in his International Union. But this was only an exceptional concession and the fundamental principle of Gompersism – the autonomy of each craft – was simultaneously reaffirmed.

Unfortunately, the militant period of John Mitchell's life was over in a flash. This new force was very quickly blunted and corrupted by big business. The industrialists had entrusted the defense of their interests to an intelligent and versatile man, Mark Hanna, the *deus ex machina* of the Republican Party. Hanna understood that workers' trade-unionism could no longer be smashed by the combined action of strike-breakers, Pinkerton detectives and the forces of Government repression. He saw organized labor as an irresistible new force with which it was wiser and smarter to compromise. He thought that by flattering it and making a few concessions to it, organized labor could be domesticated. He called its leaders 'the labor lieutenants of the captains of industry'. He succeeded in overcoming the resistance of many short sighted businessmen and winning the banker who dominated the world of Big Business – J P Morgan – to his views. By 1899 he had persuaded the master of Wall Street to deal with John Mitchell. In 1902, strengthened by his previous success, he convinced Mitchell to accept arbitration by the President of the United States, at a time when a second strike was already virtually won and a solidarity strike of all the miners, to which John Mitchell objected, would have further reinforced the position of the strikers.

This surrender generated a feeling of just anger with the President of the miners' International among the militants. In the wake of Gompersism, John Mitchell, too, was being drawn into class collaboration. In 1900 Mark Hanna had created the National Civic Federation, a mixed organization, composed of employers and labor leaders, of which John Mitchell eventually became a salaried official.

This development had serious consequences: John Mitchell, who, in terms of public opinion, had come to be almost on a par with Gompers, could no longer be the prestigious leader around whom all those who wanted to see the victory of industry-based, class-struggle trade-unionism, as against Gompersism, could unite. The miners' International could no longer serve as the jumping-off point for the organization of the unskilled and unorganized workers in manufacturing industry. Vanguard trade-unionists thought that the AFL could not be regenerated from the inside and that, if the organization of the unorganized, too long deferred, was to be carried through, it would have to be done from the outside.

In 1905 militants of various tendencies, who had all arrived at this conclusion, met to lay the basis for a new organization: the Industrial Workers of the World (better known by their initials: *IWW*). Among them were Eugene V Debs, for whom the new venture was to be[5] 'a far greater organization' than the American Railway Union; William Haywood, the leader of a metal-miners' organization in the West; Mary Jones, better known by the name of 'Mother' Jones, an exceptional woman who had devoted her life to the miners' union and, finally, Daniel De Leon, a revolutionary socialist who had long been bent on the organization of class-struggle unions.

By way of an introduction to the epic of the IWW, we shall sketch the background of several of their founders (with the exception of Debs, who is already familiar to the reader).

The Western Federation of Miners

Haywood's story is that of his organization, the Western Federation of Miners, which had been established in the West following the discovery of important deposits of gold, silver and copper in Idaho, Montana and Colorado in the eighties. The relationship between employers and employees in these distant territories was characterized by the violent ways of the frontier. Direct action prevailed over respect for the law. The bosses treated their workers like slaves. They expelled them from their camps and hunted them like wild beasts when there were strikes; they imported strike-breakers; against the miners they used not only their own armed guards, but also the local forces of law and order in their pay – the police and the State militia. The miners fought back with lead and dynamite, and mounted real military expeditions in support of their class brothers in other localities.

In 1893 the Western Federation, which had only just been created, found itself involved in a violent conflict. Following the economic crisis of 1893, the owners of the gold-mines in Cripple Creek, Colorado extended the length of the working day from eight to nine hours. At the beginning of 1894 the strike erupted. While the miners attacked certain mines and seized them in order to blow them up, the sheriff, acting on behalf of the employers, raised a private army of 1,200 men, which even included some cavalry. A long and bloody struggle ensued. The Governor had to interpose the State militia between the two belligerents.

In 1896 another battle took place, again in Colorado, but this time in the silver-mines at Leadville. The employers brought in strike-breakers who were attacked by the strikers, and a mine was destroyed. Leadville was occupied by the military. The struggle lasted for months and ended in defeat. The event had an important consequence: it led to the departure of the Western Federation of Miners from the American Federation of Labor, to which the former had affiliated in 1895. It sent delegates to the AFL congress in 1896, who asked for support for the Leadville strike and the adoption of a resolution urging workers not to enroll in the National Guard. The assembly approved of both motions, but did not decide on any practical steps to help the strikers.

But the Western miners could not remain isolated. Having broken with Gompersism, they had to find allies among the workers in their areas. In 1898 they organized a federation covering the West, from the Mississippi to the Pacific, called the Western Labor Union. Its objective was the organization, according to industry, of all wage earners, irrespective of occupation. Gompers angrily denounced this 'sectionalist' break-away enterprise. The struggle between the two trade-union federations grew acrimonious. Gompers' supporters threatened to organize all the Western States and wipe the Western Labor Union off the face of the earth if their opponents would not return to the fold and dissolve their own federation. In a self-defensive reflex the founders of the Western Labor Union decided to invade the Eastern United States and compete with the AFL. They changed their organization's name to the American Labor Union, which reached its zenith in 1903 but did not succeed in denting the AFL's influence in the East.

In 1896, William Haywood, who was working as a miner in Silver City (Idaho), began to play an active role in the Western

Federation. He soon became its secretary-treasurer and its life and soul. He took part with the organization in furious class battles between 1901 and 1904. He and his federation were to be the main pioneers of the new organization, the IWW. Fraternal links between the Western miners and the former leader of the railroad workers, Eugene V Debs, now a socialist, dated back to the time of the Western Federation's exit from the AFL. 'Big Bill' Haywood himself joined the Socialist Party in 1901.

Mother Jones

'Mother' Jones is a case all on her own. She was a sort of Flora Tristan or Louise Michel,* but magnified by the gargantuan character of the struggle in which she was involved, the size of the battlefield and the violence of the action. A personal tragedy lay at the origin of her militant career: her husband and her four children had died during a yellow fever epidemic. Finding no outlet for her feminine and motherly tenderness, she wanted to become the 'Mother' of all who toiled and suffered. Everywhere she went (and this indefatigable woman, always on the move, got around to a lot of places), men, women and children came to confide their troubles to her and ask her for advice.

But 'Mother' Jones was not a sentimentalist and she did not have the mentality of a confessor. Though she was burning with love for her brothers and sisters in poverty, she was, at the same time, an American pragmatist and a militant. She consoled not with words but with deeds. She did not provide her 'children' with vague hope. She told them how their liberation could come about: through organizing themselves. She inspired them with self-confidence and, regardless of fatigue, danger, prison and death, she stood at their head. Although, thanks to the solidarity of the lowly, she was practiced in the art of evading traps, thwarting surveillance, wriggling her way through the gaps in outstretched nets and popping up where

---

*Flora Tristan (1803-1844) was one of the earliest feminist activists in France. She campaigned for free love and the right to divorce. Among other works, her book *Workers' Unity* expressed the need for internationalist socialism.

Louise Michel (1830-1905), French revolutionary anarchist, took part in the Paris Commune as a member of the 1st International. She was deported to New Caledonia and eventually amnestied.

she was least expected, 'Mother' Jones felt the force of bourgeois repression many times.

This white-haired woman was in and out of more jails than any other American militant. But, at the same time, she commanded the respect of her enemies. She was a moral force. She compelled attention not only by her quiet courage, but also by her verve, her self-assurance and, above all, her *Americanism;* she was steeped in the democratic traditions which had shaped the United States, and she took them seriously. When she summoned these traditions to her aid, putting to shame those who brazenly violated them while speaking in their name, her opponents were at a loss for a reply to her accusations. Sheriffs, Governors and Senators stood in awe of her and could not help but admire her, even when she gave them all sorts of trouble and they put her under lock and key.

Like John Mitchell, 'Mother' Jones had been trained in the school of the Knights of Labor. She had helped John Mitchell organize the anthracite basins in Pennsylvania, giving all she had; she had commanded militias of miners' wives, armed with their oven rakes, who would move from one locality to the next to prevent men from scabbing. On one occasion she saved a group of miners who had been ambushed, by placing her hand on the muzzle of the gun-barrel and holding it in that perilous position until all the men had escaped and were safe and sound.

But, as has been said, John Mitchell's somersault revolted 'Mother' Jones and although she stayed on as organizer of the International Union, she strongly denounced the way in which its leader had accepted arbitration by President Theodore Roosevelt and fallen prey to class collaboration. Moreover, she had formed close links with the Western Federation of Miners, whose relations with John Mitchell were tense. William Haywood admired the industrial structure and the class spirit of the United Mine Workers, while disapproving of the reformist policy of John Mitchell. He dreamed of a fusion between the two organizations, which proved impossible so long as Mitchell insisted on keeping his within the orbit of Gompersism.

In the absence of unity 'Mother Jones' was the living link between the two Internationals. In addition, she represented the militant Left wing of the miners' International, one of the few unions in the AFL constituted on an industrial basis. So her presence at the founding convention of the IWW was naturally significant. As Debs remarked, 'Her very name expresses the spirit of the revolution'.[6]

Daniel De Leon

Daniel De Leon, a West Indian-born teacher, came from a totally different background. He had not risen from the ranks, like Debs, Haywood or 'Mother' Jones, and he had not come to revolutionary ideas through slow, pragmatic evolution or practical daily experience of social struggle. He was the revolutionary intellectual, the dogmatic teacher *par excellence*. A brilliant theoretician, intransigent, sharp, extremely knowledgeable, he was one of the few men in the American labor movement (together with Johann Most, the former German socialist who had emigrated to the United States and become an anarchist) who resembled the European revolutionaries. He wrote pages of vengeful articles against Gompersism and, drawing his inspiration from the militants of the Chicago group in the eighties, he developed a theory of Revolutionary Industrial Unionism which influenced an important group of militants in the American, British and Irish trade union movements. Later on Lenin paid him tribute, declaring that Daniel De Leon's industrial trade-unionism contained the seeds of the soviet system.

But Daniel De Leon had the faults inherent in his strengths. He was sectarian, narrow-minded, authoritarian, all of a piece. He lacked flexibility and a sense of reality. His mind worked logically rather than dialectically. He propagated as many incorrect ideas as correct ones. Certainly, with him lies the credit for having denounced craft and business unionism. Undoubtedly he understood that the essential task was to establish industrial unions fired by a class-struggle spirit, without which socialism would remain a mere aspiration. But, at the same time, it was he who favored the subjection of labor unionism to a dogmatic minority. He failed in the face of the fundamental problem which has plagued socialism right from the outset: he was unable to find the formula enabling revolutionary consciousness to be fruitfully linked to the elemental movement of the masses.

Unlike Debs or Haywood, Daniel De Leon did not pass from trade-unionism to socialism; he travelled in the opposite direction. Previously a lecturer at Columbia University, totally without trade-union experience, the leader of a revolutionary socialist party, the Socialist Labor Party, he tried, to no great avail, to get his hands on any section of the trade-union movement which was willing to allow itself to be colonized and help strengthen his party.

Following his group's expulsion from the Knights of Labor in December 1895, De Leon decided to create a new federation, the Socialist Trade and Labor Alliance. The organization never had more than 20,000 members. This split was not based on a mass movement and the participating organizations, in addition to the fact that they were all controlled by the socialist party, were, for the most part, craft and not industrial unions.

But the new organization's program was undoubtedly progressive and it contributed, to a certain extent, to raising the level of class consciousness of the American workers. 'The methods and spirit of the craft unions', it stated, 'are absolutely incapable of resisting the attacks of concentrated capital. The economic power of the capitalist class rests on essentially political institutions which can only be changed by the direct action of workers united economically and politically into one class.'[7]

The most constructive aspect of Daniel De Leon's militant activity was his pitiless, biting indictment of Gompers and his clique. In 1902 he wrote an essay entitled *Two Pages of Roman History*, in which he develops a scientific analysis of the reformist leaders' social role. He compares them to the leaders of the Roman plebs, who leaned on the mob in order to force the patricians to give them a share of the economic and political spoils and who, in return for the advantages they procured for themselves, contributed to the maintenance of the established order.

Gompers never forgave Daniel De Leon. But, in fact, the latter, through his sectarianism, tended on the whole to give Gompersism ammunition. Gompers and his successors used De Leon as a bogy to be taken out of the closet every time their business unionism was in trouble.

For all his shortcomings, Daniel De Leon was a useful recruit for the IWW. His brilliant pen was placed at the disposal of the new organization, for which he wrote a propaganda pamphlet arguing, with the aid of concrete examples that: 'Industrialism means Might. Craft Unionism means impotence.'[8]

The IWW of 1905

On 27 June 1905, two hundred militants met in Chicago to set up what they decided to call The Industrial Workers of the World. They intended to create a new trade-union federation in opposition to the old AFL, which they, by a play on words, called the Separation of Labor (instead of the Federation of Labor). They vehemently denounced craft and business unionism and class collaboration, to which they opposed the concepts of industrial trade-unionism, workers' solidarity and class struggle. They declared their intention to set about organizing those whom the AFL had neglected, the unskilled, whose numbers were constantly increasing due to the development of mechanization, and in whom they rightly saw the 'granite foundation of the working class'.

The founders of the IWW stood head and shoulders above Gompers. The manifesto put out by the militants who had initiated the call for the founding convention, Haywood's interventions at the gathering, the speeches made by Debs at a series of propaganda meetings held to promote the new organization, the pamphlet through which Daniel De Leon explained the IWW program – all these texts still shine today with a brightness which time has not dulled.

However, Gompersism managed to withstand the indictment brought against it and survived for a time, though only by making concessions, willy-nilly, to its opponents' ideas. Nevertheless, its historical condemnation dates from 1905.

> 'Craft divisions hinder the growth of class consciousness of the workers, foster the idea of harmony of interests between employing exploiter and employed slave . . . Universal economic evils afflicting the working class can be eradicated only by a universal working-class movement. Such a movement of the working class is impossible while separate craft and wage agreements are made favoring the employer against other crafts in the same industry, and while energies are wasted in fruitless jurisdictional struggles which serve only to further the personal aggrandizement of union officials.
>
> 'A movement to fulfill these conditions must consist of one great industrial union embracing all industries. . . . It must be founded on the class struggle, and its general administration must be conducted in harmony with the recognition of the irrepressible conflict between the capitalist class and the working class.'[9]

But, although the founders of the IWW were armed with a powerful idea, the means which they had at their disposal to realize it were inadequate. The founding convention was composed above all of people representing only themselves or a minority within the organization to which they belonged and which had not delegated them.

The only mass organization which joined the IWW was the Western Federation of Miners, with its 27,000 members, and its satellite, the American Labor Union, with 16,500 members. But, very quickly, as early as 1906, the Western miners decided to recover their freedom. They were antagonized by the faction fights which had erupted early on in the IWW. Instead of becoming the new trade-union federation to which they aspired, the organization was becoming a boxing ring in which rival sects and individuals confronted each other. In this milieu, where they constituted the only mass organization, they felt like fish out of water and left.

Furthermore, the Western Federation was beginning to undergo a transformation which was eventually to lead it back to the AFL and to blunt its militancy. The West was little by little losing the rough features of the 'Frontier'. Accounts were no longer settled with sticks of dynamite. Besides, the organization's leaders were growing old. This loss was a harsh blow to the IWW. The Western Federation was their backbone, as well as their main financial support.

The initial weakness of the IWW was that they did not succeed at the outset in taking with them any mass trade-union besides the Western Federation of Miners. The absence, in particular, of the coal-miners' International was an irreparable handicap. The founders of the new unionism were right in their belief that the prospect of the AFL's self reform was not very likely and that the initiative had to come from outside. But perhaps the IWW underestimated the occasional and partial possibilities of reform from within. Thus the creation, in 1898, of a teamsters' International affiliated to the AFL had infused the old organization with a new spirit. The teamsters had a sense of working-class solidarity hardly shared by the old craft unions.

Nevertheless, the split sought by the IWW was not as adventurist as all that. But, in order to succeed, they would have had to win the support of a sufficient number of mass trade-union organizations and wean them away from the AFL. This indispensable condition was not to be fulfilled – hence their final failure.

The 'Wobblies'

After the departure of the Western Federation of Miners, which finally took place in 1907, it might have seemed that what remained of the IWW would rapidly collapse into squabbling sects. In 1908 a break-away split the IWW in two: Daniel De Leon and his supporters created an authoritarian variant of the IWW, with its headquarters in Detroit, Michigan, while William Haywood (who, meantime, had resigned the leadership of the Western Federation of Miners) led a group known as the Chicago Group. On one side were the 'politicals', the 'doctrinaires'; on the other were the 'anarcho-syndicalists', the *wobblies,* supporters of 'direct action' alone. (It would appear that the nickname 'wobbly' was coined by the bourgeois press to deride the IWW which, on the contrary, took pride in it.)

And yet it was only after these successive splits that the IWW, under Haywood's leadership, made an effective entry into social struggles in the United States. It was no longer a matter, as in the primitive schema, of a vast trade-union federation aimed at overpowering the AFL, but of an active minority, a sort of flying squad ready to go straight away to any point of the battlefield and to take the lead in those struggles in which the workers were engaged. So, although they did not accomplish the great mission that they had originally wanted to carry out, the IWW did, in spite of everything, render an important service to the American working class. In the face of Gompersism's dereliction of duty, they were the only ones to intervene in the struggles of the unskilled workers.

At the outset, the IWW had gone for the easiest option. They had not paid much attention to the unorganized, and had turned to those already-unionized workers who were dissatisfied; they tried to detach a number of craft union branches from the AFL and, in the most advanced centers, such as New York and Chicago, they had obtained some results. In Schenectady, New York a General Electric stronghold and a fief of the AFL, they succeeded, at the end of 1906, in initiating a factory strike, one of the first of its kind in the United States. But these attempts did not get them far. So they decided to leave the craft unions alone and to concentrate their efforts on the organization of the unskilled workers. They turned, in particular, to the migrant farm workers and the lumberjacks of the West, who were predisposed, on account of their isolation and instability, to libertarian revolt – recourse to direct economic action, contempt for all political activity, inaptitude for any permanent form of organization. These 'hoboes' joined the IWW *en masse* and helped bring out the victory of Haywood's anarcho-syndicalist tendency over the authoritarian tendency represented by Daniel De Leon. At the 1908 congress the 'Western Brigade' alone provided half the delegates.

To satisfy the needs of the migrant workers and take account of their special conditions, the IWW thought up a new tactic of struggle: the Free Speech Fight. Using the town square was the only means of reaching and recruiting workers who were scattered and isolated, but who periodically came together in the towns around the employment offices, in search of new jobs. The street orators were thrown into jail, only to be replaced immediately by others. IWW flying squads came in quickly from elsewhere and were in their turn arrested. These free speech fights shook the entire West between 1909 and 1911.

In 1910 the IWW set about organizing the lumberjacks of Louisiana, Arkansas and Texas. These were neither immigrants nor migrants, but native-born Americans used to the violent conditions of life on the frontier. Suddenly turned into wage earners and harshly exploited, they were receptive to the arguments of the IWW. The strike they staged was one of the most violent in the annals of the American labor movement. But it failed, and the union which the IWW had helped organize was crushed.

In 1912 the IWW moved East and attempted to capture the textile workers. The 25,000 unorganized workers of the American Woolen Company in Lawrence, Massachusetts stopped work to protest against starvation wages. They were, for the most part, recent immigrants, belonging to 28 different nationalities. The Italians were in the majority. One of the leaders of the IWW, Joseph Ettor, ran the strike. He conducted it masterfully.

The small town was placed under siege and Ettor was

arrested. Haywood took his place. A procession of 10-15,000 strikers gave him a triumphal welcome. He undertook bold innovations. Backed by an exceptional militant, Elizabeth Gurley Flynn, he organized a European type solidarity movement, dispatching the strikers' children to the homes of friends and sympathizers in other towns. He involved women in the struggle, and they fought bravely. He ringed the factories with 24-hour picket lines made up of thousands of workers. He won over public opinion to the strikers' side. He obtained help from sections of the press. A committee of enquiry was established in Washington, and a delegation of sixteen children – both boys and girls – under the age of sixteen visited the Federal capital to describe the terrible conditions of existence in Lawrence. Samuel Gompers, who had come to testify against the strike, was branded as a liar by one of these children.

The employers eventually gave in. The workers greeted the news of their victory by singing the *Internationale* (which did not happen often in the United States) in every language. The effect of this event was tremendous, reaching well beyond Lawrence. It resulted in a wage increase for 25,000 workers.

Another strike broke out at the beginning of 1913 in the silk industry, at Paterson, New Jersey. It spread into a general solidarity strike. Haywood stood at the head of the movement. 35,000 workers of all nationalities went along to a meeting to hear him speak. He was arrested; when the AFL in its turn organized a meeting, the workers walked out in protest against the refusal of the platform to allow the IWW leaders speaking rights.

Haywood, who was very good at generating publicity, took 200 strikers to New York, where they marched through the streets. A big meeting was held at Madison Square Garden lit by an enormous bright transparency bearing, in red, the three letters 'IWW'. The strikers spoke of their conditions of existence at Paterson, sang songs which they had composed, and performed a play retracing the ups and downs of their struggle. The press published long reports. Ever the innovator. Haywood organized meetings of strikers' children and had them set up a strike committee, developing their class consciousness by telling them the fascinating tale of a children's city without adults, policemen, prisons, banks or bosses. Despite all these efforts, the battle ended in defeat.

The revolt in the textile industry had a strong impact on the imagination of the workers in mass-production industry, whom the AFL had totally neglected to organize. In 1913, in Akron, Ohio, the rubber town, the unorganized workers of the big tire factories took spontaneous action. The IWW assumed the leadership of the movement. Soon 20,000 rubber workers were on strike. The indefatigable Haywood was there in no time. Aided by James P Cannon, the future Trotskyist leader, he organized mass pickets, as he had done at Lawrence. Here the coalition of AFL unions supported the movement and considered calling a general strike. But in the end the movement failed. One of the causes of this defeat was the hostile attitude of William Green of the miners' International, Gompers' future successor as leader of the AFL and at the time an Ohio State Senator and the chairman of a legislative commission of enquiry. He denounced the IWW leaders, calling them 'outside agitators'.

Likewise, in Detroit, Michigan, another new heavy industry center, the wobblies started a strike, during the summer of 1913, in the Studebaker factory. 8,000 workers, all unorganized, struck for a week. They showed remarkable cohesion, but the action did not achieve its aim. At almost the same time the IWW organizers concentrated their efforts on the Ford factories, which they flooded with papers and leaflets, while orators harangued the workers at the factory gates. The rumor spread that the wobblies were preparing a strike at Ford for the summer of 1914. It was then that Ford, feeling threatened, introduced his famous 'high wages' policy.

Three years later, in 1916, it was the turn of the iron-miners of the Mesaba Iron Range in Minnesota, who extracted the raw material needed by the steel-mills in Pittsburgh and Chicago, to move into battle. These recent immigrants, mostly Finns, were looking for leadership. The IWW responded to their appeal. Joseph Ettor and Elizabeth Gurley Flynn went along. The strike became widespread, involving 16,000 miners. Finally US Steel granted a wage increase of 10 per cent, an eight hour day and better working conditions.

After 1914, IWW members once again focused their energies on the Western States. In spite of the successes they had had in the East, they had not managed to create a permanent organization there, and the economic crisis then under way reduced the combativity of the unskilled workers in the industrial areas of the Atlantic coast. In 1915-1916 they set about organizing the agricultural workers, particularly in Kansas, Oklahoma and Minnesota. They succeeded in unionizing 18,000 migrant workers. Then they turned to the lumberjacks of the Northwest and the copper miners of Arizona.

In 1917 the IWW reached its zenith, at least in terms of membership figures. In one year they had grown from 40,000 to 100,000. But the entry of the United States into the war provoked a storm of repression against them. All the combined forces of capitalism, the state authorities and ex-servicemen used as fascist militias were employed to crush them. Samuel Gompers, glad to be rid at last of a troublesome rival, gave President Wilson a free hand. Thousands of wobblies were arrested and given long prison sentences. The movement was quite simply decapitated. It never recovered.

Other factors – the reabsorption of migrant labor due to advances in technology, the appearance of Communism which attracted the most advanced workers, and the incapacity of the wobblies to build a permanent organization – also contributed to the decline of the IWW. The wobblies excelled in the formation of flying squads and in improvisation; they were more agitators and propagandists than organizers. They did not undertake any systematic organizing campaign, and yet this was the only way to penetrate the basic branches of industry, such as steel. For them strikes were mainly an opportunity to spread their revolutionary ideas. As soon as the battle was won, they moved on to new ground, without leaving any lasting mark. Permanent organization did not interest them. They persistently refused to sign agreements, to establish daily relations with the employers, to create a mechanism permitting the stabilization of the relationship between bosses and workers in the interval between two battles.

However, Eugene Debs was not necessarily right to attribute the wobblies' failure to their rejection of political action and their activist tactics which, according to him, did not correspond to the aspirations of the American workers. The US worker, an individualist and a fighter, shaped by the violent 'frontier' epic, has a taste and a gift for direct action, as well as a certain distrust of politicians. Far from being 'un-American', Haywood's IWW was – and this is a view shared by several observers – more in the American tradition than any other labor organization to have emerged in the United

States.

It is this which accounts for the success the wobblies had, not only among the immigrants, but also among those workers whose families had been in America for a long time, like the lumberjacks of Texas and Louisiana. Likewise, their deeply democratic spirit and structure, their distrust of leaders (which led them to abolish the title of 'President' and reduce their leaders' salaries) and their predilection for referenda helped win them the sympathy and trust not only of the migrant workers but of other groups of workers also.

This healthy conception of workers' democracy has since been trampled underfoot by the bureaucratic machine which controls the trade-union movement in the United States today, but it would be foolhardy to doubt that it corresponds to the American worker's mentality. The IWW lost its influence on the vanguard of the proletariat only when, after the First World War, it was confronted with a more important rival in the political arena: the Communist Party, supported by the prestige of the Russian revolution.

CHAPTER 2

From the IWW to the CIO

Industrial Unionism and the AFL

The reasons for the failure of the IWW had been pondered by one of its members, William Foster. In 1911, he had visited Europe and been struck by the success of the French revolutionary trade-unionists in capturing the *Confédération Générale du Travail.* The Parisians had strongly urged the IWW to engage in activity inside the AFL. (Foster became friendly with one of them, Pierre Monatte, and was a regular contributor to *La vie ouvrière* from 1911 to 1914; he wrote a series of articles for the paper on the American trade-union movement.)

In a letter to the IWW paper, Foster attacked the theory, which was accepted as an infallible dogma, that it was necessary to build a new organization outside the existing craft unions, which were considered incapable of evolving further. Haywood was not convinced, and his lieutenant, Joseph Ettor, replied that the IWW wanted not to save the AFL but to destroy it. Foster then broke with his former friends and, in 1912, created a trade-unionist League, the object of which was revolutionary infiltration within the old federation.

For his part, Debs continued to be haunted by his lifelong idea: how to promote industrial trade-unionism in the United States. In his view the IWW of 1905 had failed, in the first place, because it had underestimated the importance of action *inside* the AFL, and also, in fact mainly, because it had not succeeded in basing itself on mass trade-union organizations. In March 1914 Debs devoted an article to the problem.[1] In it he especially expressed his confidence in the future:

> 'There are sound reasons for believing', he wrote, 'that a new era of labor unionism is dawning and that in the future organized labor is to come more rapidly to fruition and expand to proportions and develop power which will compensate in full measure for the slow and painful progress of the past . . . , and the chief of these reasons is the disintegration and impending fall of reactionary craft unionism and the rise and spread of the revolutionary industrial movement.'

As for the Western Federation of Miners, which had joined

the AFL in 1911, it had just been waging a harsh struggle in the copper-mines of Michigan since the summer of 1913 and had not obtained the hoped-for financial aid from the trade-union federation. Its President publicly attacked the attitude of the Executive Council. He spoke at the coal-miners' congress and declared that if the strike was lost the responsibility would lie with Gompers and his clique. Debs understood that without the participation of the two big miners' Internationals, which had been lacking in the case of the IWW, it was not possible to lay the foundations of an industrial trade-unionism.

> 'The United Mine Workers and the Western Federation of Miners', he continued in the same article, 'becoming more and more revolutionary in the desperate fight they are compelled to wage for their existence, are bound to merge soon into one great industrial organization, and the same forces that are driving them together will also drive them out of Gompers's federation of craft unions. There are other progressive unions in the A.F. of L. that will follow the secession of the miners and augment the forces of revolutionary unionism.'

In a subsequent article Debs suggested that both miners' unions, once they had fused and left the AFL, should launch an appeal to all trade unions for a congress to set up an industrial organization for all American workers. Twenty years before its time Debs was launching the idea of the CIO.

Meanwhile, deep stirrings were shaking Gompers' organization. At the AFL congress held in Rochester in November 1912 the delegates of the coal-miners' International put down a resolution urging the federation to abandon its craft structure for industrial organization. After a long and lively debate the resolution was rejected by a two-to-one majority. However, the Executive Council had to concede some ground. It declared that the concept of the autonomy of each craft did not prevent the recruitment of the lower ranks of the working class or the amalgamation of several craft unions into one, and it strongly challenged the view that the federation had a rigid, inflexible concept and was not adapting to new conditions.

A few months later, on 1 February 1913, the AFL announced the opening of a nation-wide campaign with a view to organizing all unorganized workers and recruiting immigrants as soon as they arrived in the United States. The distribution of 500,000 propaganda pamphlets written in thirteen languages was envisaged. The plan actually began to be put into practice, particularly in the steel industry. But with the economic crisis of 1914 and then the war it was put off to a later date. Moreover, the rapid decline of the IWW in the East reassured the high-priests of the AFL and confirmed them in their comfortable routinism.

On the very eve of the war a new star arose in the trade-union firmament: the needle trades, the garment workers' unions. Two big strikes in 1910, one in New York, in the ladies' garment industry, the other in Chicago, in the men's garment industry, had given the impulse to trade-unionism in these trades, which were mainly composed of Jewish immigrants. The two Internationals had been constituted on an industrial, class-struggle basis. But, at the same time, they had borrowed from the craft unions their stable, methodical administration. They achieved a synthesis of radical and business unionism. The ladies' garment workers' union had grown up, in spite of its industrial structure, inside the AFL. But its 'male' counterpart had broken with the federation at the end of 1914 and had turned itself into an independent organization, the Amalgamated Clothing Workers. It became a pole of attraction for all progressive trade-unionists.

Organizing the Slaughterhouses (1917)

The First World War and then the Russian revolution resulted, in the United States as elsewhere, in a radicalization of the masses. A new revolutionary leadership arose, determined to organize the unskilled workers in the basic industries. So as not to be outflanked, the Gompersist clique had to follow the movement, whether it wanted to or not – aiming to bring it under control at the first opportunity.

Foster, who has already been mentioned, changed with the times. He learned from American Big Business and the new methods of mass production. He introduced the same efficiency into his campaigns to recruit the workers of heavy industry as the barons of capital applied in their industrial dungeons. While they rationalized production, he intended to rationalize the class struggle. In the face of monopolistic concentration, what was called for was a strong working-class concentration, based on the model offered by the enemy.

There was only one means of taking over the old federation from within – to gain a hold over local trade-union coalitions in some important industrial center. The local union coalitions, since they included all crafts and had to face a united front of the employers, had always been more militant and more imbued with the principle of workers' solidarity than the craft Internationals. More than once in past battles they had supported movements disapproved of by Gompers and the AFL leadership.

Foster concentrated his efforts on Chicago and turned the city's union coalition into the most progressive in the United States. The Chicago Federation of Labor was led by an honest and courageous militant, John Fitzpatrick. He had succeeded in ridding his organization of a set of gangsters who laid down the law in the construction unions. This purge, and the support given to a few wildcat strikes, had brought him into violent conflict with Gompersism.

Backed by the Chicago union coalition, Foster launched a campaign to organize the slaughter-house workers in July 1917. These workers had been completely unorganized since their defeat in 1904. They had been beaten back then on account of their division, which was a consequence of corporate egoism. Foster understood that they had to be welded into a single bloc. But, at the same time, he declined to set up a break-away organization and wanted to adapt to the structure of the AFL. He got round the difficulty, after a fashion, by amalgamating the various local craft branches into an industrial union. But, as was to be expected, the national leaderships of the craft unions concerned, far from supporting the movement, showed hostility towards it.

The AFL did not give a penny towards the campaign and, to forestall a strike, asked the Federal Government to step in as mediator. However, the Federal Mediation Commission eventually came out in favor of the workers' demands, and, all across the country, more than 200,000 slaughter-house workers, regardless of skill, nationality or color, rushed to join the dozen unions entitled to admit them.

But, later on, as soon as Foster had turned his back, the AFL leaders hastened to destroy his work. They abolished the industrial union and re-established the old craft structure, once more creating divisions among the slaughter-house workers, and not hesitating to expel those who intended to remain loyal to the industrial structure. Weakened and disheartened, the workers were unable to resist an employers' counter-offensive, and their organization was swept away in the winter of 1920-1921.

The Steel Strike (1919)

In 1918, fortified by his experience in the slaughter-houses, Foster persuaded the Chicago union coalition to undertake the organization of the steelworkers. The steel industry had become the leading basic industry in the United States since the application of the Bessemer process and the formation by Carnegie and Morgan of the huge US Steel trust. The latter had no workers' organization to contend with. The Amalgamated Association of Iron and Steel Workers (AFL) was an organization which did not admit unskilled workers to membership and took no interest in their fate. As the industrial revolution forced the implementation of new techniques, replacing skilled mechanics by unskilled laborers, so the old union showed itself more and more incapable of organizing the steelworkers.

Hence it was necessary to start from scratch. Foster was literally obliged to force Gompers' hand to get the ball rolling. The AFL leaders showed no desire to embark on an adventure. They suspected that a success in the steel industry would lead to an explosive development of industrial trade-unionism in other areas, and that it would confer considerable prestige on Foster and Fitzpatrick, turning them into dangerous rivals.

Foster finally gained Gompers' acceptance of his plan, which involved launching a simultaneous recruitment campaign in 50 to 75 steel centers. He wanted to catch the workers' imagination through mass meetings, parades and page-long advertisements in the newspapers. He asked the AFL Internationals to levy 25 cents on each of their members. But the craft union heads gave next to nothing. As for the AFL itself, once again it did not give a single dollar. Lacking the nerve of war, Foster was forced to concentrate his efforts on the South Chicago steel mills, where he had immediate success, and in no time the steelworkers, not only in Chicago, but in all the important centers, flocked to the unions. 250,000 workers were organized.

The unskilled were the first to take up the call. The despised 'foreigners' fought better and joined the unions more quickly than the skilled workers, who were generally American-born.

Foster had leaflets and newspapers distributed in order to reach them, using organizers who spoke all the relevant languages. When English was used in meetings, it was spoken slowly, clearly and very simply.

The workers, as soon as they were unionized, were split up into 24 different unions. However, they were united at factory level in an Iron and Steel Workers Council. Foster had arranged for membership fees to be uniformly fixed at three dollars, for simplicity's sake.

A strike had to be called as a result of the provocations of the steel company, which systematically laid off the newly-unionized men. Gompers and the leaders of the craft unions tried in vain to forestall the movement through the intervention of the Federal Government. 365,000 workers downed tools in fifty localities. Foster set up a co-operative organization which was administered according to strict commercial methods and provided food for the strikers. The battle lasted over three months (22 September 1919 – 8 January 1920) and was finally lost, due not just to the lack of solidarity shown by the trade-union leaders, but to their actual sabotage.

Foster drew a lesson for the future from the experience:[2]

> '. . . the whole trade-union movement won a great moral victory . . . [which] . . . more than offsets the failure of the strike itself. The gain consists of a badly needed addition to the unions' thin store of self-confidence. To trade-union organizers the steel industry had long symbolized the impossible. . . . The impossible has been accomplished. . . . If the steel industry could be organized, so can any other in the country. The mouth has been shut forever of that insufferable pest of the labor movement, the large body of ignorant, incompetent, short-sighted, visionless union men whose eternal song, when some important organizing project is afoot, is "It can't be done".'

The Communists in the Unions

In 1921, after a trip to Russia, Foster became a Communist. His conversion led him to reconsider the concessions he had made to Gompersism, but it did not modify his essential tactical conception, namely opposition to any attempt to split the trade unions. He persisted in the belief that work had to be carried out solely from within and that industrial trade-unionism could be built only through the old federation. He was encouraged in this attitude by Lenin. In his *Left Wing Communism: an Infantile Disorder,*[3] published in

1920, the Russian revolutionary had sharply attacked the ultra-Lefts, such as the American IWW, who called on the workers to leave the reactionary unions and refused to be active in them. Lenin thought that the reformist leaders had reason to be 'very grateful' to these 'left-wing' revolutionaries.

But later on, in 1928, the wind having changed in Moscow, Lozovsky, the General Secretary of the Red Trade Union International, was to criticize Foster for relying too much on the AFL leaders and neglecting the direct organization of the unorganized workers in heavy, mass-production industry.

Since it was not possible to persuade the craft unions to exchange their structure for that of industrial unionism, there remained only one last resource: the voluntary amalgamation of the different craft unions in each industry. On 19 March 1922, the Chicago union coalition adopted a resolution asking the AFL[4]

> 'to take the necessary action towards bringing about the required solidarity within the ranks of organized labor, and that, as a first start in this direction, the various international unions to be called into conference for the purpose of arranging to amalgamate all the unions in the respective industries into single organizations, each of which shall cover one industry.'

In the months that followed, about twenty Internationals, seventeen State unions, innumerable union coalitions and thousands of trade-union Locals came out in favor of amalgamation. Some Internationals, more guarded, opted for partial amalgamation. 400 railroad workers' delegate formed a Railroad Workers' Amalgamation Committee, and 200 miners' delegates, representing twelve of the thirteen districts covered by their union, created a Committee of Progressive Miners. In 1925 Foster estimated that a good half of the movement was behind the call for amalgamation.

Gompers and his Executive Council took fright. A Communist associate of Foster's, William F Dunne, the future Trotskyist, was ejected from the AFL congress held in Portland, Oregon in 1923. The Communists were expelled from union coalitions in Minneapolis, Seattle and a number of other cities. Thousands of them were expelled from the Internationals which they had succeeded in penetrating, such as the garment unions.

The amalgamation campaign fizzled out, in spite of its

promising beginnings. The labor movement as a whole, which had reached its zenith in 1919-20, had entered a period of retreat: the employers' counter-offensive was at its height; many workers who had joined the old federation and given it something of a new lease of life had already deserted it; furthermore, the era of prosperity which coincided with President Coolidge's term of office (1923-29) had stabilized social relationships and taken the edge off the class struggle; lastly, the Communists acted rashly in linking the movement for amalgamation to a political program which included the recognition of Soviet Russia and affiliation to the Red International of Labor Unions.

Foster's League* (if one is to believe Foster himself) became increasingly an appendage of the Communist Party, a pro-Soviet propaganda agency. This tactic alienated rather than attracted the young militants emerging from the ranks of the unions, disgusted by Gompers' conservatism. The way in which the Communists set about trying to gain control of the trade-union movement gave rise to a defensive reflex among these workers and its effect was to throw them back into the arms of Gompersism.

To be sure, the Communists managed to win the leadership of a number of strikes, because they were the only militant leadership available to the workers when the latter moved into struggle. Despite some ephemeral achievements, particularly in the New York garment unions, their attempts to radicalize the trade-union movement met, in short, with little success. Foster himself admits that his League gradually declined and became isolated from the masses. Yet the Communist movement in the United States after World War I possessed an able and relatively important leadership, as well as considerable resources.

John Lewis Enters the Fray

For various reasons, therefore, the organization of workers in heavy industry continued to be put off. The American labor movement seemed condemned to trail behind history for ever. Both those who participated in the movement and those who observed it from the outside eventually resigned

---

*The Trade Union League set up in 1912 had been renamed the Trade Union Educational League by Foster in 1920.

themselves to the inevitable in their own way, some storming at the 'bad shepherds' of American trade-unionism, others invoking the specific features of the labor movement in the United States. Even the least pessimistic considered the stagnation of the American Federation of Labor an established fact. No-one anticipated, predicted or prepared the tidal wave which was going to turn everything upside down and at last make possible the accomplishment of the task which had been deferred for so long.

The world crisis beginning in 1929 had to take place before the workers in US heavy industry were finally organized and the absolute monarchy of the big monopolies was brought to an end. American capitalism, whose stability and progress had seemed destined to last indefinitely, was shaken to its foundations. But, for the organization of the unorganized to be attempted at long last, the emergence of new material conditions – economic crisis, mass unemployment, a radicalization of the masses – though necessary was not sufficient. It also required favorable circumstances within the labor movement and men ready to take advantage of them. Both factors were present.

The men in question had almost all gained their initial experience in the AFL. Some of them had even belonged to Gompers' 'machine'. During the sterile decade of the twenties they had made no attempt, or almost none, to fill the void created by the historical defects of Gompersism. Although their own unions were formed on an industrial basis, they had not tried to extend industrial trade-unionism to the rest of the federation. On the contrary, they had devoted all their energies to fighting and expelling from their Internationals those who had been alone in advocating industrial trade-unionism – the Communists. But they were led to re-examine their tactics and try something new.

Among the AFL Internationals organized on an industrial basis the most important was still that of the coal-miners. Its very structure, its strategic position, its numerical importance, its financial resources and its militant traditions made it the possible backbone of a renovated movement.

It just so happened that at the end of the twenties the United Mine Workers was in a precarious position. By a curious paradox, the coal industry was in a bad way in the midst of a period of economic well-being. It was suffering from the damage wrought by competition and was plunged into anarchy. Too many mines, too many miners. The employers had not succeeded in rationalizing their activities; for its part, the union had not been able to penetrate important sectors of the industry, and was increasingly losing control over formerly organized sectors.

An agreement had been signed in 1924 between the United Mine Workers and the Northern mine-owners, by virtue of which the relatively high wartime wages were maintained. But the mechanization of the unorganized mines in West Virginia and the opening of new mines in the South using cheap labor made the situation untenable for the employers who had signed the 1924 agreement. The result was a general reduction in wages and a constant decline of the union, whose membership slumped from 600,000 to 150,000. This situation was not due merely to capitalist anarchy; it was also, to a large degree, a consequence of the incapacity and lack of combativity of the President of the United Mine Workers, John Lewis.

Everything about the mine workers' union – its structure, its past and, above all, the great suffering of the miners, their desperate struggle for life – predisposed it to be revolutionary. Yet Lewis had contrived to lead it in a conservative manner. He seemed to be a typical product of Gompersism. Samuel Gompers had honored him in 1919, appointing him to the post of AFL organizer. He ran his International according to the traditions of business unionism, did nothing to raise the level of consciousness and education of his members, abhorred socialism and communism, had no sympathy for the demand that the mines should be nationalized, supported the Republican Party in the political sphere and presided over a regime of bureaucratic dictatorship in the United Mine Workers. In 1922, at the end of a large and successful strike, he had abandoned 100,000 unorganized strikers in central Pennsylvania (Somerset County) and western Virginia who were not covered by the agreement signed with the employers. This attitude, followed by other capitulations, had weakened the International and left large sectors of the industry unorganized.

But, at the end of the twenties, the bankruptcy of the Lewis Administration was such that its only chance of survival was to turn over a new leaf. It was then that John Lewis revealed that he was made of different stuff from the craft union bigwigs. He had in reserve a genuis which combined audacity with intuition, lightning improvisations with patiently thought out long-term plans. The pressing need to save his trade-union fief led him to discover his vocation.

Roosevelt Gives Capitalism the Kiss of Life

Meanwhile, the crisis from which the coal industry was suffering gripped the country as a whole. The Great Depression had begun. At the beginning of 1933, John Lewis, on the advice of an expert, Henry Warrum, came to the conclusion that, instead of continuing to struggle for special legislation in favor of the coal industry, it was wiser and more expedient to join the clamor of the bankers and industrialists for a return to economic prosperity through Government intervention (the suspension of the anti-trust laws and the stabilization of prices and production through employers' agreements controlled by the Government).

But John Lewis placed one condition on his acceptance of this neo-capitalism: the interests of the workers were to be taken into consideration; working hours were to be reduced in order to absorb some of the unemployed; prices were to be fixed so as to guarantee the workers a minimum wage; finally, and above all, the workers' right to organize and negotiate collectively through the unions of their choice would be legally recognized. This plan, which Lewis presented to a Senate Committee on 17 February 1933, served as the basis for the famous National Recovery Act (NRA) and the main condition which he had laid down, the one concerning hours of work, became the no less famous Section 7a) of that law.

Lewis found an ally in the person of Sidney Hillman, the President of the Men's Garment International, which was organized on an industrial basis. Hillman was a former socialist who had become a business unionist and an advocate of industrial planning. He had taken his industry, which was also in a chaotic state, through an experience of worker-employer planned economy: his union had helped the employers eliminate the destructive effects of competition. His ambition was to transpose his experience to the national plane. As early as 1931 he had proposed to a Senate Committee a plan of industrial 'codes' regulating working hours and wages. In 1933 he joined Lewis when the latter set forth his views to another committee.

So the two labor leaders stood godfathers to Roosevelt's New Deal. The President's main idea was to save ailing capitalism through Government intervention and to grant the workers, at least on paper, a concession – the right to organize freely – so as to get them to accept this undisguised bolstering of the big monopolies.

But Lewis and Roosevelt were men inspired by quite different motives: one aimed, as the head of the capitalist state, to patch up the all but ruined fortress of Big Business, whatever the cost; the other, as the leader of a big labor organization, hoped to consolidate, at any price, a collapsing trade-union fief. For Roosevelt Section 7a) was a minor artifice; and, if one is to believe Lewis, it was only with reluctance that he agreed to it; for Lewis, on the other hand, it was the essential clause.

In fact the miners' spokesman had understood that his International could survive only if the other workers in heavy industry, particularly the steelworkers, were finally organized. The steel trust owned important coal-mines, known as 'captive mines', which had markedly grown in number over the previous few years. Their all-powerful owner did not recognize the labor unions. They therefore competed unequally with the organized mines and constituted a permanent danger to workers' trade-unionism. In any case, what threatened the miners' union was not simply the existence of the 'captive mines' but the very fact that the entire steel industry, that central bastion of Big Business, remained closed to trade-unionism. The miners' union would not be secure as long as the steelworkers remained unorganized.

Finally, the mechanization of the coal industry and the closure of non-profit-making mines had forced many miners to change jobs. They had found work in the other basic industries: steel, auto, rubber, metal-mining, oil, etc. Having acquired experience of and a taste for organization in the miners' union, they had been attempting, since the passage of the NRA, to establish unions in their new industries; quite naturally they turned to their old organization, asking it to come to their aid.

John Lewis started with a bold throw of the dice. He gambled all the money left in his International's coffers and allocated it for a recruitment campaign aimed at unorganized miners, which was an enormous success. The United Mine Workers became a prosperous organization once again: in the space of three months it gained 300,000 new members. Once this objective was achieved, John Lewis decided to devote the increased resources of his union to recruiting unorganized workers in the other basic industries. But here he encountered an insurmountable obstacle: the craft unionism of the AFL, its ill-will and its congenital inability to organize the unskilled.

The Defects of the Old Federation

In 1932 the AFL had not only failed to organize the unskilled (in 1930 a would-be campaign, launched by its President, William Green, to recruit the Southern textile workers had almost immediately wound up in failure), but had not even been capable of defending the positions of the skilled workers. This setback was not simply due to its lack of dynamism, but was also a result of technical factors: the unceasing progress of mechanization and industrial rationalization were tending to reduce the number of skilled workers, so causing the federation to lose ground. Its membership had fallen from around 4 million in 1920 to some 3 million at the end of 1929 and 2,600,000 in 1934.

The coming into effect of the NRA reversed the situation almost overnight. It seemed to the workers that at last, for the first time, the Federal Government was siding wholeheartedly with them and recognizing their right to organize freely. They flocked to the workers' organizations.

It was a tidal wave. All the mass-production industries were swept by the movement; not only the garment industry, but also the automobile, steel, rubber and textile industries. As early as the October 1933 congress the AFL President, William Green, estimated that, taking into account the new recruits, the federation's strength was fast approaching 4 million.

What was to be done about this throng which, so eagerly and quite without invitation, was seeking admittance to a house grown old and quite unprepared for such an influx? During the summer of 1933 William Green, under the pressure of necessity, decided to organize the new-comers into federal unions. Federal unions were factory trade-union branches, organized on an industrial basis, that is to say including all jobs within the factory. They could not therefore be attached to the craft unions. They were placed under the direct control of the federation: for this reason they were not granted an autonomous charter; they had their statutes imposed on them by the federation; they could not formulate demands, call strikes or negotiate with the employers without the approval of the federation leaders. They were no more than recruitments offices for the craft unions. The AFL made new recruits go through a course of instruction in the federal unions, then, having numbered them and handed them their individual packs, separated them and directed them to their respective regiments: the craft Internationals.

The workers grasped the absurdity of this system and called for the fusion of the various federal unions in their respective industries into industrial Internationals. The AFL refused. When, at last, no longer able to resist their pressure, it ceded to the demand, it tried to keep the new organizations under its wing, appointing – for such was William Green's desire – old, reactionary, craft-union bosses to lead them. The latter tried to break the combativity of the masses whose leadership they had usurped.

And yet never had it been more necessary to fight. The employers were doing their utmost to violate the famous Clause 7a) of the NRA, and some of the special 'codes', which were promulgated in every industry with the automatic consent of the US President, contained clauses which hindered trade-union organization.* Sometimes the workers went on strike in spite of the opposition of their leaders; sometimes, disheartened and disgusted, they began deserting the organizations which they had just joined so enthusiastically.

The Auto Industry

The drama unfolded with the greatest intensity in the auto industry, a youthful industry which had grown by leaps and

---

*Perhaps the most spectacular struggle prior to the formation of the CIO was the San Francisco General Strike of July 1934. Here all the elements which were to lay the basis for the upsurge to come were revealed: reactionary employers, grouped into the Industrial Association which held the city in its grasp, intent on denying the longshoremen regular hours, a living wage or an independent trade union – Clause 7a) notwithstanding; amazing police and vigilante brutality resulting in hundreds of injuries and at least two deaths; a wave of working class solidarity beyond simple strike action; the emergence of a new leadership from

bounds and employed half a million men, all young and dynamic. The auto bosses were, together with the steel bosses, the most solid barrier against the development of labor unionism. Immediately upon the promulgation of the NRA, 100,000 auto workers joined the AFL's federal unions. They had a mediocrity, William Collins, thrust upon them by Green, and he was soon replaced by another incompetent, Francis J Dillon. When seventy-seven federal unions in the auto industry met in Detroit, Michigan in June 1934 the delegates called for the immediate establishment of an industrial union of auto workers. William Green sidestepped the matter.

The auto workers had all too many reasons to be dissatisfied. Their industrial 'code', promulgated by President Roosevelt, contained a clause enabling the employers to lay off any worker who was a trade-union militant. Lay-offs became widespread and the workers responded with a wave of strikes.

Finally, on 9 May 1935, the Executive Councils of the AFL decided, a little late, to accede to the demand for an International Union. The new organization – the United Automobile Workers (UAW) – was set up in August. But it was only a compromise: the craft unions had retained about 15 per cent of auto workers in their respective fiefs. Moreover, William Green had reserved for himself the right to appoint the president of the new organization, and he nominated Dillon. The auto workers were sick and tired of the AFL.

The Steel Industry

Here the obstacle was not the structure of the craft unions, for a single International had full jurisdiction over the 500,000 workers in the industry: the Amalgamated Association of

the rank and file (best symbolized by Harry Bridges) capable of leading the movement and resisting the anti-Communist, strikebreaking tirades of national AFL bosses like Joseph P Ryan and Edward McGrady; and, finally, the manipulations of the AFL 'conservatives' within the General Strike Committee which succeeded in weakening the strike's total grip on the city before ending it by a vote of 191:174. Nevertheless, for a short time, the silent city had effectively been in the hands of the workers. The longshoremen emerged from it with much better conditions, hours, wages and, above all, with their union recognized. For the rest of the working class, San Francisco was a beacon of inspiration.

Iron, Steel and Tin Workers. But this organization was moribund with only between 3,000 and 5,000 members, all highly skilled. It held the unskilled in contempt and feared nothing so much as having its sleep disturbed by the intrusion of thousands of young and militant new members. Yet, as soon as the NRA was passed in 1933, the unorganized flooded uninvited into the 'Amalgamated'. They created 'lodges' (trade-union locals) to which, in their neophytes' enthusiasm, they gave names such as New Deal, NRA and Blue Eagle (the emblem of the National Recovery Administration). A year later, membership had reached 100,000.

The senile President of the Amalgamated was a certain Michael Tighe, nicknamed 'Grandmother' Tighe. His entire philosophy could be summed up in one sentence: 'You cannot fight a trust as rich and powerful as the steel trust.' Nevertheless, he put on a brave face and opened his doors to these annoying workers who were coming to disturb the last peaceful years of his life. Urged on by the pressure of the masses and also by William Green (who was subject to the same pressures as Tighe, only more so), he stretched his kindness to the point of sending out a few organizers. To be sure, his recruitment campaign was not aggressive. But those were times when the workers did not need much persuading to join a trade-union organization.

Tighe's fears were only too well-founded. He was quickly bypassed by the youth to whom he had had to open the doors. On 25 March 1934, 257 delegates met in Pittsburgh at an inter-district conference and created an organized minority, the Rank and File Movement. When the national congress of the Amalgamated was held in April in the same city, Tighe could not prevent his opponents getting a committee of rank-and-file militants elected, which was instructed to prepare a nation-wide strike.

The steelworkers indeed had reasons, just as much as the auto workers, for demonstrating their anger. The industry's 'code' had not been drawn up by Roosevelt, but by the steel trust. The employers had let it be known quite unequivocally that Section 7a) in no way altered their previous position of hostility to labor unionism. The only type of union they were ready to accept, in order to comply with the law, was a company union. The steelworkers understood that to force recognition of the trade union they would have to fight.

But Tighe was not at all keen on the idea. The rank-and-file delegates then decided to go to Washington, so as to put their grievances to President Roosevelt. In the waiting-rooms of the capital they did not allow themselves to be shown the door, and their attitude was militant. After the President made them a vague promise, they publicly said something like: 'That's good for a laugh!'. Such unseemliness had never been seen in Washington. The whole nation grasped that something had changed in the relationship of forces between capital and labor.

But a special convention of the Amalgamated was convened in June, and William Green came expressly to plead with the delegates to abandon their plans for a strike. He promised them, on behalf of President Roosevelt, a vague Steel Labor Relations Board, and they swallowed the bait. The prestige then enjoyed by the United States President among young trade-unionists was such that they let themselves be outwitted. It was a sharp blow to the 'rank-and-file movement'.

Some months later, 'Grandmother' Tighe, encouraged by his victory, went over to the offensive. He embarked on a mass expulsion of 'lodges' and union members belonging to the opposition movement.

The Rubber Industry

In 1934 60-70,000 workers had joined the AFL's federal unions particularly in Akron, Ohio, the main center of the rubber industry. William Green dispatched a wretched proconsul, Coleman C Claherty, to represent him on the spot. Like their fellows in the auto industry, the rubber workers were calling for an industrial union, instead of which Green and Claherty split them up into seven different craft unions, keeping in the federal unions only those among the unskilled who could not be consigned to one or another of the craft unions.

The workers were tired of speedups. They were impatient for action. In June 1934 they suddenly decided to go out on strike at General Tire and Rubber. Claherty was bypassed and abused. The strikers won. But the bosses did not want to submit to the NRA. Through all sorts of legal procedures they sabotaged the elections by means of which trade-unionism was seeking to get itself recognized. It would have taken nothing less than a nation-wide strike of rubber workers to force them to accept collective bargaining, but instead Green and Claherty reached a disastrous agreement in Washington in April 1935. The workers, fed up to the teeth, wanted no more talk of trade unions. By the Spring of 1935 trade-union strength had fallen once more to 3,000. The rubber workers were completely demoralized.

The Textile Industry

Here was an industry difficult to organize, suffering from especially low wages, periodic unemployment and intensive mechanization, which was constantly reducing the number of workers. Furthermore, an increasingly large part of the industry had been transplanted to the South, where wages were still more pitiful than in the North, where the ignorant and downtrodden poor white 'hillbillies' had fallen under a particularly inhuman yoke, and where the employers exploited racial prejudices to strengthen the foundations of their domination.

In the months following the coming into effect of the NRA in 1933, the textile workers flocked to the trade unions; union membership went from 50,000 at the beginning of 1933 to 300,000 in the summer of 1934. And the newly-unionized men and women quickly became militant. Although the textile Code had been presented as a 'model', and did in fact contain certain improvements, the employers violated it to a man. Working conditions remained detestable. The newly unionized were laid off in their thousands.

It was in the South that the movement of revolt began. Under the pressure of the rank and file the congress of the United Textile Workers resolved, at the end of August 1934, to call a general strike. The strike took on the proportions of a human wave. More than 400,000 workers took part in it. The movement was led by an energetic militant, Francis Gorman, who perfected the tactic of 'flying picket squads'. As soon as they had forced the closure of a factory, the workers would jump into old cars and invade the nearest textile center before the police were able to take measures to prevent the establishment of strike pickets. The strikers fought against the forces of repression. Blood flowed. The bosses and the Government initiated a reign of terror. In Georgia strikers were thrown into detention centers which were more like concentration camps.

But the AFL leaders felt they had been dragged further than they wanted. Just when victory could be glimpsed on the horizon, they suddenly brought the movement to a halt after President Roosevelt had thrown them the bait of a 'commission of inquiry and mediation'. In an atmosphere of martial law the workers had to go back to work. Thousands of them were laid off and forced to sign a pledge to leave the union which, by August 1935, had no more than 79,200 members.

The Founding of the CIO

The men who regenerated American trade-unionism were neither theoreticians nor system-builders but pragmatists. They had understood that the economic crisis, the promulgation of the National Recovery Act and the massive influx of workers into the unions at last made it possible to organize the workers in heavy industry on the basis of industrial trade-unionism. They tried at first to organize them into the old AFL, by reforming its structure and methods. And it was only when they saw that this was quite impossible that they were led to create a new organization.

In the dispute which pitted them against the last stand of Gompersism, these innovators had one crushing argument in their favor: technical progress. While industrial productivity had risen by less than 10 per cent between 1899 and 1914, it had increased by 7 per cent annually from 1920 to 1930. The Ford company declared in 1926 that 43 per cent of its 7,782 different jobs required only one day's training; 36 per cent between a day and a week; 6 per cent between one and three weeks, and only 15 per cent a longer period of time. Eighty-five per cent of Ford workers could attain maximum aptitude in less than two weeks. In the construction industry a digging machine operated by just one man and his co-driver could do the work of forty-four manual workers in the same amount of time.

Everywhere machines were simplifying operations to such an extent that the semi-skilled were replacing the skilled and, in many cases, the unskilled. In the basic branches of American industry the semi-skilled far outnumbered the other categories of workers. The structure of craft unionism was unsuited to this new situation.

And, even if it had been possible and desirable to divide

up the millions of specialized workers among the various types of job, machines and occupations changed so frequently that these workers would constantly have had to be shifted from one category to the next. Many employers themselves admitted that organizing large industrial concerns on a job basis could only generate confusion. Gerald Swope, the President of General Electric, discussed the problem with William Green as it related to his own factories. He asked if the AFL could not organize its members into a single industrial union instead of fifteen craft unions. The response was negative.

The arguments of John Lewis and his fellow-campaigners for industrial trade-unionism (Sidney Hillman, of the men's garment union, and David Dubinsky, of the ladies' garment union) were therefore based on reality.

At the AFL convention in San Francisco in October 1934 the defenders of craft unionism had to make a concession: industrial unions would be established for the workers in the auto, cement and aluminium industries and other mass-production industries to be chosen in due course. But, at the same time, the 'rights' of the craft unions were to be 'safeguarded'. How? No precise answer was given, and the actual application of the compromise was left to the Executive Council, which, in spite of its increased size, was still dominated by the leaders of the craft unions. On the platform of the convention, Daniel Tobin, the President of the Teamsters' International, repeated the insulting remarks once made by Gompers about the unskilled. He called the recently organized workers 'garbage'.

At the next Federal convention, which took place in Atlantic City in October 1935, the battle resumed. The 'industrialists' demanded that the craft unions abandon all 'jurisdiction' over the workers in industries where mass production prevailed: auto, steel, rubber, aluminum, radio, electrical goods and cement. John Lewis stated that the recruitment campaigns organized by the federation in the past had been '25 years of uninterrupted fiasco'. Daniel Tobin hit back, accusing the 'industrialists' of seeking to destroy the very foundations of the AFL.

The carpenters' representative, the obese Hutcheson, after shouting obscenities at John Lewis and making a grab at him, was dealt a hard 'left' to the jaw by the miners' leader.

This punch marked the break. The 'industrialists' had been defeated by 18,024 votes to 10,933. The moment the convention was over, they met and decided upon the creation of a Committee for Industrial Organization, which was officially set up on 9 October. Originally the CIO was to be no more than an organized fraction within the AFL for the purpose of encouraging and promoting the organization of the workers in mass-production industry. But in August 1936 the Executive Council of the old federation suspended the ten Internationals, accounting for over a million members, which had affiliated to the CIO. Thus the split in the American labor movement was consummated. In 1938 the Committee changed its name to the Congress for Industrial Organizations, giving the separation a definitive character.

The Vanguard at Work

The important thing was not the splitting off of a million workers from the AFL. The task awaiting the 'industrialists' was the organization of the unorganized. The job that had to be done was so enormous that it required the co-operation of all those willing to play a part. Whoever showed up at the yard and was ready to pitch in was given a tool. A strange alliance emerged between John Lewis and the Communists and labor radicals each with their own goals and their own methods of struggle. Who would be the dominant partner was by no means settled in advance.

The miners. – Lewis first of all drew on the men in his miners' International who had been his most loyal lieutenants, who had always obediently done his dirty work, broken strikes, dragged the most uncompromising militants through the mud and had them physically attacked – Philip Murray, his Vice-President, Van Bittner, Allan Haywood, etc. But he did not hesitate to secure the help of those very people who had rebelled against his dictatorship in the United Mine Workers, and whom he had smashed. John Brophy had been the most dangerous of his adversaries. He had fought between 1924 and 1928 for the reform of the International, denouncing Lewis's capitulations, calling for the organization of the unorganized miners, the nationalization of the mines, an end to the alliance with the Republicans and the creation of a Labor Party. At the 1926 convention of the International he had been elected President, but Lewis, having rigged the ballot, had succeeded in eliminating him.

Powers Hapgood's opposition. – Hapgood was a Harvard graduate who had become a miner out of idealism – had also given Lewis a good deal of trouble. Hapgood had been barred from entering the convention in 1927 and had been beaten up in a hotel by thugs. In 1930 the progressive opposition had held a dissident convention in Springfield, Ohio. For a while it seemed that the Lewis-Murray apparatus was going to collapse. Adolph Germer was elected Vice-President of the new organization, and was 'savagely beaten on an Illinois street'[5] in 1932. A certain Len De Caux wrote for the 'progressives'' paper.

In 1935 Lewis opened his arms to Brophy, Hapgood, Germer and De Caux. He told Hapgood: 'You and Brophy had a lot of ideas, but they were premature. A general who gets ahead of his army is no use to anybody. But now I'm ready to take over some of these ideas. Let's go, Powers.' Brophy was given the highest post Lewis could offer him, that of organizing director.

The Communists. – No one in the AFL had fought the Communists as bitterly as Lewis between 1920 and 1930. In 1923 he had one of his hack writers, Ellis Searles, write a series of articles, which were then put out as a pamphlet entitled *Communist Attempts to Capture the American Labor Movement.* These articles attacked an alleged Communist plot to amalgamate the craft unions and transform them into industrial Internationals. Lewis had persecuted the Communist miners. Not a single one was left in his International (none, at least, who declared himself as such).

But, at the 1935 AFL congress in Atlantic City, Lewis opposed a resolution which would have prevented Communist-led unions from participating in Federal conventions. He declared that anti-Communism was a pretext concealing attacks on social progress. And, when he set up the CIO, he gave Communist organizations a lot of room.

These 'radicals' who, as a result of their opposition to capitalism, had too often been isolated from the mass movement jumped on John Lewis's bandwagon, though they had been accusing him for years of being a 'murderer', a 'traitor', a 'Judas', a 'strike-breaker' and a 'bosses' agent'. They managed to introduce into his entourage a capable young lawyer, Lee Pressman, who remained the CIO's very influential legal advisor until 1948. Thanks to the hold they managed to gain over John Brophy they got one of their fellow travellers, Harry Bridges, the leader of the Pacific seamen and longshoremen, appointed regional director of the CIO for the West Coast. The Communists had already played an active role in the drive to organize workers in the key industries. They had established themselves in the auto industry through Wyndham Mortimer, the Vice-President of the United Automobile Workers, Robert Travis, who had emerged during the Autolite strike in Toledo, Ohio in 1934, and a number of others. In the steel industry they had dissolved their 'Red' International in 1934 and joined the AFL International, where their several thousand experienced militants had strengthened the 'rank-and-file movements'. Later on, when Lewis launched his great campaign to organize the steel industry, he employed a number of former members of the 'Red' International as organizers. In the rubber industry the Communists took part in the struggle against the AFL clique and played an active role in the 1936 strikes. The Communist Party secretary in Akron, Ohio, James Keller, intervened openly in strikers' meetings.

It is estimated that in mid-1937 the Communists had total or partial control of about forty per cent of the CIO's Internationals. In addition to the industries already mentioned, they had won solid positions in the electrical appliances industry (United Electrical Workers); in the East Coast Seamens's International (National Maritime Union) with Joseph Curran; in the metal mines, in the canned food industry, with Donald Henderson, a former Economics teacher; in non-railway transport; among the wood-workers and in the journalists', civil servants', office workers', and telephone workers' Internationals. In addition, they controlled the most important local union coalitions (New York, Cleveland, Detroit, Chicago, Los Angeles, etc.).

The Trotskyists. – The Trotskyists had been expelled from the Communist Party at the end of 1928. The main factor in their favor was the clear-sighted courage with which they had become aware of the degeneration of the Communist International, broken with it and begun the struggle against Stalinism on a consistent revolutionary program. But their weakness lay in the fact that they had inherited from the American Communist Party a number of its congenital defects, particularly regarding the relationships between revolutionary consciousness and the mass movement, that is to say, more concretely, revolutionary strategy in the unions. Perhaps they did not sufficiently analyze the reasons why Foster's enterprise of infiltration 'from within' had obtained such poor results. In his history of American Trotskyism, their leader, J P Cannon, who had been one of the leaders of the Communist Party, has nothing but praise for the 'progressive innovations' introduced by the Communists into the labor movement. He asserts that they led practically every strike and became the 'unrivaled' leaders of militancy within the American working class. Foster, on the other hand, in his memoirs, retrospectively acknowledges the weaknesses of his undertaking. Cannon does not engage in the same self-criticism.

The Trotskyists made hardly any contribution to the solution of the crucial problem of the organization of the unorganized workers in the key industries. Although Cannon had begun his career as an IWW supporter and, in this capacity, had led the Akron rubber strike in 1913, he and his comrades never perhaps freed themselves sufficiently from Foster's fetishistic opposition to any attempt at 'dualistic' trade-unionism. The founding of the CIO, far from having been foretold or prepared by them, took them unawares. In 1938, Trotsky himself wrote: 'No-one among us foresaw . . . the appearance of the CIO with this rapidity and power . . . We did not see this powerful trade-union movement.'[6] At the very moment when the CIO was spreading its wings, in the big sit-down strikes of 1936-37, the Trotskyists were absorbed in a futile and over-clever entry maneuver within the Socialist Party. Furthermore, they did not stay there for long and although, to be sure, they left reinforced by some valuable militants, especially young people, they had plucked, when all was said and done, a fairly scrawny foul. So they neglected the mass movement and, on their own admission, allowed the Stalinists to seize the leadership of the budding progressive movement. The only sector of the labor movement in which they intervened effectively was on the periphery of the essential battlefield: they did not concentrate their efforts in either auto, steel or rubber. But circumstances resulted in them gaining control of the teamsters' local in Minneapolis, Minnesota. The teamsters were far from the most decisive section of the American proletariat. However, in Minneapolis, the Trotskyists wrote one of the finest pages in the history of the American class struggle.

At the time of the split in 1928, the majority of the Communists in Minneapolis had followed the Trotskyists. By 1934, therefore, the latter already had an organization of long standing which was solidly rooted in the city's labor movement. As Minneapolis was above all a commercial center and a market, transport played a decisive strategic role there. Hence the importance of the teamsters' union. In May, the teamsters went on strike to force the employers to recognize their union. The conflict ended in a relatively satisfactory compromise, since the essential point, the recognition of the workers' organization by the employers, was conceded. On 17 July, after the employers had violated their pledges and sabotaged the agreement reached, the strike started off again. The Trotskyist leaders, Vincent R Dunne, a great militant working-class figure, and his brothers, assisted by Farrell Dobbs, led the movement with absolutely remarkable precision and organizational sense. Each action was meticulously prepared, and the strike strategy was worked out as if it were a military operation. In this strike, the American working class showed the signs of maturity and capacity for self-management which were to reveal themselves more completely two to three years later in the CIO's big sit-down strikes. The most modern technical means were used. The strike committee, which had a sense of publicity, published a daily paper which had an extraordinary effect on the workers. 'For the first time in the history of the American labor movement', writes Cannon, 'the strikers were not left dependent on the capitalist press.'[7]

The State Governor, Floyd B Olson, was a sort of social democrat of plebeian origin who had been brought to power by the reformist Farmer Labor Party of Minnesota. He found himself torn between the ultra-reactionary employers' association and the labor movement, the left wing of which was led by the Trotskyists. Having called out the National Guard, he swung like a pendulum, aiming his blows sometimes against the strike committee, whose headquarters he invaded and whose leaders he arrested, sometimes against the Citizens' Alliance, the employers' organization, which he ordered to be occupied in its turn. After thiry-six days of violent struggle, the movement came to an end with an agreement which was relatively favorable to the strikers. The teamsters' union had not succeeded in pulling the local union coalition into a general strike. The Stalinists, who had not been able to gain a base in the movement, reproached the Trotskyists for not extending it and complained loudly about 'betrayal'. The latter replied that the strike's essential aim – the recognition of the union – had been achieved and that 'you do not make the revolution in one town'.

When the struggle was over, Daniel Tobin, the teamsters' national dictator, tried to smash the Minneapolis union, the radical orientation and semi-industrial structure of which he disliked. But the rival union which he set up was a complete flop, and the Trotskyists retained control of the Minneapolis teamsters' union until 1941, when they were driven out by the combined efforts of Daniel Tobin and President Roosevelt.*

The Factory Occupations (1936-1937)

But whatever the influence and organizational skill of the different groups of radicals within the unions, the 1936-37 revolt gained its impetus above all from the workers themselves. Several factors contributed to it. First of all, the improvement in the economic situation; thanks to Roosevelt's New Deal and a series of measures taken to inject life into the credit apparatus and increase consumer purchasing power – in the countryside as well as in the cities – unemployment had to a certain extent been reduced, and prosperity had returned, at least partially; there were more workers in the factories and they were in a better position to demand higher wages. Then there was the ill-will of the employers, who continually violated and sabotaged the labor clauses of the National Recovery Act, refused to agree to collective bargain-

---

*In 1941 a total of 28 members of the Socialist Workers Party were prosecuted and imprisoned in the first use by the US Government of the notorious Smith Act for antiwar and labor activity. The trial was known as the Minneapolis Labor Case and temporarily smashed the Trotskyists' base in the Minneapolis Teamsters Union.

ing or to recognize the labor unions and, worse still, tried to get rid of the latter by promoting company unions. It soon became clear that there was a crucial gap in the NRA: it provided no mechanism for forcing the employers to respect the law. It was this gap that Senator Robert Wagner tried to fill when at the beginning of 1935 he tabled a bill which became law on 5 July of that year when the National Labor Relations Act, better known as the Wagner Act, was passed.

The Wagner Act confirmed the workers' right to organize freely, bargain collectively and go on strike; and it created a body, the National Labor Relations Board, whose aim was to make sure these rights were respected, both through its own interventions and through the courts. But for nearly two years the Supreme Court gave judgments which indirectly called into question the constitutionality of the Wagner Act. And this attitude encouraged the employers to ignore the law. The workers understood that they would only gain ratification of their rights through bitter struggle.

Another factor contributing to the upsurge was, of course, the industrial unions' break with the AFL and the establishment of the CIO, which gave the workers renewed self-confidence.

There was one final factor which played a part: the triumphal re-election of President Roosevelt in November 1936 gave the workers the impression that Labor had finally overcome reaction. Roosevelt's program, the New Deal, had carried the day. Imagining (with, to be sure, a good deal of self-deception) that they had an ally and a protector at the head of the Federal Government, the workers' confidence increased and they began to be aware of their own power. The factory occupations began in a political atmosphere similar to the one created in France a few months later by the victory of the Popular Front and the accession to power of Léon Blum.

The movement got underway in the rubber industry, in Akron, Ohio, the tire capital. In September 1935 William Green had failed in his attempt to impose his proconsul, Claherty, as President of the rubber workers' International, and the delegates to the founding convention, defying the AFL, had elected a man of their own choice, Sherman H Dalrymple, as President. At the beginning of 1936 the Akron workers were encouraged by the publication of a Federal

Commission of Inquiry report on the deplorable working conditions in their industry. Union recruitment shot up.

And on 29 January the Firestone workers went on strike, occupying the factory. This new technique, designed to prevent the introduction of strike-breakers, seems to have been taught them by a Hungarian or Serbian printer who had had experience of it in Sarajevo just after the outrage of 28 June 1914. It was immediately named the sit-down strike. After two days the movement was victorious. A few days afterwards analogous sit-downs took place at the Goodyear and Goodrich factories.

On 17 February there was another sit-down at the Goodyear Factory to protest against lay-offs of workers. In this case the movement turned into a normal strike, with pickets outside the factory. And, as the authorities were threatening to send in the National Guard, the Akron union coalition announced that 35,000 workers, belonging to 105 unions, would declare a general strike if the strike pickets were attacked. The struggle lasted thirty-three days and ended, yet again, in victory and the organization of the thousands of Goodyear workers.

Akron had kicked off the movement. Flint took over. After Detroit, Flint, Michigan was the biggest center of the American automobile industry and the bastion of the all-powerful General Motors company. The CIO staked its future in Flint, and won.

The sit downs there took place at the end of 1936. They spread to the various General Motors plants, while the company persisted in its refusal to negotiate with the union and the CIO. The division of labor between the different units of production at GM was so highly developed that an attack on a few key factories was sufficient to paralyze the entire system. Likewise, within each factory, action at a particular point was enough to bring production to a halt. Moreover, the workers were so used to order, the flawless functioning of a precision mechanism, and working methods where every detail was calculated and not a second was lost in useless activity that all they had to do was apply this scientific discipline to the organization of their strikes. Lastly, the fact that most auto workers were young and without trade-union experience helped them adapt easily to the new strike tactics forced on them by circumstances.

The upsurge was a closely-knit combination of spontaneity and planning; the elemental thrust of the masses complemented perfectly the experienced leadership of a minority of trade-union organizers. The movement was at one and the same time centralized and democratic. The strike committees had considerable powers. They were sometimes compelled by circumstances to take certain decisions in secret. But, apart from these exceptional cases, their decisions were subject to daily review by general assemblies of strikers.

The leaders were workers who had just recently risen from the ranks and had not yet had time to differentiate themselves from the rank and file by breathing the tainted air at the top of the ladder. The strike was led by men like Wyndham Mortimer, Robert Travis and the Reuther brothers (Walter, Roy and Victor), who had just emerged from the mass of auto workers. The two factors characteristic of all revolutionary action – spontaneity and consciousness – had come together. Though they were less politicized, the sit-down strikes were better co-ordinated than the French factory occupations. The American labor movement, which had been categorized in Europe as 'backward', thus offered a model for the proletariat of the whole world to follow. In Flint it was demonstrated that industrial concentration, mechanization and rationalization, developed to United States levels, create conditions which enable the workers to govern themselves, so opening the way to socialist self-management.

The general staff of the UAW chose two Flint plants Fisher Body nos. 1 and 2, to start with, because of their strategic importance. The employers' response in the second factory was to cut off the heating, while the police, massed at the gates, tried to intercept any food supplies. A violent battle followed. The attackers were driven off and had to retreat.

In mid-January a truce was signed after mediation by the Governor of Michigan, and the strikers were getting ready to evacuate the factories when, due to an indiscretion, their leaders discovered that General Motors was not acting in good faith. The struggle went on. In order to maintain the fighters' morale and acquire a new strategic advantage the militants then decided to point their guns at Chevrolet. But it was a difficult operation; the bosses and the forces of repression were on their guard. The militants had to resort to a ruse. While the workers in Chevrolet factory no. 9 stopped work and occupied the plant, so that the attention of the forces of the employers and the police was concentrated on them, a bold team of 400 workers seized factory no.4, which was of much greater strategic importance. The operation, planned in secret, was a success. The plant was occupied without the slightest incident.

This additional advantage, combined with the Governor's refusal to use armed force against the occupiers this time, finally led to the workers' victory. On 11 February 1937, General Motors capitulated. The auto International was recognized as the sole representative of the workers.

The initials CIO acquired mythical prestige. The union became the nerve-center of all these human beings, bowed and defrauded as they had been for so long. It was no longer just a cold agency office in the business of negotiating over questions of wages, like the AFL, but a home, a school, a place to relax and have fun. The American workers, whom capitalist society had made into self-interested individualists and cynics, suddenly discovered that unknown treasure: comradeship. It was as if a new world, a new existence, had begun. The women, doubly exploited, as workers and as women, were doubly delivered. They had fought with heroism against the police, led by Trotskyist militant, Genora Johnson.

The sit-downs not only gave the workers in the key industries confidence in themselves and in their collective strength, which they had lacked in the past, and which, once acquired, would never leave them; they also shook the notion of private property. To be sure, the American strikers had scrupulously respected their exploiters' property: they had not seized it, they had only 'occupied' it for a short period. Nevertheless, Big Business yelled bloody murder. The lawyers in its pay described the sit-downs as 'revolutionary', 'subversive' acts 'destructive of law and order', 'illegal property seizures' and 'a step towards pure and simple expropriation'. The AFL added its voice to the outcry. After using every means to try and sabotage the auto sit-downs, it attacked the very principle of factory occupations. William Green declared that they were 'a weapon of the CIO likely to open the way to a fascist dictatorship'. The Federal Congress and the legislators of various States rushed to pass laws prohibiting sit-down strikes. The workers responded by invoking a new notion: the right to own their jobs. In this way a first breach was made in the wall of private property. The consciousness of the workers was slowly awakening to the idea that the big factories where they worked as producers were their collective property.

But the sit-downs in Flint and other places had more immediate consequences on the trade-union and political level. The epidemic of factory occupations reached its apogee in March 1937; at that point nearly 200,000 workers were involved in the movement. And, as we shall see, it was on 2 March 1937 that US Steel signed an agreement with the CIO.

The sit-downs also provoked a favorable ruling on the Wagner Act handed down by the Supreme Court on 12 April. For nearly two years this body had allowed a doubt to hang over the constitutionality of a law which forced employers to treat the labor unions as equals. Now that the auto workers had asserted their rights through direct action, the judges admitted that the law in no way violated the United States Constitution.

The Unionization of the Steel Industry

The factory strikes in the auto industry had been neither foreseen nor desired by John Lewis. But he was quick to see the advantages that could be gained from this movement. The upsurge of the auto workers could, if successfully kept in hand, compel Big Business to give in to the CIO. Lewis conducted himself for all the world as if he had prepared, ordered and authorized everything. As soon as the Flint sit-downs began, he cabled the strikers, promising them the CIO's complete and unanimous support in the conduct of the strike. Addressing a press conference in Washington, he recalled that the CIO had just recently helped the United States President to repel the attack of the 'economic royalists' who had tried to use their money to get him out of the White House. 'The same economic royalists', he added,[8] 'now have their fangs in Labor. The workers of this country expect the Administration to help the strikers in every reasonable way.'

When, a little later, the President called the CIO leaders to the White House and insisted that negotiations for a settlement of the dispute should begin only after the factories under occupation had been vacated, John Lewis replied with a categorical 'no'. And when the Governor of Michigan, Frank Murphy, threatened to send in troops, Lewis succeeded in forcing the Governor to back down. In the negotiations, which resulted in a surrender by General Motors, he showed his qualities as a negotiator.

As soon as the storm had passed, John Lewis returned to the plan which he had thought out so thoroughly and which was his essential objective: the unionization of the steel industry. The coal-miners and the two garment workers' unions, led by Hillman and Dubinsky, supplied the funds required for the campaign. A team of 433 organizers was established and sent into action. They operated in accordance with a meticulously prepared strategy. Thirty-three regional offices were opened in steel centers. A newspaper was published and an advertising manager, experienced in modern techniques, engaged.

The Steel Workers Organizing Committee (SWOC) directed its attention not only to the unorganized, but also and above all to those workers organized in the scab company unions. The steel magnates had in fact developed this type of organization so as to counter the rise of labor unionism without overtly violating Clause 7a) of the National Recovery Act. They had even encouraged the formation of a 'Central Council of Employees' Representatives', consisting of delegates from different factories, in the hope that this Council would be dominated by conservative, anti-CIO elements. But what happened was just the opposite. On 20 December 1936, 200 'employees' representatives', delegated by forty-two steel mills, met in Pittsburgh and decided to affiliate to Lewis's Organization Committee. By the end of 1936 125,000 steelworkers had joined SWOC.

On 2 March 1937, Lewis signed an agreement with Myron C Taylor, representing the steel trust. SWOC was officially recognized. At the beginning of September, on Labor Day, 200,000 steelworkers took part in a giant demonstration in Pittsburgh.

John Lewis Contains the Movement

Yet the founder of the CIO had not changed his spots. He remained a conservative, wedded to class collaboration. The CIO had more than one feature in common with the old AFL. The basic principles of revolutionary industrial unionism, as the IWW had conceived of them – the notions of class solidarity and class struggle – were foreign to it.

At the very moment he was taking the leadership of the movement, Lewis was obsessed by the idea of containing the radicalization of the masses. Had it not been for him, the rebellious industrial workers might well have followed their leaders into a class-struggle trade-union federation.

The founders of the CIO – Lewis, Hillman, Dubinsky – wanted to set limits to a movement which, at bottom, disquieted them. The respective objectives of John Lewis and William Green were not fundamentally different. They just disagreed about methods.

Moreover, John Lewis's relatively conservative venture would have failed had it not been for the attitude of the radicals themselves, most of whom gave him their backing. Some of them sobered down with the offer of a good job.

In the auto industry the rift between the rank and file and the leadership appeared the moment the battle with General Motors ended. The contract signed by the UAW with the trust was not wholly satisfactory. The union was only recognized as the representative of the workers in the seventeen plants which had gone on strike, and then for a period of six months only. The bosses continued to hire non-union labor. In addition, there were gaps in the contract in relation to speedups, seniority, shop stewards and minimum wages. Lewis's deputy, John Brophy, had to defend the deal against an opposition which was demanding, among other things, that the contract should be put to a vote.

The split was revealed more clearly during the Chrysler strike, a sit-down which followed the one at General Motors in March 1937 and lasted seventeen days. The company had agreed to recognize the union's right to represent its members, but refused to grant it exclusive representation of the work force. Lewis made a truce with Chrysler of his own accord; the workers were to vacate the factories without having won what they had gone on strike for. Chrysler publicly congratulated John Lewis on his intervention, while the workers demonstrated their displeasure. Five votes had to be taken before the workers at the main Dodge factory would agree to leave the shops.

From this moment on, Lewis and his spokesmen made repeated statements condemning factory occupations. But, for all that, they did not disappear. The rank and file continued for many months to make use of this weapon, whose efficacy they had learned. The sit-downs became wildcat strikes, that is to say, strikes disapproved of by the trade-union leadership. They flared up again here and there all the way through 1937, generally in response to some employer's provocation. The most notable was the one at the Pontiac plants at the end of November. The President of the UAW, Homer Martin, in agreement with Lewis, intervened harshly in these different disputes. He declared the strikes illegal, threatened the strikers with the withdrawal of all financial or other support, and finally forced them back to work.

The movement was much more easily controlled in the steel industry, since it had never been as spontaneous there as in the auto industry. It was muzzled from the moment it achieved victory. Lewis and the steel trust reached agreement without the workers having been consulted or even informed of what was afoot. Whereas the auto International had grown from the bottom up, the steel International was brought into being from above, administratively, by means of a general staff with a lot of money at its disposal and made up of former leaders of the miners' International who had never been noted for their respect for internal democracy.

To cap it all, the steel International absorbed even scab unions. In short, used to being lorded over, the workers easily switched from the dictatorship of their employers to that of their new union leaders.

In the textile industry Sidney Hillman organized the workers without any real trade-union agitation, his sole objective being to bind them to their employers by contract. This entire procedure was carried out from above, without real rank and file participation.

There were several industries in which the CIO appointed the members of the organizing committee. The latter had a monopoly of all decisions concerning strikes and contracts, and controlled most union locals' funds.

CHAPTER 3

The war and its aftermath

The War and National Unity

The young CIO had barely reached adolescence when it was absorbed into the apparatus of the American Empire. Strikes were outlawed, not through an order from above, à la Hitler or Mussolini, but through a 'no-strike pledge' by the trade-union leaders.

Although the wage freeze meant that wages fell behind the inflationary rise in the cost of living, the workers at first accepted these fetters fairly submissively, since war production had not only absorbed chronic unemployment, but given jobs to those who had never before worked in factories, especially women. All members of the family got jobs, and their combined earnings improved the standard of living of the family unit. In addition, they all put in overtime.

Besides, President Roosevelt still enjoyed a certain prestige among the workers which he used to get them to accept sacrifices, in the name of a deceitful 'Equality of Sacrifice'. In fact Big Business was supposed to make its contribution in the form of increased taxes. But the workers, for their part, had not been forgotten by the taxman. They discovered that their buying power was dwindling, while the monopolies were amassing profits. In the end, to get the workers to accept a wage freeze, Roosevelt set up the Office of Price Administration (OPA), whose job it was to control prices. But this body was unable to stop the rise in the cost of living.

The union leaders had sacrificed an excellent strategic position without getting anything much in return. The demand for labor far outstripped the supply. The workers were in a position to make the bosses dance to their tune. Had they not been deprived of the right to strike, they could have made considerable advances; however, compulsory arbitration by the War Labor Board completed their disarmament. In order to create an illusion of impartiality, the Board was established on a tripartite basis composed of equal numbers of trade-union, employers' and public representatives. But the public was represented by the Government, the self-styled guardian of the 'general interest'. And the Government was nothing more than the executive agent of Big Business. The trade-union representatives, reduced to the role of an impotent minority, helped to sustain the illusion that the Board was an impartial agency. The judgments which it delivered were not favorable to the workers. Later on Roosevelt issued a decree enabling the Board to take punitive measures against recalcitrant unions. In one of his rarely lucid intervals, Matthew Woll, one of the most conservative bureaucrats in the AFL, declared that the War Labor Board had become 'a policeman's stick'.

At the beginning of 1942 the President got the trade unions to renounce 'voluntarily' their right, guaranteed in their contracts, to receive double pay for work done on Sundays and holidays. On 16 July the War Labor Board froze wages by promulgating the Little Steel formula. (The 'formula' drew its name from the fact that it was first applied in the steel mills not connected with the steel trust, united in an association nicknamed Little Steel.) The formula was then applied to industry as a whole. Evaluating the rise in the cost of living between January 1941 and May 1942 at 15 per cent, the Board prohibited any wage increase in excess of this percentage. From May 1942 onwards, prices were supposed to remain stable; wages, according to the authorities, should therefore follow suit. In fact, prices rose in a spiral, in spite of the OPA, and wages remained static.

The representatives of Labor also became involved in the War Labor Board, in this way lending credibility to the Executive decree issued by President Roosevelt on 17 April 1943 on the recommendation of this Board, which bound workers to their jobs for the duration of the war.

When the workers finally got angry, the Government did not hesitate to send in the Army against them. When the workers at North America Aviation in Inglewood, California stopped work in June 1941, Roosevelt ordered the troops to occupy the plant and threatened to draft the strikers. Philip Murray condemned the strike on behalf of the CIO and delegated a representative who was mandated to remove the leaders of the trade-union local and bring the conflict to an end. Sidney Hillman gave his approval to the President's intervention.

Later, when the struggling miners challenged the no-strike pledge and the Little Steel formula, Congress passed the

Smith-Connally Act (25 June 1943), which banned work stoppages in Government-run concerns and introduced various procedures designed to counteract strikes. Thereafter it was enough for the Government to seize a concern to make a strike in it illegal. For the sake of appearances Roosevelt used his right of veto against the new law. But Congress was undeterred and the President did nothing to sway the few Southern Democratic votes which could have nullified the proposed legislation. In fact, he had promised the Southern reactionaries back at the end of 1941 to bring in anti-labor laws in exchange for their support for the United States' entry into the war.

As a consolation for the sacrifices they had agreed to in the name of the workers, the trade-union leaders obtained a few meager concessions. One of them was the introduction into employment contracts of the so-called maintenance of membership clause, which stipulated that all employees belonging to the union at the end of a certain time (generally two weeks) following the signing of a contract, and all those joining the union after this period had elapsed, had to retain their membership for the duration of the contract. The trouble with this formula was that it left it up to the worker to decide whether or not he joined a union. He was therefore vulnerable to pressure from the employer who tried to discourage him from union membership. More than one worker reasoned: 'Why should I pay dues to the union when I can get just as much without belonging to it?'. At first Philip Murray protested, but he eventually accepted the bone which the War Labor Board threw him to gnaw.

Another consolation offered to the trade-union movement was the check-off system, whereby the employer deducted the amount payable in trade-union dues from the payroll stubs of unionized workers and gave it to the union. This service was appreciated by the trade-union bureaucracy, since it was assured of regular receipt of funds without having to lift a finger; but it alienated the union member by making the employer the union treasurer.

As compensation for the sacrifices made by Labor, the trade-union leaders were allowed to sit on innumerable bodies concerned with the running of the war, and were entrusted with settling questions of production, man-power and wages. In this way their vanity was flattered. But they never had a real say in things. The representatives of the capitalist state and Big Business reigned supreme. Contrary to what happened in Britain, where the Conservatives had to admit the Labor Party into a coalition government, the American trade-union bureaucracy was not placed on an equal footing with the men of Big Business, even in appearance. It gained neither Cabinet rank nor important Government posts. It only entered the White House through the service door. Sidney Hillman never became more than a secret adviser to the President.

At the congress of the miners' International in October 1942 the delegates agreed with John Lewis that 'the officials of the trade unions were in danger of becoming unofficial representatives of the Administration, disciplining the rank and file and shifting from militant independence to pliant dependence upon the good will of the Government administrators'.[1]

As the war went on, President Roosevelt packed Government agencies still further with men of Big Business. So it was that, under the pressure of the Southern industrialists, he appointed the reactionary Fred Venson 'economic stabilizer'. The President of the textile International, Emil Rieve, one day had a stray impulse to act independently; he resigned from the War Labor Board and declared that the workers in the cotton industry would call off their no-strike pledge: 'We agreed to the no-strike pledge', he declared, 'in exchange for an impartial Board, not in order to get Vinson.' He withdrew his resignation in next to no time.

The only one not to complain about the overly small share given to the workers in the war-time economy was Sidney Hillman. The 'trade-union statesman', as he was dubbed, had become the semi-official ambassador of the Administration to the labor movement, much more than Labor's ambassador to the Administration. He ran the Office for Production Management together with the General Motors magnate, William S Knudsen. In this capacity he passed war orders to Ford and Bethlehem Steel despite the fact that these companies continued to defy the Wagner Act openly and to provoke the workers. Not only John Lewis, for whom he became a *bête noire,* but even Philip Murray, with whom he remained on the best of terms, found that Sidney Hillman was going a bit too far.

The Communists Go Patriotic

Hillman found competitors and allies. The Communists vied in patriotic zeal with him. During the period between the Nazi-Soviet Pact of August 1939 and the German aggression against the USSR in June 1941, they had been fierce adversaries of American imperialism and national unity. But with the Wehrmacht's eastern drive they became war-mongers. The American Communist Party went out of business of its own accord. 'The workers', Foster wrote in 1942,[2] 'have to take the lead in accepting willingly every sacrifice necessary to prosecute the war; they must be tireless in carrying out the multitudinous tasks of the war; they must make the defense of the nation in this crisis their supreme lodestar in all their activities.' And Earl Browder, going one better, wrote that same year that, if the war was to be won, 'the main sacrifice' had to be made by the workers.

No-one gave more ardent backing to the no-strike pledge than the Communists. They branded all those who went on strike or declared their support for strikes as traitors. In March 1944 the employees of the big Chicago mail-order firm, Montgomery Ward, stopped work when the management refused to renew a contract – in spite of the fact that the CIO-affiliated union had been victorious in regular elections. It was the first official strike since Pearl Harbor. Practically every tendency in the labor movement formed a common front. The teamsters (AFL) and railroad workers (AFL or independent) respected the picket lines. Every tendency, that is, except the Communists.

Harry Bridges, whose longshoremen's International had organized the workers in Montgomery Ward's warehouses, cabled President Roosevelt to the effect that despite the provocation by the employers the members of his union would not take part in the strike. The Chicago union coalition appealed in vain to these workers to disobey their trade-union leadership's orders, calling on them to respect rather than break the strike. Samuel Wolchock, the President of the CIO United Retail, Wholesale and Department Store Employees of America, was subjected to the most violent attacks by the Communists, who bitterly accused him of sparking off the dispute.

The Communist fraction within the Chicago union coalition attacked the secretary of the coalition for 'being more concerned to support the workers at Montgomery Ward than to reaffirm and defend the no-strike pledge'. The communists advocated all-out production and even speedups. In the auto International they gave their approval to piece-work, to which the organization had always been opposed, and supported a wage freeze. (They did not, it must be added, succeed in getting the backing of the International for these two measures, in spite of all their efforts.)

Many employers did not hide the fact that their preferences went to trade-union leaders of Communist allegiance. A journalist writing for the Chamber of Commerce wrote that some employers directed their workers to unions controlled by the Communists, since they were more reasonable on matters of wages and working conditions and maintained more discipline among their members than 'anti-Communist' unions. Philip Murray condemned the leaders of certain Communist-dominated unions for the support they gave to a militarization of the workers, which, in spite of everything else, Labor did have the decency to oppose. The Communists offered to prolong the no-strike pledge. Albert Fitzgerald, the President of the International representing the workers in the electronics industry, which was controlled by the Communists, declared in 1945: 'The no-strike pledge was not declared only for the duration of the war.'[3]

The Communists' attitude during this period had a lasting effect on the American workers; their standing in the workers' eyes, which they had earned by the militancy they had shown in former times and their active participation in the founding of the CIO, had taken a big dive. It was to facilitate their subsequent exclusion from the ranks of Labor.

Lewis Goes It Alone

For his part, John Lewis fell out with President Roosevelt and consequently with the CIO. Although his intransigence may well have been inspired by considerations other than the interest of the workers, it nevertheless had important consequences: it created a fissure in the edifice of national unity and helped the disoriented workers to regain confidence.

From the start, as has been pointed out, the Lewis-Roosevelt partnership had rested on a temporary and limited community of interests. They went part of the way together because they needed each other, but they were not pursuing the same goals. The unforeseen growth of the CIO altered the relationship of forces between capital and labor to a greater extent than Roosevelt had wanted. Things deteriorated when, in the spring of 1937, Big Business tried to test the CIO's strength by forcing it into a strike in the steel mills belonging to the Little Steel group. The militant bosses of Bethlehem and Republic Steel mobilized the police together with fascist militia-type bodies (citizens' committees) to terrorize the strikers and smash their movement.

Although a pro-Labor President was in office in Washington, the police opened fire, on 30 May 1937, on an open-air meeting being held in the neighborhood of the Republic Steel plant in South Chicago, killing ten workers and wounding a hundred. More striking steelworkers were killed in Massillon and Youngstown, Ohio. The Governors of the States which had sent in the National Guard against the strikers were Democrats and supporters of Roosevelt, and the man responsible for the Chicago massacre was none other than the Democratic Mayor Edward J Kelly, one of Roosevelt's lieutenants, elected with Labor's backing.

While workers' blood was flowing in the streets of the steel centers, President Roosevelt, speaking at a press conference, quoted a famous line from *Romeo and Juliet*:

> 'A plague on both your houses!'

heaping opprobrium on both camps at once, Labor as well as capital. Lewis replied a few months later in a speech broadcast on radio and television. Recalling the battle of Little Steel, he exclaimed:[4]

> 'Labor, like Israel, has many sorrows. Its women weep for their fallen and they lament for the future of the children of the race. It ill behooves one who has supped at Labor's table and who has been sheltered in Labor's house to curse with equal fervor and fine impartiality both Labor and its adversaries when they become locked in deadly embrace.'

Relations between Lewis and Roosevelt cooled. From 1938 onwards the President ignored the union leader's opinions and no longer took account of his recommendations when he was making appointments to Government posts.

Another reason for the break between Lewis and Roosevelt which, to a certain extent, flowed from the first was the more and more pronounced war-mongering of the President.

Lewis was opposed to America's entry into the war: firstly out of hatred for the President; secondly because this hatred brought him closer to the isolationist wing of the Republican Party; and finally because Lewis had nothing to gain from a war which would confer dictatorial powers on the Executive, increase the influence in the councils of state of both the military and the magnates and reduce Labor to a still more subordinate position. He was too proud to accept the servile role that was to be played by men of lesser stature such as Philip Murray, Sidney Hillman and William Green during the period of national unity.

On the night of 25 October 1940, without informing any of his CIO associates of his intentions, Lewis stated in a radio broadcast:[5] 'I think the re-election of President Roosevelt for a third term would be a national evil of the first magnitude. He no longer hears the cries of the people.' After endorsing the candidacy of the Republican, Wendell Wilkie, Lewis placed the question of confidence before the members of the CIO: if they were not going to follow his advice and recommendations, he would quit the Presidency of the federation at the next convention.

Lewis's move underestimated Roosevelt's popularity among the workers. Called upon to choose between him and the author of the New Deal, the workers opted for the latter. Lewis had imagined that, after weaving the myth of Roosevelt as Labor's deliverer for seven years, he could, from one day to the next, without any prior explanation, order his troops to go over to the Republican camp – the camp of ex-President Hoover, who was associated in people's minds with the Great Depression.

Roosevelt was easily re-elected. And Lewis, keeping his word, did not stand for the Presidency of the CIO at the November 1940 convention; he handed it over to his lieutenant, Philip Murray. However, Murray had meanwhile split from John Lewis when the latter accused Roosevelt of 'plotting' the United States' entry into the war; and Philip Murray's candidacy had been keenly supported by Sidney Hillman.

Lewis Versus Roosevelt

In his struggle against Roosevelt and war John Lewis had initially enjoyed the support of the Communists, who were, at the stage of the war, defeatist to a man. When Lewis endorsed Wilkie, the CIO's legal adviser, Lee Pressman, warmly congratulated him; Harry Bridges praised him for showing 'the courage of a lion'. While expressing reservations about his political choice, the Communist leader Earl Browder wrote that among Lilliputians who were grovelling at the feet of the war machine Lewis stood out like a giant. At the CIO congress in November 1940 the Communists, reinforced by the cheering-section of the miners' International, gave Lewis a 43-minute ovation.

But, on 22 June 1941, Hitler attacked Russia, and the American Communists reversed engines. They deserted John Lewis and went over to Sidney Hillman. Lewis was isolated. He was bitterly disappointed, for, in his conceit, he had not understood that his erstwhile allies were devoted body and soul to a deity far more exalted than himself. Yet he made one last effort to defeat the interventionist forces in the CIO, led by Sidney Hillman and the Communists. On 18 October 1941, a few weeks before the federation's congress, he went to Philip Murray and asked him, in vain, to remain faithful to him. There was a rupture between the two men.

In these circumstances Lewis preferred action to speeches: he thumbed his nose at Roosevelt and Philip Murray by calling a strike in the 'captive' mines. On 14 September the 53,000 miners in the coal-mines owned by the steel trust had stopped work. They wanted higher wages and union control of hiring, a justified demand, since 95 per cent of them were unionized. The steel magnates continued to employ non-union labor. If they gave in to their miners, they would not be able to avoid making the same concession to the workers in their steel plants.

By provoking this conflict, the aim of which appeared to be limited, Lewis was thus opening a battle which involved the entire steel industry. After a short truce the strike flared up again and soon gave rise to a solidarity strike by 100,000 miners in non-'captive' mines. Roosevelt threatened to call out the military while rumour had it that 50,000 men would be mobilized to maintain public order.

Philip Murray was placed in an embarrassing position. On the one hand, the dispute upset his plans for integrating the CIO into the national inter-class bloc which was being prepared in order to fight the war; on the other hand, he could not, as the Vice-President of the miner's International, disown his own organization, and it was difficult for him, as the chairman of the Steel Workers Organizing Committee, to come out against a movement which closely affected the steelworkers. Moreover, the delegates to the CIO congress, which had just begun in Detroit on 17 November 1941, took up the strikers' cause enthusiastically. Murray resigned himself to protesting against the judgment of the National Defense Mediation Board which was unfavorable to the strikers. But at the same time he prevented any solidarity action by the steelworkers. Only the Communists dared to oppose the strike openly.

Roosevelt had to beat a retreat when, despite the decision, Lewis called the 'captive' miners out again. To save face, he submitted the conflict to a three-man arbitration commission, which granted the miners in the 'captive' mines union control of hiring. It was a setback for the President and national unity. The following year, 1942, the miners' International withdrew from the CIO and dismissed Philip Murray from his position as Vice-President.

The Miners' Four Rounds

Having regained his freedom, Lewis could show just what he was made of. He behaved as if America was not at war, defied the Little Steel formula, the no-strike pledge and the War Labor Board, confronted Roosevelt and dealt with him as one Power with another. He dared to cripple a huge country engaged in an armed conflict unprecedented in history. For a moment he caught the greatest Power in the world off balance bringing it down with a national miners' strike in four rounds.

In the end, alone against everyone, he won.

He won because he had discerned, with his sure instinct for the mood of the masses, the dissatisfaction and impatience at the grass roots. He was the spokesman first of his miners and then, when the miners' example spread, of the American workers as a whole. He was able to challenge and defeat the White House because he had the invisible support of a power almost equal to that of the President, the power of Labor.

In quitting first the AFL, then the CIO, Lewis had isolated himself (at least in appearance) from the main body of the labor movement. But he remained the leader of the miners, the most militant organization of American Labor. Apart from their traditional grievances, the miners had recent and pressing motives for complaint. Their wages, which had always been lower than those in other key industries, were frozen even more solidly than those of other groups of workers by the Little Steel formula. And during this time the cost of living was shooting up in the mining basins. In some cases the prices of essential foodstuffs had risen by 100 per cent since 1941.

In March 1943, on the eve of the expiry of the various contracts of the coal and anthracite miners, Lewis announced the wage claims of his men. The advisers to the White House were afraid that the slightest concession to the miners would encourage the workers in other industries to put in claims too. In addition, they hoped to isolate and compromise Lewis by forcing him into a fight which, in their view, given the circumstances, could only end in defeat. On 8 April the President signed an executive order strengthening, rather than softening, the wage freeze, and on the 29th, after miners' wildcat strikes had broken out here and there, he delivered an ultimatum to the strikers, ordering them to resume work immediately, failing which he would use all his vast powers against them. Two days later he decided to requisition the mines and place them under temporary Government management. The threat of military intervention was in the air.

The miners responded on 1 May with a general strike. But it lasted no more than a morning. Lewis, humoring public opinion, agreed to a two-week truce, which was extended until the end of May. And on 1 June, since his demands had not all been met, he again threw the miners into the fray. A further truce, to expire on 20 June, was accepted by Lewis. When zero hour came, without any results to show from the negotiations, the miners, still with the same unanimity, went on strike for the third time. The action lasted 48 hours, but this time the strikers were less easily controlled: six days after the order to go back to work, 150,000 miners had still not responded.

With Lewis accepting a lengthy new truce – it expired on 31 October – wildcat miners' strikes broke out over the summer in western Pennsylvania, Alabama and Indiana. The miners were obviously exasperated. On the morning of 1 November the 530,000 strong miners' army was out on strike again as one man. The fourth round was beginning. Roosevelt finally backed down. The choice was either to break the miners' strike by force or to grant concessions.

The first solution was risky. The presence of the troops would not have made the miners go back to their pits; the dispute would have dragged on and the steel industry, essential to the conduct of the war, would have been crippled by the lack of coal. The use of force would furthermore have scandalized working-class opinion, which Roosevelt needed to take account of. So he yielded and, over the head of the War Labor Board which had persisted in turning a deaf ear, he agreed to make a number of concessions to the miners.

During the battle the trade-union leaders had stabbed the miners in the back. Philip Murray had declared: 'I shall not break my pledge to the President to refrain from strike action.' The leaders of the auto and rubber Internationals had publicly condemned the movement. The Communists had organized mass demonstrations against Lewis. But the subordination of the War Labor Board to Big Business had been so clearly revealed that even the most servile of trade-union leaders had to dissociate themselves from that body and threaten to resign from it.

Lewis had scored only a partial economic success, but had won a resounding victory on the political front. The whole edifice of national unity was shaken as a result. Finally, and above all, the miners' struggle restored courage and self-confidence to workers in other industries. The no-strike pledge had never been popular among the workers. But, for want of a new pole of attraction, they had initially expressed their discontent passively. Since Pearl Harbor, attendance at trade-union local meetings had fallen and the workers seemed gripped by a sort of lethargy. John Lewis's bold action snapped them out of it.

Right at the beginning of the miners' strike the delegates to the Michigan State CIO congress, representing 500,000 auto workers, passed a resolution in support of the strikers against the wishes of their leaders. In June 29,000 auto workers, swept by the contagion, stopped work for four days at the Chrysler plants in Detroit, and 50,000 Akron rubber workers struck for six days. At the end of 1943, 200,000 steelworkers went out on strike and Philip Murray quickly had to force them back to work. The railroad workers threatened to follow suit, and Roosevelt ordered the Army to seize the networks in order to forestall conflict. A million railroad workers received a wage increase, so putting the Little Steel formula under further strain.

Walter Reuther's Hour Strikes

It was not, however, until the end of the war that the workers in the key industries returned to the stage. For them the war had been only a compulsory interval after which the movement picked up again with increased strength and maturity. The auto industry was once again in the forefront. Hundreds of thousands of young men had been absorbed by the industry during the war and had joined the International, whose membership now exceeded a million. Although the organization had sobered on the surface, it had developed in depth. It had consolidated its structures and its system of shop stewards.

In 1941, a few months before Pearl Harbor, the UAW had won a victory over Ford, the only auto manufacturer which still persisted in excluding the trade union from its factories and terrorizing unionized workers. After a spontaneous ten-day strike at the beginning of April 1941, preceded by an intense and effective organizing campaign, the 'lord' of River Rouge had had to back down and agree to elections in his factories, which resulted in a big majority for the CIO. Seeing that he was beaten, Ford reversed his position and gave his workers privileges which were not granted by any of his competitors.

During the period of national unity a strong minority in the auto International had been opposed to the no-strike pledge and the renunciation of double pay for Sunday and holiday work. This minority became more numerous and more vehement in the course of 1943. And in September 1944, at the UAW congress, under the significant name of the 'Rank and File Tendency', it played, for the first time, the role of an organized opposition, endowed with a consistent program and an experienced leadership. Its resolution demanding the setting aside of the no-strike pledge was supported by nearly 40 per cent of the delegates; and, two months later, when the proposal was put to a vote, about the same proportion of the membership gave it their backing.

This powerful current arising from the grass roots was tapped by an energetic and ambitious young man, Walter Reuther. He belonged to the generation of activists forged by the Great Depression who had come to the fore during the sit-downs of 1936-37. He had kept in contact with the ranks and had a keen understanding of their psychology. His personality had original features which distinguished him from all other American labor leaders. He was not a product of either Gompers' or Lewis's 'machine', nor of Stalin's. He was truly a new man and he embodied the CIO better than any of its founders. He was the son of a socialist working-class militant of German origin. He had himself belonged to the Socialist Party until 1938. He had both a proletarian background and a university training, having attended Wayne State University in Detroit while he was working as a tool and die man at Ford. He knew the world outside America, having worked as a mechanic in Germany and the USSR. His travels round the world had taken him as far afield as India and Japan.

Reuther was possessed of a brilliant, methodical and realistic intellect, in which the agitator combined with the businessman, a remarkable capacity for work and a youthful, winning exterior. Moreover, he did not lack physical courage, as he proved in May 1937 by handing out leaflets at the gates of the River Rouge factory, an act which earned him a beating from Henry Ford's goons.

Although he was influenced, to a greater or lesser extent, by European social democracy, he was still thoroughly American and attached to the capitalist order. He did not even maintain his links with as moderate a progressive group as the Socialist Party. He followed in the wake of the Left of the Democratic Party.

The General Motors Strike (1945-1946)

The resentment which had built up among the auto workers during the years of war and national unity exploded as soon as the war came to an end. In July 1945, at a meeting of eighty-seven Presidents of trade-union locals in the Detroit area, a resolution was carried calling upon the leaders of the International to account for the negative balance-sheet of their period of office. The workers had not had a raise since 1942. The wage freeze had led to wages falling behind prices by almost 20 per cent. Immediately after the end of the war the employers, on the pretext of reconversion, had sharply reduced wages, cut down on overtime, abolished bonuses, laid off many workers and shifted those they kept on to lower categories. General Motors in particular gave the signal for an offensive which was designed to reduce the power of the unions.

Walter Reuther, feeling the wave of discontent rise, grasped that it was in his interest to take the leadership of it. He did so, however, after a considerable delay. During the period of national unity he had supported the renunciation of the strike weapon, although in a more nuanced (and also more skillful) way than the Communists, and had fought the 'Rank and File Tendency', which was calling for the abrogation of the no-strike pledge. He understood that by taking a combative attitude now he had a chance of winning over the most restive workers. He advanced the slogan of a 30 per cent wage hike without a rise in prices. Support came to him from the workers and also from none other than the White House. President Truman, who had succeeded Franklin Roosevelt in April 1945, signed an executive order on 16 August, authorizing wage hikes if they did not result in price increases. The new President's idea was not so much to give the working class a present as to prevent inflation.

Reuther, who had already, in June, proposed to the authorities a plan for wage hikes without price increases, seized the opportunity. He proposed his program as being relevant not only to the auto workers, but to the entire American working class.

General Motors spurned the demands which were presented to it. Then Reuther launched the watchword: 'Open your books!'. Capitalist America hid its face in horror. By demanding that the company should publicly divulge its secrets, the auto International was driving a wedge into the status quo: it was not merely a question of establishing whether or not General Motors was capable of granting a substantial wage increase without raising its prices; the call for the opening of the books contained in embryo the demand for workers' control of production and the socialization of the monopolies. Naturally Reuther did not intend to go as far as that; and he stated this publicly. He only wanted to arouse public opinion and swing it in favor of his wage demands.

Since General Motors persisted in its refusal, 225,000 of its employees, at 96 different plants, began a strike on 21 November 1945, which was to last 113 days and finally draw nearly two million workers in its wake. Not only did three powerful industrial organizations, the steelworkers, the workers in the electrical appliances industry and the meat packers, join forces with the General Motors workers; for the first time an auto workers' strike also enjoyed the support of social groups outside the industrial working-class: white-collar workers, the middle class, war veterans.

The solidarity was more effective than is usually the case in the United States. From the beginning of the struggle a united workers' support committee was set up, with the participation of both the AFL and the CIO, as well as a national committee for aid to the strikers' families composed of prominent liberals, among them Eleanor Roosevelt. In the course of January proletarian reinforcements appeared on the battlefield. On the 15th, 200,000 workers from the electronics industry; on the 16th, the meat packers (CIO and AFL together); on the 21st, the 750,000 steelworkers. President Truman, after enjoining the General Motors strikers to return to work, decided to appoint a committee of inquiry which concluded that the company could concede an increase of 19.5 cents per hour without having to increase its prices. GM persisted in its refusal.

But the reinforcements made separate deals. Philip Murray accepted an increase of 18.5 cents for the steel industry. The Communists did likewise for the electrical appliances industry, and the meat packers settled for 16 cents. The other sections of the auto International agreed to 18.5 cents from Chrysler and 18 cents from Ford. And all the while the General Motors workers were still in struggle.

Finally, on 13 March, the fighters in the last ditch, those at General Motors, won the equivalent of the 19.5 cents recommended by the committee of inquiry, as well as a few other benefits. It was a little over half the 30 per cent increase sought originally.

The battle at General Motors was far from a defeat. To be sure, the wage hikes won were quickly cancelled out by sky-rocketing prices, but on the whole the trade unions emerged strengthened from the struggle; the morale of the workers and their self-confidence, at least in the weeks following victory, were reinforced.

The Battle of the Railroads

The 1945-46 strike galvanized the railroad workers among others. The railroad Brotherhoods, independent of the rest of Labor, were bastions of the most reactionary trade-unionism to be found in the United States. By their corporate exclusivism and friendly-society mentality they outdid the AFL itself. The two railroad organizations which threw themselves into the battle, the railroad workers' Brotherhood and the mechanics' Brotherhood, had not been involved in a strike for over 50 years. They were autocratically run, the former by Alexander Whitney, the latter by Alvanley Johnston. Both of them trampled democracy underfoot and had become advocates of industrial peace. Yet they had to fight, whether they liked it or not.

The railroad workers were especially dissatisfied in fact. Their organizations' lack of combativity and solidarity had led to a decline in their wages and working conditions in relation to other industries from first place in 1928 to twentieth in 1945. In the autumn of 1944 the five big Brotherhoods had drawn up a common list of demands, which included a 30 per cent wage increase and a reduction in working hours. Rank and file pressure was so strong that Whitney was afraid that if he called a strike his men would refuse to go back to work when he instructed them to do so.

The Brotherhood leaders, however, were at daggers drawn with each other, and every one of their actions (even an action as important as a strike) was inspired by a concern to gain special advantage for themselves while doing the greatest possible harm to their rivals. Whitney and Johnston waged a costly guerrilla campaign against David B Robertson, the dictator of the Engineers' Brotherhood (an organization with 120,000 members, including not only engineers but also 40,000 mechanics). The result was that Robertson refused to take part in the struggle, as did the other railroad organizations, and tried to break the strike. Although the mechanics had stopped work, he cabled his members (including his own mechanics), urging them to 'get transportation moving'.[6]

However, the railroad workers who did not belong to the two Brotherhoods officially in struggle refused to act as scabs. Although only a third of the workers ensuring railroad traffic were officially on strike, the American railroad system was brought to a complete halt.

In the end the movement came to nothing, thanks to its two initiators, Whitney and Johnston. They had allowed themselves to be forced into taking strike action, but, placing their faith in the relations Labor had enjoyed with the White House in Roosevelt's time, they were convinced that the President would get them out of their fix at the right moment. They were wrong. Truman was very much out of patience with the labor unions at that point. Advised by an entourage in which the influence of Big Business predominated, he let Whitney work himself into a corner and did not make the expected gesture. The strike, which had first been planned for 18 May, was postponed till the evening of the 23rd. On that date it broke out. Truman, who had ordered the seizure of the railroads a few days beforehand under the Smith-Connally Act, declared on the radio that if the railroaders did not resume work by the following evening railroad traffic would be ensured by Federal troops. Whitney and Johnston did not dare to confront the forces of Government repression. After two days of struggle they ordered their members back to work, making do with a wage increase of 18.5 cents per hour.

Whitney blamed President Truman and announced that he would devote all the financial resources of his organization to beating him at the next elections. (Later, on 20 January 1948, he was to make amends by joining in the chorus of support for Truman's candidacy.)

The Battle of the Coalfields

The example of the General Motors struggle also roused the miners and pushed them into struggle again. Their contracts expired at the end of March 1946. John Lewis called for the creation of a relief and pension fund, to be financed by the employers, by means of a tax of 7.5 cents on wages paid, and administered by the International. The mining bosses refused to take a single step in this new direction. On 1 April 400,000 miners stopped work. For forty days the pits were deserted and the coal stocks ran out.

Since negotiations proved unsuccessful, President Truman ordered the Attorney-General to take possession of the mines on 21 May, still in pursuance of the Smith-Connally Act, so as to have a legal pretext for breaking the strike if need be. But the miners were so determined that the Government thought it wiser to compromise. On the 29th Lewis came to an agreement with the Attorney-General by which the relief and pension fund was to be set up and financed by the employers through a tax of 5 cents for every ton of coal produced. The miners also got substantial wage hikes. A few months later the battle was resumed. On 21 October John Lewis asked for negotiations to review wages and working hours to be reopened and then proclaimed that the contract in force was at an end. On 20 November the 400,000 miners stayed above ground for the second time that year. Shortly before the strike began the Government had had a Federal judge issue an injunction to force Lewis to suspend his action. On 4 December he, along with his International, was very heavily fined.

This penalty angered the entire labor movement. The AFL (to which the miners' International had reaffiliated) and the CIO both sided wholeheartedly with the miners. Among the workers there were many voices raised in favor of a general strike in protest. But the trade-union leaders were afraid of their own power and did not dare to unleash the forces under their control. Lewis, for his part, locked in isolation and ignoring the rest of the labor movement, did nothing to encourage a current of proletarian sympathy. And on 7 December he suddenly ordered a return to work just as he was initiating an appeal to the Supreme Court. Three months later the original judgment was confirmed, although the size of the fine was reduced.

But the November 1946 strike was not actually a defeat. Lewis, in accordance with his usual tactics, had only waved the white flag in order to catch his breath. A few months later, in June 1947, he won greater concessions from the coal magnates, who had regained possession of their mines, than those obtained by any other labor union. In his duel with President Truman he had the last word.

The Southern Drive

It is not possible, within a few pages, to give an overall picture of the South and to explain why a whole area of the United States with a population at that time of 27 million* remained historically underdeveloped compared with the rest of the country. The South was long a backwater; even after the war, William Green of the AFL could compare it to China, India and Mexico, and Baldanzi of the CIO, could describe it as a '"foreign colony", whose struggles recalled the first attempts

---

*36 million, if Texas and Oklahoma, which are more properly part of the Southwest, are included.

at emancipation of the colonial peoples'. To account for this anomaly, we would have to go a long way back, as far as the Civil War, from which, after more than 80 years, the South had still not recovered. Here we shall make do with briefly mentioning that the South was then still exploited in colonial fashion by Big Business in the North. Its industrial development had been systematically held back. Its industrial, commercial and banking concerns were controlled by Wall Street. Wages there were distinctly lower than the national average (78 per cent of the latter in 1944), as was the average per capita income (69 per cent in 1945) while the lower cost of living did not match this drop in wages. The South had the highest rate of illiteracy, disease, death, infant mortality and slum housing in the whole of the United States.

For a long time, the organization of the Southern workers had been considered an almost impossible task: their backward mentality, their total domination by a reactionary paternalist boss class, the division resulting from their racial prejudices, and the extreme distrust which the Southerners felt toward any venture which came from the North seemed so many obstacles to the extension of trade-unionism to the South. A white observer with liberal leanings, W J Cash, expressed his doubts in 1941 as to trade-unionism's chances of victory:[7] 'In spite of slow changing,' he wrote, 'the old pattern is still too powerfully stamped upon the minds of most of the workers'. The black writer W E Burghardt Du Bois considered in 1935, that[8] 'there can be no real labor movement in the South; their laboring class is cut in two . . . Labor can gain in the South no class consciousness'. But these over-pessimistic forecasts were proved at least partially wrong by the relative success of the Southern drives.

It was in the month of May 1946 that the CIO decided to launch into the venture. A fund of a million dollars was established, to which the main industrial unions (steel, autos, textile, electrical industry, etc.) contributed. Philip Murray's steel union made the highest contribution.

The participating unions were not inspired by purely philanthropic motives, but by self-interest. The capitalist firms which had been forced to recognize them in the North continued to apply the *open shop* in their factories south of the Mason-Dixon line.* It was urgent to put an end to this situation. The Northern industrialists had to be prevented once and for all from invoking the unfair competition of low wages in the South to oppose wage raises. And it was also necessary in order to put a stop to their threat to move their firms to the South rather than pay decent wages in the North. As David J McDonald of the steel union declared,[9] 'As long as there is a single non-union man living in America, that non-union man is a threat to the standards of all union men in America.'

The unionization drive in the South was to confront formidable obstacles; it found itself in conflict with the entire social, economic and political system which was rotten to the core. If the contours of the class struggle were sometimes relatively blurred in the North, the CIO's initiative was to lay them bare in the South. As soon as its intentions were made public, the Southern capitalists and their fascist-minded agents threw up a chorus of curses against the invasion of the South by the 'Communists', 'Reds', 'carpetbaggers' and 'nigger-lovers'. If Labor compromised with the adversary, if it, too, fell into 'anti-Communism', if it made concessions to racial prejudice, it would weaken the whole undertaking and jeopardize, from the outset, its chances of success. In such a situation, all progressive forces ought to have made a common front and sunk their differences.

Unfortunately, that was not what happened. As soon as the AFL became aware of the CIO's initiative, it lost no time in calling a conference, amid great publicity, of its organizations in the South. And it declared war on the rival federation's recruitment campaign. William Green came in person to Asheville, North Carolina to accuse the CIO of being a Communist organization. 'The Southern workers', he declared, 'are patriotic Americans. They cannot feel at home in an organization which seems incapable of co-operating with industry and which devotes most of its time to trying to destroy private industry. They have nothing in common with the alien philosophies of the CIO.' And he gave this warning to the Southern industrialists: *'Walk with us, or you will have to defend your life against the Communist forces!'*.

In order to discredit the CIO, the AFL had seized on the pretext of a mass meeting organized a few days earlier by the Communist-controlled New York union coalition, at which a

---

*The demarcation line between the Northern States and the slave States at the time of the Civil War. It cannot be found on any map, but it dies hard.

'Committee to Support the Organization of the South' had been set up. The CIO felt compelled to counter this scurrilous attack by chiming in with Green's 'anti-communism'. The director of its organizing campaign, Van Bittner, a 'carryover' from the miners' union, then (after John Lewis had bequeathed him to Philip Murray), of the steel union, immediately called a press conference to disavow the New York initiative. In a speech which was widely distributed in leaflet form, he exclaimed: 'God knows that Philip Murray . . . and I have dedicated a great part of our lives to fighting Communism in the United States!'. Reverend Charles Owen Rice publicly congratulated the CIO for rigorously keeping the 'Reds' out of the Southern drive.

These statements not only broke up the bloc of 'progressives' at a time when they should have backed one another up in order to take on the Southern counter-revolution. They not only constituted a bad action, but also a lie and an injustice. For it is an undeniable fact that the pro-Stalinist trade-unionists, despite what one might call their 'congenital defects', took a very active part in the organization of the Southern workers and played a vanguard role in the area's main industrial centers.

In spite of the CIO's repeated declarations condemning all racial discrimination, the leaders of the Southern Drive did make concessions to color prejudice; and it is a fact that the pro-Stalinists were about the only ones in the South to tackle openly and unreservedly the organization and education of the black workers. Van Bittner's team adopted the tactic of organizing the white workers *first* while the pro-Stalinists did not hesitate to receive all the Blacks with open arms, even if the whites in the same firm were still reticent toward the trade-union movement, or even hostile to it. For example, in the Camel cigarette factories at Winston-Salem, a magnificent union local was formed, in which Blacks predominated. Its leaders hoped, by example and by proving the union's effectiveness, to win to it little by little the white workers, who were still suspicious, or, more precisely, terrorized by their employer. On the other hand, in Baton Rouge, Louisiana, where the campaign was in the hands of Van Bittner's machine, Standard Oil's huge refinery, which employed nearly 10,000 workers, was still not even partly organized in April 1948, because the organizers persisted in deferring the recruitment of black workers (who were only too keen to join the union), on the pretext that they wanted first of all to recruit the whites (who were still holding back).

The same opportunism was observable in the other issues dealt with by the CIO's official propaganda. The head of publicity for the drive, Ed Stone, congratulated the Southerners for their 'heritage of independence and militancy', forgetting that this 'independence' and 'militancy' consisted in unleashing a bloody civil war for the maintenance of slavery. George Meany of the AFL recalled that the South had given the United States some of its greatest military leaders (whereas, as it happens, the Southern origin of a good many US Army officers accounts for the officer corps' highly reactionary character, analogous to that of the German *Wehrmacht*, which was dominated by the Junker caste).

The CIO undertook the defense of the Southern capitalists against those from the North. 'The CIO', stated a leaflet, 'supports Southern capital in its efforts to promote industries owned and controlled by Southerners.'

The CIO presented itself as being opposed to strikes: 'The strike weapon must be used only to remedy extreme injustices', declared one of its leaflets. George Meany of the AFL praised to the skies the 'perfect' way in which the Southern workers had observed the no-strike pledge during the war.

The CIO thought it smart to counteract the poisonous attacks which religious ministers in the pay of the employers launched from the pulpit against trade-unionism by joining in the prayers itself. A leaflet which was widely distributed reprinted a speech made by Van Bittner in the Episcopalian Cathedral in Boston.[10] 'God', it reads, 'is the Lord and Master of each section of our lives. He is a jealous God. He demands from us each moment of our lives and our breath. He reigns as Lord over your business and he reigns as Lord over my union. He wants Christian economic institutions and, if you please, Christian unions.' Not only did this trade-unionist fawn upon the clergy, but he tried to convince the workers that they were wrong to be distrustful of the latter: 'Frankly speaking', he added, 'a number of American workers are suspicious of established religion. They believe it to be more interested in the piles of bricks and stone in which we worship than in the destruction of the hovels in which the poor man is forced to live. They believe, in other words, that the Church is in favor of the status quo . . . *You and I know that it is not so.'*

In its desire to 'adapt' to the reactionary South, the CIO recruited a number of regional directors still imbued with Southern prejudices in addition to being insanely 'anti-communist', such as Charles L Cowl for Florida, Fred C Pieper for Louisiana and Robert W Starnes for Mississippi. Starnes was a close friend of the Governor of Mississippi, Fielding L Wright, the most reactionary Governor in the United States and one of the main inspirers of the 'revolt' against Truman's 'civil rights' program. Pieper was linked to the 'machine' of the ex-Governor of Louisiana, the aspiring dictator, Huey P Long.

The AFL leaders were, if possible, still more reactionary. The official 'co-ordinator' of the old Federation's recruitment campaign, George L Goodge, was a front man. His role lay in concealing under a 'liberal' and 'humanitarian' veneer the real face of the AFL in the South (craft exclusivism, alliance with the worst reactionary elements, collaboration with the employers and discrimination against Blacks). The real leaders of the AFL in the South were a nasty bunch indeed. In Georgia, they had disturbing relations with the Klu Klux Klan. In Savannah, their paper openly attacked President Truman for his program of 'civil rights' for Blacks. In Louisiana, they were devoted to the corrupt machine of the former boss of New Orleans, Maestri, and that of the Long family. In Memphis, Tennessee, they were allied to the corrupt and corrupting machine of 'Boss' Crump. In Florida, they distributed leaflets urging citrus fruit workers to report immediately to the FBI the appearance of organizers from the rival CIO union. In Dalton, Georgia, they handed to the employers the names of workers who had joined the CIO, and the latter were immediately fired; and so it went on.

And yet, in spite of all these reactionary features, the CIO's Southern Drive, and even the AFL's, were none the less *progressive.* Never had the Southern 'liberals', prompted as they were by the best intentions but heterogeneous and timorous, succeeded in organizing themselves into a coherent force to drag the area out of its backwardness.

The CIO certainly did not possess a consistent social or political program. It accepted and defended the existing economic system. It rejected all socialist ideologies. It continued to cling to one of the two big capitalist parties and refused to set about creating a labor party. But the very necessity of organizing the workers in the key industries gave its program a relatively radical character. It was born in struggle. It successfully confronted the most powerful monopolies in the United States. It condemned and went beyond craft exclusivism and opened its doors to all. In spite of its bureaucratization over the years, democracy had not disappeared from its grass-roots organizations in the late forties and early fifties. Finally, it had to organize the most heterogeneous proletariat in the world, and it was able to do this only by solemnly affirming the equality of all workers, irrespective of race, sex, color or origin. When it 'raided' the South and spelt out the points of this program in a leaflet, this simple enumeration assumed a *revolutionary* character.

The same Van Bittner, whose reactionary statements may have shocked the reader a while back, trumpeted the news of human progress when he declared, in that same Episcopalian Cathedral in Boston, that 'the CIO is devoting all its efforts to breaking the economic power of the giant monopolies'. And the head of publicity for the drive was suddenly transfigured when he stressed that the CIO was 'awakening the men and women workers of the South from the lethargy which has kept them on the lowest rung of the economic ladder'.

The staff who were entrusted by the CIO with the task of organizing the South also reflected this dialectical contradiction. Though some regional directors were, as we have said, openly reactionary, others were distinctly progressive, and the goodwill, perseverance, spirit of sacrifice and physical courage with which they carried out their thankless task, more often than not lost and isolated in the face of decades of stagnation, compels admiration.

Even the most reactionary CIO organizers like Robert W Starnes were progressive without knowing it. Starnes would very much like to have organized *first* and *above all* the white workers, who, in a State like Mississippi, were stuffed full of conservative and racial prejudices. But *it is a fact* that Starnes succeeded mainly, at least initially, in organizing *Blacks* – who, in a racist State like Mississippi, were in the vanguard of human progress, since they had nothing to lose, but everything to gain from a social transformation. This poor Starnes reminds one of those sad men or women who manage to attract only the type of partner they do not like. And it was perhaps in this backward State of Mississippi, under the reactionary leadership of Starnes, that the CIO achieved the greatest miracles. The town of Natchez was one of the worst bastions of obscurantism and anti-Labor and anti-Black terror. A team of sociologists published a detailed description of it in 1941 which leaves an almost heart-breaking impression. But the CIO revolutionized Natchez. The rubber and wood workers there set up solid union locals, where whites and blacks both had their place. The general level of wages was considerably increased. The counter-revolution beat a slow retreat. Natchez began to live.

The same thing happened at Laurel. Here, the 2,500 workers, black and white, of the Masonite Corporation established a strong union local and obtained large wage raises, paid holidays, free medical care, life insurance, etc. And, by opening a co-operative grocery store themselves, they succeeded in containing the rise in the cost of living. Laurel, previously one of the most backward towns in America, gave a pioneering impression after the Southern Drive.

And the same miracle can be found, although much more rarely and in a more attenuated form, in the AFL itself. Thus, in Florida, 3,000 phosphate miners, black and white, were organized *on an industrial basis*; their district published a paper with progressive leanings, the moving spirit of which was a young Protestant minister who at the same time worked as a miner.

The CIO encountered the most obstacles and had the least success in the textile industry, which was the most important industry in the South, employing between 25 and 30 per cent of the total labor force. In 1946, there were 578,300 textile workers in the South. Most of them lived in company owned housing, where the pressure of the bosses and the hold of their agents, including the clergy, were extremely strong. All means, including violence, were used to bar the way to the CIO.

Early in 1949, the textile union claimed to have unionized 125,000 workers in the South, that is to say a little under a quarter of the industry's total work-force. The best results were obtained in North Carolina, but they were a lot less brilliant in South Carolina, Tennessee and Georgia. 'I agree that there have been obstacles in our path that are terrific', declared George Baldanzi in November 1948.[11]

Despite these difficulties and the relatively undistinguished numerical results and despite the heavy handicap with which it burdened itself by trying to compromise with Southern reaction, the CIO nevertheless helped to change the face of the South. Just as after the great victory of 1936-37, one could say, without risk of exaggeration, that the world was no longer the same place.

CHAPTER 4

The blacks and the labor movement*

The time has come to analyze, in terms of the United States as a whole, the antagonism which has existed between white workers and black workers for as long as some men there have sold their labor power to others.**

As early as the beginning of the 19th century, emancipated Blacks flocked into big cities like New York and Philadelphia, putting up with the lowest wages and competing with unskilled white workers for jobs. The result was race war. There was an increasing number of brawls. In Cincinnati, in 1829, a white mob injured and killed freedmen and runaway slaves. In Philadelphia there was a series of racial conflicts between 1828 and 1840. The one in 1834 assumed the proportions of a pitched battle and lasted three days. This was repeated in 1835, 1838 and 1842.

The white workers used every means to limit or prevent the employment of Blacks. At the same time they showed little inclination to support the abolition of slavery, for fear that such an event would substantially increase the number of black workers. The behavior of the abolitionists did nothing to help dispel this distrust. They had little sympathy for the workers and condemned the nascent class struggle between capital and labor. William Lloyd Garrison, speaking at a

---

*This chapter, with minor alterations, was drawn from a full-length account by Daniel Guérin of the struggle of the Black people in the USA: *De L'Oncle Tom aux Panthères,* Editions 10:18, Paris 1963. This was published in an earlier version in the USA under the title *Negroes on the March,* George Weizman, New York 1956. It will be noted that while the present book begins only with the advent of monopoly capitalism, for this chapter Guerin's account of earlier parts of the 19th century is retained. This is because on this question more than on any other aspect of US labor history the crucial events and political alignments which were to mark many aspects of the subsequent relationship between the two major components of American Labor occurred prior to, during and in the years following the Civil War [Ed.] .

** It should be added that research on the relations between the Blacks and the Labor movement ran into a serious obstacle: the spokesmen of Labor unionism and those of the Black race, each concerned to defend their respective group, presented sharply differing versions of this history (D.G.).

workers' meeting in Boston at around the time the first issues of his newspaper, *The Liberator*, were being published in January 1831, denounced the labor movement as an organized conspiracy to 'inflame the minds of our working classes against the more opulent'.[1] According to him, the unions were 'in the highest degree criminal'.

The workers were angry to see the abolitionists[2] '"stretch their ears to hear the sound of the lash on the back of the oppressed black", at the same time as they were deaf to the cries of the oppressed wage workers in the North'. The defense of the wage earners seemed to them to be more important than the emancipation of the slaves and they feared that a campaign centered mainly around abolition would divert attention from their own condition. 'The primary cause of slavery,' they affirmed, 'lies in the very state of industry; it was a matter of changing that before anything else.'

Thus, from the beginning, the movement for racial emancipation and the movement for social emancipation took divergent paths. 'The abolitionists', wrote Du Bois,[3] 'did not perceive the new subordination to which the worker was subjected by organized capital, whilst the workers did not understand that the exclusion from the working-class program of four million workers was a fatal omission.' And yet, notes the author of *Black Reconstruction*, unity between the two movements would have made them 'irresistible'. 'They exhibited fundamental differences instead of becoming the single big party of free labor and free land.' These were irrevocable choices, which were to pit the black and white victims of exploitation against each other for generations.

The most underprivileged white workers in the North were Irish immigrants. Their condition was hardly less deplorable than that of the slaves. They had landed on the shores of the United States in order to escape a centuries-old oppression which was almost as harsh as that suffered by the Africans. Like them, they were on the lowest rung of the social ladder and had to settle for the lowest and worst-paid jobs. But, instead of uniting, these two battalions in the army of the disinherited engaged in cutthroat competition with each other.

In 1863, at the height of the Civil War, a workers' insurrection broke out in New York. The mostly Irish white workers were in control of the city for a few days. The violence of this uprising and the savagery with which it was repressed bore some resemblance to the Paris Commune. Some of its features make it possible to regard it as an episode of the class struggle. The workers were tired of a war, almost all the financial burden of which was being borne by them, and hostile to compulsory military service, which led to their blood being spilt for the sake of the rich. Unfortunately this social conflict was coupled with a racial pogrom. Big Business in New York (which was moreover losing money because of the war with the South) lost no time in diverting the workers' indignation onto their black brothers. Thus stirred up, the Irish workers blamed the Blacks for the war and at the same time satisfied an old resentment against their competitors on the labor market; they killed all those they could lay their hands on.

When Lincoln was assassinated in 1865, the Irish organizations in New York refused to march with the Blacks and the City Council would not let Blacks join the funeral procession.

As the International Workingmen's Association stressed, in an address bearing Karl Marx's signature, the War of Secession had had 'as its immediate result a deterioration in the condition of the American worker'. While Big Business had made fabulous profits from it, inflation had increased the workers' suffering. However, the war had 'offered a compensation in the emancipation of the slaves and the impulse thus given' to the workers' class struggle.* There was hardly any response from the labor movement to this appeal for proletarian internationalism. With a few rare exceptions, it failed to grasp the revolutionary content and significance of Reconstruction. It was too busy fighting the new industrial oligarchy. For their part, the radical white Republicans like Charles Sumner and Thaddeus Stevens showed little interest in or sympathy for Labor.

---

*In this remarkable Address the respective as well as the joint interests of the working-class movement and the Black liberation movement were appraised exactly. However, Karl Marx did not always have such a felicitous position. In November 1864 he had got the International to endorse an extravagant letter to Lincoln, congratulating him on his re-election and calling him (inaccurately) 'a son of the working class'. 'The European workers', it declared, 'feel distinctly that the Star-Spangled Banner bears the destiny of their class.' In presenting Lincoln as the champion of the proletariat because he had emancipated the slaves, Karl Marx was losing sight of the bourgeois and capitalist class character of the Northern regime. The New York Communist Club protested the letter.

As for those black leaders who supported the Republican Party, they did not understand to what extent the new political regime established in the South was under the domination of the Northern capitalist oligarchy and, preoccupied by the political emancipation of their race, they did not notice the mortal threat which hung over the whole nation, and over themselves, from the lightning rise of capitalism.

Labor, thinking that in this way it was taking on the capitalist oligarchy, joined hands with the Democratic Party, the party of the Southern counter-revolution. For their part, the Blacks, thinking that in this way they were fighting the Southern counter-revolution, joined hands with the Republican Party, the party of triumphant Big Business. Neither of them seized the opportunity which had been theirs, shortly after the War of Secession, to bring about a vast concentration of democratic and progressive forces, grouping together the supporters of the political emancipation of the Blacks, the labor unions, the small farmers in the West and the poor whites in the South. It was one of the great missed opportunities of American social and political history.

The trade-union federation in the 1860s was called the *National Labor Union.* There were radical and internationalist tendencies within it. It had forged relations with the International Workingmen's Association. It was waging a struggle for the Eight-Hour Day. Its leader, William H Sylvis, had a relatively progressive position on the race question. He was an advocate of unity between black and white workers. He was conscious of the need to win the Blacks to the cause of Labor. 'If we can succeed', he declared on a trip to the South, 'in convincing them that it is in their interest to make common cause with us, we will have a power in this part of the country which will shake Wall Street.' But he was not able to offer the Blacks a program in conformity with their democratic aspirations. His position on Reconstruction was extremely timorous. He showed himself sharply hostile to the policy of the radical Republicans and blind to the revolutionary content of the experience. And he heaped insults on Congress, which was forcing this immense social change on a refractory South with an iron hand.

Following Sylvis, the National Labor Union, at its 1867 convention, understood that only the organization of the Blacks into labor unions could prevent the bosses using them as strike-breakers:[5] 'Either we shall make them our friends or capital will make use of them as a weapon against us.' Yet the attitude of the white workers toward their black brothers remained hostile, and the burning question of the admission of the Blacks was deferred from one convention to the next. It was only at that of 1869 that black delegates were admitted and the organization of the black workers began to be carried out. But, tired of waiting, the freedmen set up a Black union federation at the end of the same year as a protest against the discrimination which the white unions continued to practise against them. This new organization considered itself part of the National Labor Union and sent delegates to its convention.

At its 1870 convention, the rapprochement between the workers of the two races, which had barely begun, stopped dead. The white union federation certainly took a step forward when it freed itself from the domination of the Democratic Party and decided on the creation of a labor party; but it did so on a program of working-class reforms which ignored the specific demands of the Blacks, such as the defense of their civil rights and the abolition of all discrimination in employment and pay.

For their part, the black workers made the mistake of not grasping this opportunity to unite with the white workers for independent political action. They clung to the Republican Party, which retained in their eyes the prestige of having emancipated them. The congress of the National Labor Union refused to admit one of the black leaders of Reconstruction, not because of the color of his skin, but because he was an official of the Republican Party. A black speaker, likewise a Republican, vehemently opposed the formation of a third party and urged the congress to affiliate to the Republican Party, which amounted to asking the workers to join the party of the bosses. The Black union federation, having lost its fight, broke with the National Labor Union and became a Black branch of the Republican Party, a move which was to bring about its disintegration. Through both sides' fault, the divorce between Labor and the racial emancipation movement became complete.

We now enter the dark years when triumphant Big Business established its unrestricted domination. In the South, the Blacks were betrayed by the Republican Party and the counter-revolution swept away their conquests. In the North, large-scale industry built its bastions into which it threw successive waves of unskilled and unorganized immigrants; it exploited and fostered their national differences, isolating them from and setting them against each other. And, to break their rebellious inclinations once and for all, it brought up wagon-loads of black workers from the South who were prepared to put up with lower wages than the whites and to break their strikes.

The gulf created between the two races by the advocates of slavery served the interests of modern capital perfectly; on the one hand racial prejudice prevented the spread of class solidarity between black and white workers; on the other hand discrimination in employment prompted the black worker to accept like a shot any job enabling him to get a foothold in industry, even if it was at the expense of the white workers. Strike-breaking was his only chance of knocking down the barriers of discrimination.

Where an employer showed himself ready to employ him permanently, as was the case with the railroad magnate Pullman, the Black had more sympathy for the boss to whom he owed his job than for the labor unions which did their utmost to prevent him getting it. When Eugene Debs' American Railway Union was dragged into a serious social conflict with the Pullman Company in 1894, the black workers, instead of siding with the strikers, acted as strike-breakers. They did not forgive the organization, which was on other matters very progressive, for excluding Blacks under its statutes. Debs later acknowledged that the discrimination practised by his union had been one of the main reasons for its defeat.

This pioneer of American socialism had been gravely mistaken in claiming that 'there is no Black question independently of the working-class question, the proletarian class struggle'. 'We have nothing special to offer the Negro,' asserted 'Big Gene',[6] 'and we cannot make separate appeals to all races. The Socialist Party is the party of the working class, regardless of color'. 'When the working class has triumphed, the race problem will have disappeared for ever.'

The error was both theoretical and practical. It showed an incorrect understanding of the relationship between the 'base' and the 'superstructure' – that is to say the manifestations of racial prejudice.

In practice, Debs' conception was likely to confirm the Blacks in their passivity. They might draw from it the conclusion that they had only to stand idly by and wait until Labor had carried out its historical task on their behalf – a conclusion which was nothing but a proletarian transposition of the bourgeois notion that the Blacks were too backward to be capable of independent action. Moreover, an abstract position of the type put forward by Debs alienated a lot of Blacks from working-class socialism, since they did not find in it any immediate response to their racial concerns.

However, not all the labor unions were hostile to black workers. The Knights of Labor, those forerunners of the industrial unions (page 52), believed in the unity of the one great human family. All nationalities, races, creeds and professional categories were welcome in their organization. At their Richmond convention it was a black delegation which introduced the Grand Master of the Order, Terence V Powderly. Black workers joined in droves, and at their height, in 1886, the Knights had some 60,000 black members.

But this attempt to organize the unskilled workers in large-scale industry did not last long. Neither was it long before the Knights of Labor disintegrated, to be superseded by the craft and business unionism of Samuel Gompers, which was as selfish as it was particularistic. The American Federation of Labor (AFL) systematically refrained from organizing those sectors of production which Blacks had succeeded in getting into, jealously barring unskilled whites as well as Blacks from membership of its skilled workers' unions. For several decades relations between black and white workers were locked in a vicious circle: the discrimination practised by one side gave the other side no alternative but to play the role of strike-breakers; and this strike-breaking was seized upon by the craft unions to justify the ban which they placed on Blacks.

Nevertheless, when trade-unionists took the trouble to win the Blacks' confidence, their efforts were not always fruitless. Thus, during the 1901 steel strike, 300 Blacks were brought from Alabama by a steelmill on the outskirts of Chicago. AFL activists made contact with them and explained to them what was really at stake in the strike. As a result the arrivals refused to betray the cause of their class brothers and the employer had to send them back to their place of origin. In the same way, in 1919 in Bogalusa, Louisiana, the employers in the lumber industry played a part in bringing black and white workers together by having three whites coldly gunned down and killed. The reason? They had bravely protected a black man who was guilty of recruiting members to the mixed union among his fellow-Blacks and had escorted him through the streets of the town. One of these three whites was the President of the AFL local.

However, these were exceptional cases. When, shortly after World War I, under the impulse of the Chicago union coalition, the AFL decided or resigned itself (for a short period only) to undertake the organization of the unskilled masses in large-scale industry, it ran up against the obstacle of black labor. The recruitment campaign launched from 1917 onwards in the Chicago slaugher-houses met with little success among the black workers, even though they accounted for a little over 20 per cent of the industry's overall workforce. An Afro-American in the service of the employers organized a scab union composed solely of Blacks. It enjoyed the support of the Black petty bourgeoisie and its various organs (newspapers, churches and the professions). The AFL organizers made the mistake of confining black trade-unionists in separate locals. They nonetheless succeeded in recruiting a number of Blacks, but the race riots which broke out in Chicago in June 1919 brought this incipient reconciliation to an abrupt end.

The unionization of the steel industry came up against the same difficulties. During the great 1919 strike, the employers had 30-40,000 black strike-breakers come up from the South. While a class war was taking place between the workers and the bosses, a race war pitted black workers against white workers on the picket lines. The strike committee showed little understanding of the specific problems involved in recruiting black workers. It seemed to go without saying that they would join the labor unions. To foster this illusion was to ignore the ABC's of the Black problem. Racial tension reached such a pitch that a conference had to be held between Labor leaders and leaders of the Black community. But the prejudice which the discriminatory attitude of the AFL had planted in the minds of the black workers proved stronger than these attempts at fraternization. The hostility of the Blacks contributed, to a considerable extent, to the failure of the strike.

In vain did the Black defense organizations repeatedly intercede with the old Federation to get it to adopt a more liberal attitude. In 1918 and 1920, the Urban League urged Samuel Gompers to admit black workers to the unions on an equal footing. In 1924, the National Association for the Advancement of Colored People (NAACP) addressed an open letter to the AFL Congress: 'For years and years', it stated, 'the American Negro has been requesting his admission into the ranks of the trade-union movement. The Negro movement as a whole is outside the ranks of the organized labor movement. The white labor movement will not have the Negro movement within it. If we come to allow the formation in America of a powerful bloc of non-unionized black workers, workers who would be entitled to hate the trade-union idea, all workers, black and white, will suffer the consequences. Is it not time for the two proletariats finally to unite?'[7] And the Association proposed to the AFL 'the formation of an interracial workers' commission to promote systematic propaganda against racial discrimination in the unions'. A similar approach was made again in 1929. But the Federation did not even deign to reply.

However, from 1934 onwards, the fight against trade-union discrimination was conducted, within the federation itself, by A Philip Randolph, the fiery President of the sleeping car employees' Brotherhood, a purely black organization. Randolph, ignoring the criticisms of the Black intelligentsia, understood that his union should join the organized labor movement, in spite of Labor's racial prejudice. For his part, William Green, the AFL President, hastened to accept the Brotherhood's request for affiliation, since this fake concession to the black workers enabled it to disguise the discriminatory practices of the craft unions; moreover, the trade organized by Randolph did not compete with whites for any jobs.

For years, at every congress of the old federation, Randolph preached in the wilderness amid general indifference. He was received with supercilious smiles and sometimes even aroused the open hostility of the white delegates. His proposals were always put off indefinitely.

At the 1940 convention, Randolph took the offensive again. Basing himself on a set of overwhelming facts, he urged in vain that an interracial commission be set up in order to eliminate the various forms of discrimination practised by the unions. There was a further scandal at the 1942 convention, when, in a bold innovation, the black trade-unionist tarred American racism with the same brush as European colonialism. The President of the Teamsters, the ultra-reactionary Daniel J Tobin, who combined this office with that of Vice-President of the AFL, howled, quite beside himself:[8] 'Sooner or later, this kind of stuff will have to be stopped.'

However, Randolph did not lose heart and continued to exhort his fellow-Blacks to join the labor movement, even where racial prejudice survived, and to combat racism within the AFL. In the long run the results of his persistence were not wholly negative.

The United Mine Workers was one of the few organizations in the AFL which, from the outset, adopted a liberal attitude toward black workers. The Knights of Labor, from which it had emerged had left its mark on the union, and had taught it about the brotherhood of man. Also, it had been established on an industrial basis and was never tainted with the exclusivism of the craft unions. Its statutes specified[9] that it proposed 'to unite in one organization, regardless of creed, color or nationality, all workmen . . . employed in and around coal mines'; other clauses assured black and white miners of equal pay; black and white were organized in the same locals; the union employed black organizers to facilitate the recruitment of black miners; in a number of locals Blacks held the positions of President and secretary. The Black community appreciated this attitude and always showed itself favorable to the union. When 'Mother' Jones, the heroic and legendary 'grandmother' of the miners, could find no meeting hall for her strikers, she held her meetings in Black churches.

In Alabama, the union had some trouble gaining a foothold. During the 1908 strike, a so-called 'citizens' committee', inspired by the employers, informed the union that[10] 'no matter how meritorious the union cause, the people of Alabama would never tolerate the organization and striking of Negroes along with white men.' 76 per cent of the strikers in the area in 1920-1921 were Blacks, a fact which brought the anger of the founders of US Steel to bursting point. All the same, under the energetic and generous impetus of William Mitch, the union did eventually take root in the area though it had to take the bull by the horns. For example, the Ku

Klux Klan was a fierce adversary of the union, so the white miners joined it, gained control of it, and in this way rendered it harmless! In Birmingham, Alabama, in 1948, 45 per cent of the union's members in the district were black.

However, the mechanization of the mines has tended to lower the social position of black labor since then, and the union has not reacted adequately to this situation.

The example of the Mine Workers inspired the CIO, its offshoot. From the moment of its creation, on the basis of industry and no longer of craft, the CIO adopted a totally different policy on race from that of the corporatist unions of the old AFL. It opened its doors to Blacks, without worrying about the so-called 'accident of color'. It won them equal pay with whites. It involved them in the leadership of its organizations at every level. It even succeeded, particularly in the North, in doing away with all social segregation between its black and white members and getting them to take part together in leisure activities and dances. In addition, it actively propagandized, by means of both the written and spoken word, against racial prejudice, not only among its members, but also outside. Thus it campaigned in favor of the program for civil rights.

In a pamphlet dedicated to black workers,[11] the CIO explained that at its foundation it had had 'to banish racial discrimination, just as it had [had] to banish craft discrimination'. 'The modern labor movement', it added, 'has been convinced by its own experience that one can no more exclude workers on account of the color of their skin than one can exclude them on account of their trade differences.' 'The very nature of industrial unionism', observed Irving Howe and B J Widick in their book on the United Automobile Workers,[12] 'made impossible the racial divisions prevalent in the AFL. . . . The new industrial unions could not have consolidated their power without winning some support from Negro workers.'

When the Committee for the Organization of the Steel Industry embarked on its recruitment campaign in 1936-1937, it received active assistance from the National Negro Congress, which helped to dispel the traditional hostility of the leaders of the Black community toward Labor. The black workers, at first somewhat distrustful, backed up the white workers. During the Little Steel strike, in 1937, the blacks fought alongside the whites on the picket lines. And one of the ten Republic Steel strikers shot down by the police was a black man.

The leadership of the powerful UAW, which was to embrace one and a half million workers, was for a long time, at least while it was led by Walter Reuther, in the vanguard of the fight against discrimination and racial prejudice. According to Howe and Widdick,[13] 'In the UAW, many Blacks have learned that the whole white world is not a conspiracy against them, but that there are unionists ready to risk their careers to help them.' In March 1946, the union set up a special department at national level to fight discrimination. Its object was to see to the enforcement of the organization's policy on racial matters through actions either against employers or against union members themselves. Each local had to form a local committee with the same duties. The department in question was placed under the direct authority of President Reuther, assisted by a black co-director.

The UAW did not hesitate at that time to penalize those of its members who engaged in acts of discrimination:[14] 'By penalties against acts of discrimination, by education against discrimination it is possible to end prejudice and discrimination.' To this end the Anti-Discrimination Department published a whole series of lively, well-presented bulletins which struck the workers' imagination and ceaselessly denounced the 'economic roots of discrimination'. The UAW's activity was not confined to the field of production. Thus, after the black delegates to the union's 1940 convention in St. Louis, Missouri had been subjected to discrimination in the city's hotels and restaurants, the union decided that in the future it would hold its conventions only in cities where black trade-unionists would be treated on an equal footing with whites. By bringing its influence to bear upon its white members the auto union played a great part in curbing the terrible race riots which broke out in Detroit in 1943.

But these results were not obtained at the drop of a hat. For many years, the UAW had to struggle both against the racial prejudice of its own members and against the deeply rooted distrust of the Blacks toward white trade-unionists. During the sit-down strikes of 1936-37, many black workers took a wait-and-see attitude, although this was not true of all of them, since a black man was elected as a member of the strike committee during the Chrysler strike in March 1937. But most black workers simply remained at home until the end of the conflict. While they did not co-operate with the strikers, neither did they act as scabs. For them, the union was nothing more than an association of white workers, which they had good reason to suspect.

The strike at the Dodge factory, in a suburb of Detroit, in 1939, almost gave rise to a racial brawl. A number of workers, most of them black, crossed the picket lines under police protection in order to resume work. The union had the good sense not to send its pickets after them and instead pinned the responsibility for this return to work on the employers. Racial conflict was thus avoided, and the way was open for the subsequent unionization of the Blacks.

The unionization of Ford, in 1941, presented particularly serious obstacles from the racial angle. The 'Lord' of River Rouge had always opened his doors to Blacks. On the eve of the strike, they numbered 11,000, that is to say 12 per cent of the total work force. This employment policy was certainly not inspired by humanitarian considerations. The admission of the Blacks was aimed at preventing the unions from gaining a foothold in the factory; in addition, black workers were assigned the most deadly dull work. Finally, the jobs were obtained through church ministers and other leaders of the Afro-American community, whose activities and good works were closely dependent economically on Ford. The Blacks flocked to the churches and Sunday schools in the hope of being taken on by Ford. In contrast, black trade-unionists or black academics favorable to the labor movement were refused the right to speak in the Black community's churches.

When Ford understood that he could not immunize his factories for very much longer against the flood tide of labor unionism, the black ministers in his pay publicly extolled the merits of the AFL and claimed that that organization had always acted in the best interests of their fellow-Blacks. But a minority of independent and progressive Black leaders, led by the NAACP, whose secretary went specially to Detroit, campaigned on behalf of the CIO auto union. Later on, the strike was eventually won without over serious racial clashes. The Ford local, the famous Local 600, held the foremost place among those American unions practicing racial harmony and electing Blacks onto their leadership.

During the Second World War, the influx of Blacks into

the armaments factories and their promotion occasioned a whole series of racial conflicts from 1941 to 1943. These incidents were in large part stimulated, if not instigated, by the Ku Klux Klan, which was very active in Detroit owing to the presence of many white migrant workers from the South, and by the employers themselves. At Packard's, on two occasions, in 1941 and 1943, the white workers staged sit-down strikes to protest the introduction or regrading of Blacks. The UAW local took a soft, equivocal attitude. But the national leadership intervened more vigorously.

When a similar incident occurred at Chrysler in February 1942, the union insisted to the employers that all workers refusing to go back to work for racist reasons should be laid off. At an interracial public meeting jointly organized by the UAW and the NAACP in April 1943, Walter Reuther declared straight out that his union 'would tell any worker that refused to work with a colored worker that he could leave the plant because he did not belong there.'[15]

However, neither the CIO as a whole nor the auto union in particular had really resolved the problem of interracial relations at the work-place. In the case of incidents like those which have just been described, the national leaders did not always intervene promptly and energetically. They occasionally felt obliged to make concessions to the racial prejudices of their members.

Sometimes even the trade-union leaders exploited racial tension to organize a firm. That is what happened in 1941, at the Curtiss-Wright aeronautics plant in Columbus, Ohio. A strike broke out, partly because a Black had obtained a more qualified job. But in reality the CIO organizers seized on this pretext in order to launch a battle to obtain union recognition by the employer.

Undoubtedly the CIO did bring reconciliation between the two races a step closer. It obtained appreciable results both by getting Blacks equal pay for equal work and by securing them access to jobs which till then had been closed to them. But in both these fields – and above all in the second one – the situation was still far from brilliant, in spite of the advances made.

Most Blacks in the industries organized by the CIO were still allocated unskilled jobs. At a hearing before a Senate Commission in 1947, Walter Reuther was pressed by a senator to indicate the percentage of Blacks with skilled jobs in certain big firms such as Ford. After attempting to evade the question several times, the President of the UAW finally had to admit that the vast majority of Ford's black workers were still employed at the foundry; he had to acknowledge that that type of job was hard and ranked among the least skilled.

In the steel industry, the results obtained were no more encouraging. In spite of the slight progress made, the Black continued to come up against rigid limits above which it was impossible for him to rise in the hierarchy.

To sum up, the founding of the CIO in the thirties contributed to forcing back racism at the work place. For the first time in many decades, since the heroic times of the Knights of Labor, the black worker had a strong hand extended to him, inviting him to join the army of industrial unionism. In response to this call, a million and a half Blacks joined the labor unions where they showed themselves to be among the most devoted and combative militants.

What is still more important, the CIO, by virtue of its very existence, indirectly acted as a support and a bulwark for the black community as a whole, enabling it to consolidate its forces, pluck up the courage to formulate new demands, take a more independent attitude and prepare the ground for the mass struggles it has fought since then.

But hardly had it done the Black liberation movement this service when industrial unionism became atrophied. Engaged in class collaboration rather than class struggle, it has shown slight signs of life only when it has been a question of protecting the conditions of the oldest, most privileged workers, those most attached to the advantages conferred on them by seniority. The privileges of this labor aristocracy can be safeguarded only at the expense of the most disadvantaged and exploited workers, of whom the Blacks constitute the majority.

When, in 1955, trade-union unity was re-established, two hypotheses could be advanced: either the ex-CIO leaders would succeed in converting the old craft-union leaders to their liberalism on the race issue, or, on the contrary, the traditional racism of the reformist bigwigs would rub off on the relative radicalism of the industrial unions. It was this second hypothesis which became reality. The bureaucrats of the reunified federation certainly committed themselves to eliminating racism, but the words had to be wrung from them.

For many years they swept the civil rights program under the carpet. Nor did they eliminate racial prejudice from their own ranks. So much so that the President of the AFL-CIO, the ultra-reactionary George Meany, had sharp exchanges on the subject with Philip Randolph as well as with an NAACP committee specialized in labor issues.

It took the anti-racist explosion of Summer 1963 and the security of President Kennedy's backing for a civil rights bill for the powerful trade-union federation, with a membership of over 15 million, to make up its mind, a little late, to give its support to this program. Support of a purely platonic kind, however, since it almost immediately refused to give official backing to the March on Washington for Freedom Now on 28 August 1963, leaving 'its members full liberty to participate in it as individuals'. Only the auto union (UAW) joined the organizing committee for the march.

In accordance with an old custom, the trade-union bureaucrats find it convenient to blame the rank and file for their own failure. The most reactionary of them hardly conceal their racist prejudices, while the least conservative show a temporizing paternalism toward Blacks, constantly appealing to them to be 'patient'. Basically the Blacks interest them only when it is a question of collecting their subscriptions, keeping them tied to the Democratic Party, or, as was the case at the time of John Kennedy's election, getting the absolutely necessary support from them to enable their Presidential candidate to squeeze through.

In the 1960s, the hostility of the white workers toward their black brothers, far from abating, had only increased. The main reason for this was, of course, economic. The introduction of automation and the threat of unemployment had led the workers of ethnic America to believe that their conditions of existence were threatened by the few advances made by Afro-American* along the road towards equal rights.

---

*Furthermore, the massive migration of black workers into the industrial North and Midwest transformed the demography of the big cities. Urban America redivided along ethnic and class lines over issues not immediately connected with the work place: schools, housing, declining services, neighborhood questions. The last migration, that of many working class and most middle class whites to the new suburban sanctuaries, had left the inner cities, already decaying and with fewer amenities, to the black and latin community. [Ed.]

In addition, as the AFL-CIO grew more and more socially conservative, it put into mothballs that struggle against discrimination which had been waged when industrial unionism was on the rise. While the racist Meany kept a firm grip on the AFL-CIO, the anti-racist Walter Reuther was eliminated, first by the split which took his union out of the federation, and then by his accidental death.

This baleful evolution finally convinced the Black liberation militants that they could expect nothing from a trade-union movement that was increasingly integrated into the established order, and contributed to the birth of a Black nationalism which often took the forms of reverse racism. At the same time it prompted the black workers, especially in Detroit, to organize outside the labor unions while denouncing their counter-revolutionary role. To be sure, those black revolutionaries most inclined to a joint struggle with white revolutionaries, such as the Black Panthers, agreed to ally themselves with a white student and intellectual youth in revolt against a vicious American imperialism.* But they were more skeptical as to the possibility of joint action with the organized white workers. The gulf between the two groups, both victims of exploitation at the hands of Big Business, has become, for the moment anyway, wider than ever.**

---

*It is unfortunately true that between 1968 and 1970 many formerly integrated black action groups threw out their white members. [Ed.]

**The explosion of Black struggles in the sixties was not without result. Whole categories of jobs, once closed to blacks (and latins), have opened up to them. The struggles in the mid to late seventies, taking place as they have during a period of generalized recession in America and the world, have focused on cutbacks. The worst hit have been the last-hired, first-fired minorities (blacks and women) – not only in the stagnating private sector, but in the public sector as well, as one city after another confronts the specter of bankruptcy. [Ed.]

CHAPTER 5

From anti-labor legislation to anti-Communism

The Taft-Hartley Act

After the strikes on the railroads and in the coal-mines Big Business felt the time had come to move onto the counter-attack and get Congress to pass some anti-Labor legislation. The employers' organization, the National Association of Manufacturers, found accomplices for this purpose among the big farmers, who, closely linked in any case to industrial and banking capitalism, were disturbed by the growing influence of Labor and were fearful, above all else, of the unionization of the farm workers.

President Truman had himself prayed for such anti-working-class legislation. On 6 May 1946, during the railroad strike, he addressed a message to Congress in which he called for a law which would enable him to break any strike which, in his estimation, was vitally affecting the country's economy. He asked for the right to conscript strikers under penalty of martial law, to impose heavy fines and long jail sentences on leaders of such strikes, and to make use of injunctions. In another message, in January 1947, Truman requested Congress to draw up legislation outlawing 'jurisdictional' strikes and 'unjustified' secondary boycotts.

The Republican victory in the November 1946 Congressional elections, their first victory since the Great Depression, was the final touch in the creation of a climate favorable to the passage of anti-working class legislation.

On 23 June 1947, the new law, named after its promoters, Senator Taft and Representative Hartley, was passed. First of all it restricted trade-union organizations' rights. It forced them, under penalty of not being recognized, to supply so many particulars about their financial affairs, their dues, their relations with their members, etc., that John Lewis could warn:[1] 'I assert without qualification that there isn't an organization in the American Federation of Labor that can make that report in a manner that it can feel assured will be satisfying to the labor-hating, labor-baiting General Counsel of the National Labor Relations Board.' The Act furthermore made the unions liable to heavy fines and damages if they violated one of its countless clauses.

Next the Taft-Hartley Act mutilated the right to strike. Notice of sixty days now had to be given before strike action was taken, under penalty of dismissal and imprisonment. Solidarity and wildcat strikes were outlawed. Trade-union leaderships against whose will wildcat strikes were declared were liable to penalties. Any strike considered by the President to endanger 'national health and security' could be postponed for 80 days (on top of the 60 days' notice) by a court order. The Federal courts could issue injunctions against any strike which was declared illegal.

The closed shop, that is to say the obligation to hire only union labor, was banned. This prohibition destroyed with one stroke of the pen the system of union-controlled hiring which the seamen's, longshoremen's and printers' organizations among others, had won in bitter struggle. The union shop, that is to say the obligation for new employees to join the union within a certain time, was only tolerated if 30 per cent of the workers requested a vote on it and a majority came out for it in factory elections. But even then a trade union could not demand the dismissal of a worker whom it felt necessary to expel from its ranks.

In States where special legislation was adopted prohibiting not only the closed shop, but even the union shop, these laws had priority over the Federal law. We will come back later to the calamitous consequences of this clause ('section 46') of the Act.

The bosses had the right, at least once a year, to start proceedings challenging the right won by a union to represent their workers. President Truman himself acknowledged that this provision put 'a powerful weapon into the employers' hands by allowing them to force union elections at a moment strategically favorable for them'.

The Taft-Hartley Act also included certain provisions aimed at preventing the politicization of the trade unions and restricting freedom of opinion. If the law is taken to the letter, it is illegal for a labor organization to support a candidate in a national election. Moreover, no union can use the services of the National Labor Relations Board, that is to say, among other things, gain, by means of elections, the right to represent the workers in a concern, unless its leaders have signed an affidavit swearing that they are neither members of the Communist Party nor 'affiliated with that party', and that they have no relations with any organization whose objective is 'the overthrow of the United States Government by force or by any illegal or unconstitutional method'. Any trade-union leader professing advanced ideas ran the risk of falling foul of this clause of the Act.

Finally, the Taft-Hartley Act contained certain provisions designed to prevent various abuses indulged in by the AFL craft unions, such as high dues, 'jurisdictional' strikes, strikes to compel an employer to affiliate to an employers' organization, the necessity for the boss to take on surplus workers whom he did not really require *(feather-bedding)*, etc. The Act also included measures for the protection of the rights of the rank and file against the union leaderships, for example the ban on employers deducting trade-union dues from pay roll envelopes without the individual authorization of each employee.

But these measures were only adopted in order to pacify the workers and appease public opinion in general, which was unfavorably disposed towards the abusive practices of craft and business unionism. The measures in question served to mask the anti-Labor character of the Act's essential provisions.

The Taft-Hartley Act was an extremely sharp blow to the labor movement. Applied literally, in particular by a reactionary-minded National Labor Relations Board, it locked the American unions in a strait-jacket. It proposed, at the very least, to clip their wings, undermine them and weaken them. The Act hit both the AFL and the CIO. Some of its provisions, like the one which laid down the division of a concern into job units for the purposes of union elections, bore particularly unjustly on the CIO, which was constituted on an industrial basis. Other provisions, like the ban on the closed shop and the various measures intended to prevent abuses by the craft unions, were felt more especially by the AFL.

The Act was injurious to the trade-union leaders and tended to curb their privileges, so breaking with the policy followed by Roosevelt, who had always been clever enough to win over the trade-union bureaucracy.

The Taft-Hartley Act might have provoked fierce opposition from the whole of the labor movement and united the ranks with the leadership, since the workers' interests coincided, at that juncture, with those of their leaders. Furthermore, the labor movement had the means to stand up to the Act. It was at the height of its power. It organized more than 15 million wage-earners. It possessed a vast apparatus, real estate, headquarters, newspapers and enormous resources. It had never yet suffered a serious defeat. Its fighting ability remained intact.

In the event, Labor's response was weak. No important action was taken either to prevent the passage of the Act or to support President Truman when, worried about his re-election, he vetoed its legislation, even though he had been one of its inspirers the year before. Since the passing of the law the struggle for its repeal has been sporadic, haphazard, and without significant results.

How can this failure of the labor movement be explained? Firstly in terms of the divisions in American trade-unionism and the selfish exclusivism of its leaders; then, and above all, by Labor's relative weakening and demoralization due to the constant rise in prices – a consequence of inflation – and the inertia of the trade-union hierarchies.

A Masked Resistance

It looked for a moment, just after the Act had been passed, as if the trade-union leaders were preparing to resist. The trade-union correspondent of *New York Times* wrote that Labor's battalions were deploying for the 'battle of the century'. But the AFL, for its part, confined itself to covering the pages of the daily papers with publicity bills calling for the abolition of the 'slave labor bill'.

Yet a few public demonstrations were organized. Only one of them assumed any real significance. That was because the initiative for it came from the rank and file. The Detroit auto-workers were urged by their International, influenced by Communist and Trotskyist militants, to leave the factories on the afternoon of 24 April 1947 and converge on Cadillac Square, in the heart of Detroit. In spite of the efforts of Walter Reuther's men to undermine the demonstration, it was a success.

In New York, on 4 June, the AFL organized a big meeting at Madison Square Garden, which drew 50,000 demonstrators, and the CIO, having declared Tuesday, 10 June Veto Day, got a crowd of 60-100,000 workers marching through the main thoroughfares of the city, carrying protest placards. Among the workers the idea of a general strike to protest the Act arose spontaneously. It found a spokesman in April 1949 in the person of a New York Representative, Arthur Klein, who proposed a one-day general strike so as to demonstrate Labor's determination to obtain the repeal of the Taft-Hartley Act. This politician even sent the main trade-union leaders telegrams insisting on such action. But his suggestion fell on deaf ears. Delegate John de Vito vainly took up the proposal again at the auto International's convention in July. It was rejected.

There was another means besides a general strike of putting pressure on the Federal legislators: the traditional tactic of the 'march on Washington'. The Los Angeles unions, both AFL and CIO, organized an auto 'cavalcade' in August 1947 which crossed the huge continent and ended up in the Federal capital, where it protested the Taft-Hartley Act. But this initiative was coldly received by the national leaderships of the two trade-union federations and it remained limited in scope.

The labor movement took up the struggle against certain particular provisions of the Act, notably the obligation to fill in affidavits certifying that their leaders were not 'Communists'. Many organizations, including some with a solid anti-Communist reputation, were opposed to this obligation. John Lewis, for the miners, and Philip Murray, for the steelworkers, refused to sign the affidavit. As Lewis was Vice-President of the old federation, his refusal to sign meant that federal unions, that is to say trade-union locals not affiliated to an International but placed under the direct control of the federation, were deprived of the possibility of using the services offered by the National Labor Relations Board, and could not therefore take part in factory elections.

At the federation's convention in San Francisco, on 14 October 1947,[2] Lewis exclaimed: 'How much heart do you think [it] will give the members of our organizations out in the industrial centers of this country when they see their great leaders, with all the pomp and ceremonials of a great convention, kneeling in obeisance before this detestable and tyrannical statute? Do you think that that will encourage them?' And he added, 'If we have the courage to stand together we are strong enough and powerful enough to protect our members, our unions and our country from the detrimental effects of this most despicable act.'

But Daniel Tobin, the teamsters' leader, who had already taken on Lewis at the 1935 convention, replied:[3] 'Some people say "defy the law". This is a law that we shall resent, but there is a certain legal procedure to change the law, and it isn't by revolution.' Another delegate declared, '[As] behooves an American citizen . . . I shall respect the Taft-Hartley Act'. Lewis lost his position as Vice-President and, in December 1947, the miners' International – for the second time – left the AFL, slamming the door behind them.

It was obvious that as soon as one big trade-union organization decided to sign the affidavit required by the Taft-Hartley Act, the other Internationals, despite their reluctance, would end up following suit. The first organization to sign would in effect find itself in a privileged position: it would have a chance of being recognized as the legal representative of the workers in concerns where elections were held.

However, those opposed to signing the affidavit pointed out that participation in the National Labor Relations Board's elections was not of such great importance for the unions, and that the gains made in 1936-37 and the organization of millions of workers had been the fruit of struggle and strike pickets, and not of elections. But these men spoke the language of another time and went unheeded.

The International Association of Machinists (independent) voted to be the first to capitulate early in September 1947. None of the CIO-affiliated organizations had yet complied with the formalities laid down by the new law. At the beginning of December the Executive Bureau decided to maintain its position of non-co-operation. But, on 6 October the textile International signed the affidavit.

Philip Murray, obviously influenced by the attitude of Lewis and the miners, still refused to sign on behalf of the steelworkers. But he did not dare impose the attitude taken by his own International on the different Internationals in the CIO.

On 31 October the President of the auto International, arguing that this was the final date fixed by the National Labor Relations Board for signing the affidavit, picked up the pen of surrender. Little by little the ranks of those opposed to signing disintegrated. The seamen's International announced, on 15 November 1948, that it would submit. On 27 July 1949

Philip Murray declared in the name of the steelworkers that his organization would sign too. Apart from the miners (independent) and the printers (AFL), only three important Internationals, all affiliated to the CIO and all controlled by the Communists, still held out against the Act: the longshoremen, the electrical industry workers and the workers in the fur trade. On 21 October the President of the United Electrical Workers announced that his organization was also throwing in the towel.

The Final Convulsions

Only one trade-union organization defied the Taft-Hartley Act, at the cost of a long and expensive struggle: the printers' International. The Act affected this organization particularly harshly by banning the closed shop, which was rigorously adhered to in the trade, by throwing into question the traditional practice of hiring according to seniority, by prohibiting 'secondary boycotts', that is to say the refusal to undertake work involving 'scabs' in another branch of the industry, and, last but by no means least, by laying down Draconian penalties for violating contracts and demanding the signing of written agreements between bosses and workers.

On 27 March 1948 the courts issued an injunction against the International, instructing it to cease its tactics of resistance to the Taft-Hartley Act. The strike which it called lasted twenty-two months, cost enormous sums of money and ended on 18 September 1949, in relative victory. The employers conceded a substantial wage increase and a type of contract which contained a certain number of protective clauses, but not, however, the most important one: the closed shop.

The printers' struggle did not receive any effective support from the labor movement as a whole. The AFL, to which the union was affiliated, showed itself lukewarm, and the CIO was content with passing sympathy resolutions. The International had proposed to all other unions that a special national convention of Labor be held in Washington for the purpose of drawing up a plan of united workers' action against the Act. No trade-union leadership, not even that of the miners, responded to this call.

President Truman had promised that, if he was re-elected in the 2 November 1948 elections, he would repeal the Taft-Hartley Act. Instead of waging the 'battle of the century',

Labor merely endorsed the Truman candidacy and black-listed the outgoing Congressmen who had voted for this anti-working-class legislation. But, after his re-election, Truman did not keep his promises. The reactionary general adviser to the National Labor Relations Board, Robert N Denham, whom Truman had appointed to the job in place of a liberal, declared that 'the Taft-Hartley Act would continue to be strictly applied'.

The Expulsion of the Communists

Capitulation before the Taft-Hartley Act was followed by the expulsion from the CIO of those Internationals which were influenced by the Communists. There were several reasons for the relative ease with which Philip Murray's 'machine' prevailed over the one controlled by the American CP.

First of all, the atmosphere of anti-'Red' hysteria, a consequence of the 'Cold War', was created and maintained in the United States by all the means used to condition public opinion. The success of this red-baiting was rooted in the chauvinism of the oldest, the most backward and the most corrupt strata of the American working class, their attachment to order and the established political system, and their traditional prejudices against any vanguard parties with a European ideology. The communists' dependence on Moscow reinforced these prejudices and reaction exploited the situation very astutely.

The Communists were easily defeated because they did not do battle frankly, on a clear and coherent program. They never, or almost never, attacked their trade-union opponents at their weakest point: their failures in the social struggle in the United States. When they did dare to speak out, they were only aggressive in the field of foreign policy, thereby confirming the charge brought against them of being in the service of the Kremlin; although even on this level their opposition was not very consistent: they were compromised by their pro-Rooseveltian past. For a long time they tried to use trickery and conceal their views. They camouflaged themselves and lied. They claimed, for example, that they were not affiliated to the Communist Party, whereas everyone knew that they were. Up till the last minute they attempted to negotiate and make deals with Murray's 'machine'. Their expulsion, far from raising their prestige, reduced it to zero. They suffered an inglorious defeat.

According to different estimates made in 1946, the communists at that time controlled between 30 and 35 per cent of the CIO's membership. In 1949, on the eve of their elimination, this percentage was down to 20 per cent, about a million members, following various defections. Their main bastion, in terms of Internationals, was the United Electrical Workers, an organization with some 500,000 members; in terms of areas, they were strongest in the unions in California, which were led by Harry Bridges, who was the West Coast District Director of the CIO as well as the President of the West Coast Longshoremen's International.

The communists also dominated a number of industrial Internationals like the metal-miners', the food and tobacco workers', the non-railroad transport workers', the agricultural machine workers' and the fur workers', as well as various seamen's Internationals (on the East and West Coasts) and, lastly, some skeleton 'white-collar' Internationals: clerks, civil servants, telephone workers. The Communists also possessed considerable influence, which did not, however, extend as far as control of the organization, in the auto and meat Internationals. Finally, at the height of their influence they controlled a number of local union coalitions, some of them important, like those in New York, Chicago, San Francisco, Los Angeles, Cleveland, Minneapolis, Seattle, Denver, Newark, etc.

At the top the Communists were quite strongly entrenched in the national leadership of the CIO, where one of them, Lee Pressman, had remained the federation's respected legal adviser, and another, Len de Caux, had kept his position as the editor of its official organ, the *CIO News*. Moreover, they had far from negligible support on the National Labor Relations Board, thanks to the presence, in that strategic position, of sympathetic officials.

As early as the end of 1946 Philip Murray was broadcasting his violent hostility to the Communists. But he did not want to launch a frontal attack on them just yet, since he feared a split which would weaken the CIO; in addition, he was using the Communists as a counterweight to the most aggressively anti-Communist elements, social-democrats or ex-social democrats like Walter Reuther of the auto International, Emile

Rieve and George Baldanzi of the textile International, and John Green of the shipbuilders' International. In particular, Walter Reuther's ambitiousness offended Murray, and he protected himself against it by granting favors to R G Thomas, the former President of the auto International, who had been defeated by Walter Reuther at the UAW congress in March 1946. R G Thomas was more or less in league with the Communists in his International.

At the CIO convention held in Atlantic City from 18-22 November 1946 Murray fought an initial skirmish against the Communists. He put down a resolution condemning and rejecting the efforts of the Communist Party and other political parties 'to interfere in the affairs of the CIO'. Avoiding the struggle, the Communists maneuvered behind the scenes and decided to vote for the resolution, figuring that the phrase 'and other political parties' made it easier for them to go along with it.

At the next CIO congress, which took place in Boston from 13-17 October 1947, the struggle continued with kid gloves on. After listening to a speech by Secretary of State, Marshall, in which the old soldier presented his famous 'Plan', the opponents and supporters of the Marshall Plan agreed on an equivocal resolution which endorsed 'healthy post-war recovery programs' and which everyone was free to interpret in his or her own way. The Communist leaders took care not to break this facade of unanimity. Harry Bridges remained silent throughout the congress. They showed the same reserve in relation to domestic policy. The only person who dared to speak out was Mike Quill of the public transport International (see p.208), who denounced President Truman's reactionary, anti-working-class Administration.

At the beginning of 1948 the struggle against the Communists in the CIO burst into the open. Two circumstances brought about the break – the increasingly strong opposition of the pro-Communist unions to the Marshall Plan and the backing they gave to Henry Wallace, the Progressive candidate who ran against Truman for the White House. At the meeting of the CIO's Executive Bureau, held in Washington on 22-23 January 1948, there was a sharp clash between Harry Bridges and most of the other leaders. Bridges refused either to support the Marshall Plan or to withdraw his backing for Wallace's 'third party'. The Communists lost by 33 votes to 11. On

5 March Harry Bridges was dismissed from his position as the CIO's Area Director. On 6 February Lee Pressman resigned from his job as the CIO's legal adviser in order to dedicate himself to organizing publicity for Wallace's party. A few months later, on 27 June, Len de Caux quit editing the *CIO News* in his turn.

The Communists Lose the Seamen

The pro-Communist tendency in the CIO was considerably weakened by sudden turns in several important Internationals. One of the first occurred in the East Coast Seamen's International, an organization with about 60,000 members. Under the energetic leadership of Joseph Curran it had emerged victorious from two strikes which had taken place in March and November 1936. Curran had established his International and retained control of it with the participation and support of the Communists.

Together Curran and the Communists had created a bureaucratic dictatorship and crushed all opposition in the International. The marriage lasted ten years. But in July 1946 it suddenly broke up. Curran, feeling strong enough to fend for himself, separated from his partners. A fratricidal struggle, which was punctuated by violence, began. Curran attacked the Communists for the 'totalitarian' methods he had practiced hand in hand with them, and turned these same methods against his erstwhile allies.

In September-October 1947, during a stormy convention which lasted 24 days, he ended up winning out over his opponents. He pushed through an amendment to the statutes submitting all important decisions to a referendum, which considerably reduced the powers of the International's national council, still dominated by the Communists.

Curran was cheered at the CIO convention in October 1947. In July 1948 fresh elections gave him complete victory: the Communists were driven out of all their positions. But Curran, intoxicated by his triumph, hastened to make ill use of it. He proceeded, using the most arbitrary methods, to purge his International, suspending and expelling members suspected of pro-Communist sympathies.

In April 1949 the national council passed a resolution barring entry to any individual adhering to a Communist or simply 'subversive' doctrine, or committing anti-union acts, such as making criticisms of the Federal leadership. The resolution was rejected by a meeting of seamen in the port of New York and aroused strong opposition in other sections of the International. Finally a slightly different text was carried by the convention held in September 1949: Communists, Fascists and Nazis were barred from membership of the International.

But Curran took his witch-hunt so far that a strong opposition grew up again, especially in New York, whose port was the International's principal bulwark. On 16 November 1949, following the arbitrary dismissal of the official for the port of New York and his assistants, violent incidents broke out between supporters and opponents of Curran, during which the latter called on the police to rescue him from the opposition. But anti-Communism had the last word.

Reuther Purges the Auto International

The Communists suffered a shattering blow when they lost the strong influence they had within the auto International. (They had, in particular, dominated the Ford section of the union since 1941.) For years the UAW had been the scene of a bitter fratricidal struggle for control of the International between the pro-Communist tendency led by the secretary-treasurer, George Addes, and the anti-Communist tendency led by Vice-President Walter Reuther. The President, R G Thomas, had tried to bridge the gap between the two groups and preserve the unity of the organization.

This tendency struggle was, to a certain extent, harmful to the International, since it did not take place on the basis of clear programs. Neither the Communists nor the former social democrat Walter Reuther were fighting for principles. It was essentially power that was at stake in the fight. It involved two groups equally eager to control the organization. The quarrel did, however, have some beneficial side-effects: it preserved the democratic life of the union and prevented the formation of a monolithic bureaucracy.

At the 1946 convention Walter Reuther just succeeded in ousting R G Thomas from the Presidency of the organization, although he did not secure a majority on the Executive Bureau. Resentment drove R G Thomas towards the pro-Communist camp, to which he had already offered pledges. And at the November 1947 convention, Reuther had to face a bloc between Addes and Thomas, which was not, moreover, composed only of Communists.

Instead of fighting Reuther in a militant fashion, the opposition exercised its wits in order to discredit him through personal attacks, in which slander played its part. Reuther was triumphantly re-elected and won an overwhelming majority on the new Executive Bureau. The way was open for the elimination of the pro-Communists.

At the following convention held in Milwaukee, Wisconsin from 10 to 15 July 1949, Reuther consolidated his victory and was given new weapons to get rid of his tendency opponents. He got an amendment to the statutes carried which took away from locals their existing right to take sanctions against their members. From then on it was the national Executive Bureau which was to have the right to penalize a member for 'unworthy conduct'. In this way Reuther could eliminate his opponents (Communists or others), whereas previously this had been impossible for him when the local was controlled by his adversaries.

Applying the new rule straight away, the congress voted for the expulsion of the two leaders of the pro-Communist tendency. They had laid themselves open to repression by committing an irregularity. But the punishment did not fit the crime. Reuther wanted to make an example of them and to intimidate his opponents.

Catholic Infiltration

In order to defeat the pro-Communist tendency, Reuther had made an alliance with the most reactionary elements in his International, particularly with the Association of Catholic Trade Unionists (ACTU). Now Catholicism, being the religion of the great wave of immigrants (Irish, Italians, Poles, Czechs, etc.), was consequently the religion of a large number of unskilled workers in the key industries. (Cleveland, for example, a vast industrial center, was a Catholic city, in which each ethnic minority had its own special churches.)

The very fact that the CIO had organized these immigrants, that is to say the workers in the basic industries, made it much more vulnerable to Catholic influence than the old AFL. Its late President, Philip Murray, belonged to the Church more than to Labor and represented the hierarchy within the working-class movement. God always came into his speeches and he did nothing without taking the advice of a Pittsburgh clergyman, the Reverend Charles Owen Rice.

The Church had not succeeded in influencing the Catholic workers during the period of the CIO's growth. Furthermore, the role played by Catholicism in the fascist countries of Europe had led to a fall in its prestige among the workers. But after the war, when the US Government and the Vatican established an anti-Communist partnership, the Church made an effort to implant itself in the trade-union movement. It was careful not to make the mistake of setting up Christian unions and preferred instead to infiltrate the CIO.

The ACTU was the Catholic answer to the Communist fraction in the unions. The Catholic trade-unionist was quite strictly subordinated to a priest, who was vested with the leadership of the ACTU branch by the statutes, and without whose approval nothing could be done. The literature published by the ACTU was subject to an *imprimatur.*

The Catholic trade-unionists had learnt from the Communists not only the art of propaganda but also, and above all, the art of infiltration. They knew how to extend their influence and burrow underground. They organized cadre schools; then, when their new recruit was considered up to it, they sent him into such and such a sector of the trade-union movement which they were intent on conquering, providing him with precise instructions and making sure that he was flanked by some Jesuit Father skilled in the art of beating the Communists at their own game.

A Lost Bastion: Public Transport

The ACTU was the moving spirit behind a dramatic turn which suddenly put an end to Communist control of a relatively important organization, the Transport Workers Union, which had a membership of 100,000. The nucleus of this International was Local 100 of the New York City subway employees. Created in 1934 during the mass influx into the unions which followed the enactment of the NRA, this organization had obtained a national charter from the CIO in 1937 and had been led since that time by a fighting Irishman, Mike Quill. The subway employees were almost all Irish Catholics, but at that point in time they did not care for their Church's interference in temporal affairs, and their rebellious temperament, made more aggressive by the Great Depression, had led them to follow the most advanced trade-union leaders. For ten years Mike Quill governed the International hand in hand with the Communists. He was appointed President of the union coalition (CIO) and became a New York City Councilman.

But in 1946 the Catholic Church felt that the time had come to reassert its authority over the Irish employees of the New York City subway. A nucleus of militants was organized and given appropriate training at the Xavier Labor School, a workers' cadre school run by a Jesuit Father, the Reverend Philip Carey. Then the new trade-union missionaries were thrown into the fray. They were so successful that by March 1948 control of Local 100 had been wrested from the Communists.

Mike Quill, who had been dreaming for some time of shaking off the yoke of his demanding allies, grasped the opportunity. He resigned from the union coalition. A very sharp struggle began between him and his pro-Communist ex-allies for control of the transport International. At the Federal convention, held at the beginning of December 1948, he won an overwhelming victory, eliminating all the Communists from the Executive Bureau. Sixteen trade-union officials, representing more than half the organization's staff, were fired.

The National Split

At the CIO convention in Portland (22-26 November 1948) the struggle between the two camps was waged in the open for the first time. The Communists finally attacked the Marshall Plan openly, for which they were bitterly reproached by Philip Murray. Walter Reuther called on then to choose between the CIO and the Communist Party. Murray declared that under no circumstances would he permit them to infiltrate the CIO. He particularly attacked the 'rickety' Internationals dominated by the Communists. He had the convention pass a resolution giving full powers to the CIO's Executive Bureau to open an inquiry into the position of those Internationals affiliated to the CIO which had failed in their recruitment tasks. (This failure was due on the whole to the specific characteristics of groups of workers who are difficult to organize in all countries on account of their petty-bourgeois mentality, their individualism and their close links with the bosses.)

Lastly, Murray came away from the convention with exorbitant powers: from now on the federation could take away affiliated organizations' constitutive charters, dismiss their leaderships and transfer their jurisdiction to other Internationals.

The Communists defended themselves quite ineptly. Their efforts to reach a compromise, even at the cost of humiliation, were obvious. The congress was hardly over when the first repressive measures were taken by the Executive Bureau of the CIO. It revoked the constitution of the New York union coalition, one of the broadest in the United States. The grounds: 'having adhered in a servile fashion to the line and the orders of the Communist Party.' Its records and assets were taken over by a temporary administrator, pending the creation of a new union coalition. The New York Communist unions, forgoing all resistance, yielded to their enemies. After the one in New York the other union coalitions controlled by the Communists were purged in their turn.

The final act was played out at the CIO convention which took place in Cleveland, Ohio from 31 October to 4 November 1949. It carried a whole series of amendments to the CIO's statutes. One of them prevented any member of the Communist Party, a Fascist organization or any other 'totalitarian' movement, or anyone carrying out activities on behalf of these organizations, from occupying a leading position in the CIO. Another gave the Executive Bureau full powers to expel those members of the union to whom the previous amendment applied. And yet another authorized the Bureau to expel a trade-union organization whose policy was geared to the goals and based on the programs of the political organizations mentioned above.

Next the convention voted for the expulsion of the electrical workers' International, the third most important union in the CIO, and the agricultural machinery workers' International. It decided to set up a new International for the electrical industry headed by James Carey, the CIO's young secretary-treasurer. The convention gave the CIO Executive Bureau full powers to summon the other ten Internationals under Communist hegemony and expel them.

The result of this purge was to aggravate the division, which was already so deep, within American Labor. Yet another split had occurred. The expelled Internationals became the object of 'raids' by rival organizations still in the CIO, who tried to take away their members, and a powerful organization like the United Electrical, Radio and Machine Workers of America, born out of the great tidal wave of 1937, split in half, much to the amusement of the magnates of General Electric and Westinghouse.

In the Service of the Cold War

The Communists were only kicked out for reasons of foreign policy – because they opposed the Cold War and the Marshall Plan which was then its instrument. Through their presence and their opposition, for all that it was discreet, they could have prevented the CIO from placing itself entirely at the service of the State Department. After their expulsion Labor was free to become the champion and the drummer for the plan to turn Western Europe into an anti-Communist colony.

The only one in the labor movement to sound a dissonant note was John Lewis. It was the time of the insurrectionary strikes in France. On 27 October 1948, he wrote to William Green:[4]

> 'You are supporting Truman. I assume you have his ear. Just as one miner to another, why do you not have him stop the shooting of French coal miners who are hungry?
>
> 'Truman controls the money bags of the Marshall Plan, upon which the tottering French Government subsists. . . . The future of France will be dark indeed in every economic, social and political sense if American money, American guns and American bullets are to be used to shoot, starve and oppress French citizens, while the bureaucrats and the financially powerful in France subsist on American resources and deny the human element of the population any participation in the largesse of the Marshall Plan. . . . Truman could aid the cause of humanity and perhaps do himself a good turn by using some of the vast power in his hands in the control of the Marshall Fund by requiring the French Government to abandon its police-state methods and cease making war on its own citizens who are coal miners, at the expense of the American tax payers.'

The CIO and AFL bureaucrats not only gave wholehearted support to the Marshall Plan, but also volunteered to participate in administering it. They pointed out that no-one was better placed than they to dispel the European workers' distrust of the Plan. In November 1947 the AFL Committee for International Labor Relations decided to insist that representatives of Labor, chosen by Labor itself, should be appointed to all echelons of the Marshall Plan's administration, including high diplomatic posts in important countries. In this way the

European workers would be shown that American foreign policy was not run by and in the interests of Wall Street. At the AFL congress in November 1948 President Truman's assistant, John Steelman, declared:[5] 'American Labor representatives are among our best ambassadors of goodwill abroad.'

I saw one of these 'ambassadors' at work in France. I had met a propagandist for the textile union (CIA) in Atlanta, Georgia in 1948. He was trying, sometimes at the risk of his life, to organize the workers in an area where the bosses were fiercely hostile to labor unionism.

When I was back in France I found myself one day in the square in front of Amiens Cathedral. I noticed the presence of a number of gentlemen standing still, bundled up in stiff collars, with their hands encased in black gloves. Suddenly a whistle went off and a line of cars appeared at the corner of the square: *'Le plan Marshall, messieurs, le plan Marshall!'*, shouted one of these officials, who bore an expression of servile gratitude.

A man got out of the first car and the authorities bowed and scraped to him unceasingly. I recognized the trade-union militant from Atlanta. He had become the 'Marshall Plan'.

CHAPTER 6

Trade union unification

The Struggle in the Steel Industry

In spite of the foregoing symptoms of decay, the internal dynamic of Labor still had some surprises in store. Rank and file pressure, stimulated by the constant rise in prices, continued to exert itself, counterbalancing the growing hold of the bureaucracy. It succeeded in finding expression even in Internationals run as undemocratically as was the steelworkers'. In June 1949 the steelworkers asked for a wage increase of 12.5 per cent, pensions of $125-150 a month at the age of 65 and, lastly, a system of health insurance.

The steel companies rejected these demands out of hand. The rank and file was so impatient that spontaneous stoppages broke out here and there. On 1 October 1949 the International had to call its 500,000 members out on strike.

John Lewis made a gesture towards unity. Although the International on strike belonged to the CIO, he appealed to the AFL to show solidarity. On 14 October he wrote to William Green:

> 'One of the biggest battalions of the workers' movement is engaged in a vital economic conflict.... Its adversaries are strongly entrenched. They have limitless financial credit at their disposal and wield unequaled power. Allied to the steel-producing companies in this huge, barbarous attack on the steel workers are the main forces from various other industries such as the insurance companies and the financial empires of Du Pont and Mellon. These formidable allies have set their sights on crushing the power and destroying the structure of the steel workers' federation. We've got to stop that.'

And he asked Green and his associates to 'relegate to second rank all other considerations' and to 'prepare to shape up to the giant adversaries who, otherwise, would decimate the main sections of the organized workers' movement one after the other'. He proposed that nine of the main AFL Internationals, together with the miners' International, should each extend $250,000 worth of credit a week to the steel International. But William Green and the craft union bosses did not budge.

On 25 October the CIO Executive Bureau decided to levy a war fund of 'many million dollars' to support the struggle of the steelworkers. At the beginning of November the first cracks appeared on the employers' side. Bethlehem and Republic Steel, followed by a few other firms, signed contracts instituting pensions of $100 at the age of 65, after 25 years' service, and a system of health insurance to be financed in equal proportions by workers' and employers' contributions. On 11 November US Steel, isolated and humiliated, had to give way in its turn.

The concessions won fell well short of the International's demands. It did not secure a wage increase. The principle that the employers alone should finance social benefits was not recognized. Dave MacDonald, then the secretary-treasurer of the International, was exaggerating somewhat when he declared that it was 'the greatest step forward in the history of American Labor'. Nevertheless, the steelworkers had shown fighting spirit. They had thwarted an arrogant monopoly which was seeking to smash the workers' organization.

The Unification Process

The idea of trade-union reunification, healing the wounds of the split which had given birth to the CIO, had been in the air for some time. At the beginning of 1949 the CIO left the Communist-controlled World Federation of Trade Unions (WFTU), to which the AFL had always refused to affiliate, and together the two federations established the International Federation of Free Trade Unions (IFFTU), which had an anti-Communist orientation.

Unity negotiations had been under way for a long time. If they had not borne fruit, it was both because of John Lewis's intransigence and his rivals' fear that he would dominate a reunified labor movement.

However, at the end of 1946, the specter of the Taft-Hartley Act led to a resumption of talks between the two federations. The initiative came from the CIO. William Green stressed the need for organic unity, which to his mind meant 'the return to the fold' of the 'lost sheep', while Philip Murray, as a shrewd tactician, gave priority to united action against the anti-Labor legislation. On 15 May 1947 Green announced the imminent fusion of the two trade-union federations. But he was only bluffing. The CIO had shown itself to be much more cautious. It declared that it would not sacrifice any of the principles in the name of which it had been founded for the sake of unity.

However, the feeling for unity was very strong at the grass roots. The workers hoped that the reunification of working-class forces would add to Labor's power. But the main obstacle to unity lay at the top. The Labor leaders had carved themselves personal fiefs which they sharply defended against their rivals, and none of them seemed prepared to sacrifice a scrap of their prerogatives.

However, something changed in the behavior of John Lewis, the number one trade-union boss, who had brought his miners back into the AFL at the end of 1945, left the old federation again in October 1947 and locked himself and his International in wait-and-see isolation. He soon began to make repeated gestures toward unity. At the beginning of 1950 he proposed to Philip Murray that the steelworkers, the coal-miners and all other workers should conclude a 'pact of mutual aid and joint defense' against the generalized offensive of the employers. Murray turned down the proposal but suggested, in his turn, in a letter addressed to the AFL, the railroad Brotherhoods and the two largest independent unions, the creation of a committee concerned, in the first instance, with bringing about unity in action, and then with laying the basis for organic unity. The personal antagonism between Philip Murray and William Green prevented the move from coming off at that point.

On 9 November 1952 Philip Murray suddenly died. Four months later William Green followed him into the grave. The almost simultaneous disappearance of both federations' Presidents, whose egocentric obstinacy had been a far from negligible stumbling-block on the road to unity, created a new situation. Their two successors, George Meany, for the AFL, and Walter Reuther, for the CIO, were a little more accommodating. Having together thrust aside John Lewis, who was a terrible nuisance to both of them, they began long and laborious negotiations. In August 1953 they achieved their first result with the signing of the Non-Raiding Agreement, by which the two federations pledged to desist from all attempts to poach each other's members. The text of the agreement alluded to future possibilities of organic unity.

A fact to remember: the document was not ratified unanimously, but by a simple majority of International unions

– 65 AFL Internationals out of 110 and 29 CIO Internationals out of 32. The proportion of those who continued to hang back was much higher in the old craft unions of the AFL than in the young industrial unions of the CIO.

One of the organizations most hostile to the agreement was the teamsters' International, which was increasingly recruiting workers in any and every trade and was therefore walking over rival Internationals' flower-beds.

Once this first step was taken, the conventions of the two federations, meeting immediately before the reunification convention, voted for organic unity on 1 December 1955. The new organization was significantly named *The American Federation of Labor and Congress of Industrial Organizations* (AFL-CIO). The ten million-strong AFL agreed to cohabit with the CIO, which had half as many members. George Meany took the Presidency of the reunified federation, and Walter Reuther had to make do with one of the Vice-Presidential posts.

In vain had the President of the auto workers sought to pose effective guarantees for the protection of industrial trade-unionism, the rigorous application of the 'non-raiding' agreement by all Internationals, the elimination of racial discrimination in the unions, etc., as conditions of reunification. Unfortunately his efforts had been thwarted within the ex-CIO itself: the President of the steelworkers, Dave MacDonald, had well and truly committed himself to a hurried and unconditional merger. Reuther had had to resign himself to this, while hoping that the dynamic of the unions from the CIO would finally prevail within the reunified federation.

And so the dispute which had led to a split in Labor's ranks nineteen years earlier was patched up by a compromise. The agreement stipulated that craft unionism and industrial unionism were both 'appropriate, equal and necessary as methods of industrial organization'.

Moreover, the AFL, in spite of the numerical weight of the craft unions within it, had ended up organizing a fairly large number of workers on an industrial basis as well. They were assigned to a department of industrial unions which consisted of thirty-one former CIO Internationals with 4,528,000 members and twenty-five former AFL Internationals with 2,629,000 members, totalling fifty-six Internationals with 7,157,000 members. The teamsters transferred 400,000 of their members to the new department of industrial unions.

Walter Reuther was made its President. The craft unions were George Meany's fief, the industrial unions Walter Reuther's. There was a situation of dual power.

The new federation comprised the following leadership bodies:

- an *Executive Council,* composed of a President and a secretary-treasurer, both from the AFL, assisted by seventeen Vice-Presidents from an AFL background and ten from a CIO background. It was to meet at least once a month;
- an *Executive Committee,* composed of the President, the secretary-treasurer (both ex-AFL) and six Vice-Presidents, three from the AFL and three from the CIO. It was to meet every two months and was entrusted with the important function of discussing and drawing up recommendations for the Executive Council (in fact it soon ceased to be convened, which enabled the Executive Council to exercise undivided domination over the new federation);
- a *Convention* to be held every two years (instead of every year, as had been the case in both federations prior to reunification);
- a *General Bureau* which was to meet at least once a year between conventions acting as a sort of miniature convention and composed of a representative from each affiliated International.

By way of transition the area and local unions of the two federations were to continue to exist side by side for two years before merging. Actually, the fusion of the two bureaucratic apparatuses was sluggish and required more time.

An important innovation was the creation of a large number of specialized *permanent committees*, which had not existed in the statutes of the two old trade-union federations. All the employees of these fourteen committees were appointed in dictatorial fashion by President Meany. As none of the staff of the two federations was laid off, there was both a juxtaposition and an extension of the bureaucracy.

A number of *departments*, whose functions sometimes overlapped those of the permanent committees, were superimposed on this committee structure.

Although the principle, which was of Federal origin, of the autonomy of each International within the new federation was respected and, at *grassroots* level, each local in turn enjoyed relative autonomy, the bureaucratic apparatus formed by the area and local unions on the one hand, and the permanent committees and departments on the other, was strictly subject to the directives of the Executive leadership. This out-and-out centralization stood in contrast to the old AFL structure and, even in relation to the ex-CIO, which had been more centralized from its founding, it marked an intensification of authoritarian trends.

One department, the one dealing with organization, which was responsible for the recruitment of unorganized workers, was subdivided into twenty-two geographical areas in the United States and one in Canada, each with a director and an assistant director (one from the AFL, the other from the CIO). This department, quite unjustifiably in view of its inactivity, employed twice as many people as the area unions, so reinforcing the trend toward centralization.

In addition to its departments, the AFL-CIO set up a 'Central Agency for Investment Policy' for the purpose of advising affiliated Internationals on the best way of investing their vast financial resources. The reunified federation spawned a bank. Eleven years after reunification Walter Reuther was to stigmatize[1] those labor leaders 'who have a banker's mentality' and who 'think that the success of their organization is measured by the enormous deposits that they have invested in the bank'. And he recalled that the labor movement in Weimar Germany had been the strongest and the richest in the world. 'Now what did Hitler do with this movement with all its millions in the banks? He destroyed it.' At the same time Reuther stressed the contrast between this gold mine ('millions and millions and millions') and the derisory sums set aside by the unions for solidarity campaigns and solidarity with strikers across industrial boundaries.

On the ideological plane the preamble to the statutes was a step backwards in relation to those of the old trade-union federations. As reformist as it was, the old AFL still spoke in its statutes of a 'struggle . . . going on in the nations of the civilized world between the oppressors and the oppressed of all countries, a struggle between capital and labor'.[2]

The CIO, created more recently and therefore less prone to the old class-struggle language,[3] nevertheless aimed 'to bring about the effective organization of the working men and women of America regardless of race, creed, color or nationality, and to unite them for common action into labor unions for their mutual aid and protection'. It further served notice that the CIO had 'forged the instrumentality whereby labor will achieve and extend industrial and political democracy'.

In the preamble to the reunified federation's statutes all this had gone; objectives were now to be pursued prudently[4] and to remain 'within the framework of our constitutional government and consistent with our institutions and traditions'. The *New York Times* commentator did not fail to express satisfaction that there was no more talk of oppressors and oppressed – reference was made instead to the 'general interest of the whole American people' – and that the document was impregnated with a 'healthy Americanism'.

This was a state of mind which was to be commented upon by Federal President George Meany in these terms:

> 'To be frank, we American trade-unionists like the capitalist system. Naturally we well intend to preserve it in our efforts aimed at bettering the standard of living of the workers by improving the system itself. But we do not intend to abandon it for some pipe-dreams or some ideological fantasies invented by those who do not understand the workers' real needs and aspirations.'

Anti-Communism Sanctioned

The new federation placed itself at the service of the American Empire. Arthur Goldberg, the former American delegate to the United Nations, summed up the principles of the AFL-CIO's international policy as follows:[5]

> '[To contain] Communist penetration among the free nations and areas of the world and the elimination of Communist domination where it exists. They were also agreed that the means to be employed must be:
>
> 1. To maintain our own armed strength at a level consistent with a tough-minded evaluation of Communist potentialities for aggression.
> 2. To strengthen the economic and military capacities of the free world to resist Communist aggression of the military or propaganda type.
> 3. To invigorate the United Nations as a major instrument for the achievement of world peace and security.'

The CIO fell into line with the AFL's anti-Communism. As Goldberg recognizes, there had in fact been differences of 'temperament' and 'tone' in matters of foreign policy between the AFL and the CIO before reunification. We shall see later that these slight differences persisted.

Meany was in the hands of the former director of the AFL's 'Committee of Free Trade Unions', Jay Lovestone, a repentant Communist who had become a corruptor of so-called 'free' trade-unionism throughout the world on behalf of the CIA. Meany and Lovestone took anti-Red hysteria well past the limits set by the American Empire. Even the White House and the State Department could not defend 'America's' interests so avidly. Thus they publicly criticized the admission *en bloc* of thirteen new member states to the United Nations and condemned the policy of 'bridges to the East' inaugurated by President Johnson: 'Why', they argued, 'allow the Communist leaders to profit from our technical competence and help them in this way to forge still newer chains of tyranny?'.

This anti-Communism found expression in the new federation's statutes in a grossly excessive clause (Article 8, Section VII) by virtue of which the Executive Council could,[6] after holding an inquiry, suspend by a two-thirds majority any International if it was found that its 'policies or activities are consistently directed towards the advocacy, support, advancement or achievement of the program or of the purposes of the Communist Party . . . '. The suspension took effect from the day it was decided on, but could be appealed against to the national convention.

Against Corruption

Article 8, Section VII was also applicable to trade unions 'dominated by corrupt influence', in other words unions where racketeering was rampant.

It was not mere taste for virtue that finally impelled the Labor leaders to wage war on practices which, particularly in the AFL, they had put up with for a long time. If the workers' movement was led to purge itself, it was above all to ward off the danger of growing Government interference in its affairs on the pretext of 'morality'.

Indeed, several commissions of inquiry – either at State level or at Federal Congressional level – were going to investigate the scandalous actions which certain unions were guilty of. The first of these was set up in 1952 under the name of the New York State Crime Commission and concerned itself with the racketeering practices in the longshoremen's International, especially in the port of New York. The second was the commission of inquiry appointed by the Senate, which sat for two years – from 1957 to 1959 – under the chairmanship of Senator McClellan. It had been initiated by that ranting witch-hunter, the deceased Senator Joseph McCarthy. It was he who had tabled a resolution in the Senate in January 1957 asking for the formation of such a commission. And it was because young Robert Kennedy had been McCarthy's associate that the future Attorney General was promoted to chief counsel to the McClellan Commission.

John Kennedy, then a Senator, made common cause with his younger brother. The two Kennedies committed themselves fully to a demagogic fight against trade-union corruption which, at the time, won them favor in the eyes of bourgeois public opinion and brought them curses from Labor. John Kennedy was to be one of the main promoters of the Landrum-Griffin Act of 1959, of which more will be said further on and which, on the pretext of performing a 'moral' function by dealing severely with racketeering, in fact restricted trade-union freedom.

The fight against corruption was, under its 'moral' cloak, suspect in more than one respect. Racketeering, to the reactionaries, was a convenient word which could be used to curb trade-union action. The bosses feared the militancy and the strength of the teamsters. This was especially true of the Southern bosses, since they knew that the teamsters' International was the only one capable of smashing the open shop, that is to say putting an end to the exclusion of labor unionism in the Southern States. The Democratic Senator Frank G Lausche, of Ohio, revealed the ulterior motives of the promoters of these 'morality' investigations on television: 'The teamsters have become too powerful and must be throttled.' Through the teamsters it was Labor as a whole that was the target.

If corrupt trade-union bosses had to be got rid of, that should have been the task of the members of the Internationals concerned and not that of the Federal leaders (for example, the International Typographical Union voted against the expulsion of the teamsters in order to defend the principle of trade-union autonomy). In fact, Meany and the central AFL leadership used the issue of corruption to whittle away the independence of the Internationals affiliated to it and to effect that centralization the absence of which had always distinguished it from its younger rival, the CIO.

The Purge of the Unions

The Federal leaders, pressed by the authorities and knowing how much harm was being done to the labor movement's prestige by racketeering, reluctantly agreed to clean out their own backyards – but from above.

The purge of the International Longshoremen's Association, which organized longshoremen on the East Coast and in the Gulf of Mexico, had begun in 1953 before reunification and after the conclusions of the New York State Commission of Inquiry had been made public. The International had become infamous through the exploits of its gangsters, particularly in the port of New York (which is the subject of the film *On The Waterfront,* with Marlon Brando playing the lead). Its officials, a number of whom were hardened criminals, accepted bribes from the employers and demanded money from non-privileged longshoremen who were trying to obtain work.

The AFL had its work cut out for it in the struggle against corruption among the longshoremen. The International was called upon to mend its ways, and, since its President, Joseph Ryan, turned a deaf ear, the old federation decided to grant a constitution to a new longshoremen's International, into which it sank nearly a million dollars to help with recruitment. In vain: in the National Labor Relations Board elections Ryan's old International managed to defeat its newly-born rival three times.

The fight against racketeering in the port of New York even gave rise, in September 1955, to a general strike of longshoremen on the Atlantic coast to protest the intrusion of the New York State Commission of Inquiry. Here public morality found itself in open contradiction with the imperatives of the class struggle. The commission's objective was to deprive the union of control of hiring, which was its most precious conquest. The refusal to give work permits to 600 longshoremen because of their criminal records, the elimination of one of the most popular union leaders, MacLoughlin, and the blunders of the commission, which ventured to ask indiscreet questions about the income and private lives of longshoremen, lit the fuse. The port workers made it a point of honor to remain loyal to their leaders. Finally, a compromise solution ended the strike: the longshoremen's grievances against the commission of inquiry were referred to a special commission.

Subsequently, the ILA was purged, at least of its worst elements. Ryan was succeeded by the more acceptable Captain William Bradley. In November 1959 the longshoremen's International was readmitted, on a provisional basis, into the AFL-CIO, but on condition that it carried through the purge in its ranks. It was not finally reinstated until December 1961.

The teamsters' Brotherhood was also, in its way, a hotbed of corruption. As a matter of fact, there was at least a slight difference between the racketeering of the longshoremen's leaders, who extorted gratuities from their members, and that of the teamsters' leaders, whose major sin consisted in violating the law and cheating the taxman, while they defended their members' interests quite well. True, they did 'borrow' substantial amounts from the union kitty for their private use a little too often.

Their President, Dave Beck, was sentenced to five years in jail for tax fraud. His successor, James Hoffa, was prosecuted for getting hold of confidential documents from the McClellan Commission through a lawyer, and then for bribing two members of the jury to vote for his acquittal. After interminable proceedings he was eventually sentenced, at the beginning of 1967, to eight years' in jail with no possibility of parole. The conditions in which this conviction was secured did no credit to American justice: it was proved, in effect, that the Government resorted to the services of an informer against whom there were far more serious charges than those laid against Hoffa, and who obtained his release by testifying against the accused.

But, above all, what made the AFL-CIO hostile to the teamsters' Brotherhood was not so much its 'immorality' as its habit of defying the union federation and competing with it. In November 1955 Dave Beck had rushed to the help of the longshoremen's International, offering it a loan of $400,000 by way of compensation for its expulsion from the AFL-CIO. The trade-union federation had become angry and had threatened the teamsters with expulsion, so forcing them to withdraw their offer.

Worse still (from the point of view of the AFL-CIO), Dave Beck had established alliances with trade-union organizations not affiliated to the AFL-CIO like the engineers' International and unions thrown out of the CIO, before reunification, for their Communist loyalties, like the metal-mineworkers' International, as well as Internationals expelled from the AFL for corruption, such as the bakers' union. The thinly veiled ambition of the teamsters' leader was to combine with these different elements into a new trade-union federation which would compete with the AFL-CIO.

In December 1957 the AFL-CIO congress expelled the teamsters' Brotherhood, thus depriving the reunified federation of nearly two million members. The latter has continually refused since that time to readmit the teamsters. It allowed Hoffa to be jailed without lifting a finger.

Hoffa, on the other hand, was re-elected President of his International for five years in 1961, and his salary went up from $50,000 to $75,000; he was again re-elected in 1966, with the figure being raised this time to $100,000, which made him the highest-paid trade-union leader in the United States (the salary of George Meany, the Federal President, was far below this record figure: it was originally set at $45,000 but was later increased to $75,000).

The hostility of the AFL-CIO leaders toward the teamsters' International was most certainly justified, but in that sprawling organization corruption was not always the rule at the grass roots: a number of Locals were quite free of it. Moreover, the teamsters' International was really militant, even though it was run in absolutist fashion. Owing to its traditions and the very fact that it had, in part, an industrial structure, it suffered less from the narrow craft consciousness of the other unions formerly in the AFL.

The harsh rectitude of the AFL-CIO proved harmful to labor conflicts on more than one occasion. For example, in May 1961 the longshoremen's International signed a pact (of which more will be said later) with the seamen's and teamsters' Internationals. When a strike by 82,000 seamen broke out in June of that year the longshoremen felt compelled to withdraw from the pact, fearing that, by allying with the teamsters, they would be compromising their chances of being permanently reinstated a few months later by the AFL-CIO. Thus a powerful united front against the shipowners was weakened.

Two Internationals were expelled in December 1957 at the same time as the teamsters: the bakers and the bleachers. Five others were suspended after being convicted of corruption by the McClellan Commission; they included the ex-AFL auto and textile Internationals and the distillery workers. These Internationals had to accept monitorship, under the terms of which they were forced to expel their corrupt leaders. They were then readmitted into the federation.

It should not, however, be thought that corruption has infected the entire American labor movement. The efforts made to stir up public opinion against racketeering and the rumpus kicked up around Congressional commissions of inquiry and legal actions should not lead to a mistaken assessment: in spite of the bureaucratic defects of the top brass, the labor movement, in its vast majority, retains a certain moral well-being: there are, to be sure, flagrant abuses, such as the exorbitant salaries of the trade-union leaders and their well-heeled lifestyles. Walter Reuther denounced with verve those working-class leaders who every February, at the height of the tourist season, check into the poshest hotels in Miami Beach, such as the Americana Hotel. He slammed the leading body of the AFL-CIO, which met in the roulette room at the Hotel Monte Carlo in Miami to decide on measures against corruption. But at least these abuses are 'legal'. Furthermore, they are approved of by a considerable section of the rank and file, who are flattered by the ostentatiously luxurious lifestyles of their representatives.

Nevertheless the lifestyle of 'honest' Labor leaders bears a strange resemblance to that of the corrupt leaders. Thus in Europe a trade-unionist would be easily found out if, by chance, he had a second (illegal) income. But in the United States, expense accounts for trade-union officials are so commonplace that none of them could be accused of 'immoral earnings' merely by reference to these 'extras'.

Finally, as we shall see, the stink given off by some trade union leaderships goes virtually unnoticed by some nostrils doubtless inured by the whole of the surrounding capitalist society to financial scandals, purulent malpractices, misdemeanors and even criminal acts. These days there is a close relationship between trade-union gangsterism, where it flourishes, and the sort of delinquency exhibited by Watergate.

The Balance Sheet of the Union Merger

The direct consequence of the disciplinary action taken under Article 8, Section VII of the reunified federation's statutes was a severe limitation of the autonomy of the constituent Internationals and, consequently, a considerable growth of centralization. The old AFL abandoned its federalist tradition. While William Green had never dared to question the autonomy of the craft unions, his successor George Meany was not held back by the same scruples. In a speech made just before the federation's December 1957 congress, which was to decide on the expulsion of the teamsters, he made a fairly heated attack on the building trades Internationals and reprimanded them for taking their 'jurisdictional' demands too far by seeking to claim for themselves workers in trades already organized into industrial Internationals.

As for the ex-CIO, it reinforced the authoritarian trend which had already been dangerously exemplified when it expelled the various unions under Communist control.

Trade-union unity was both a blessing and a curse. First of all, it amounted to a simple juxtaposition of craft unionism and industrial unionism. It was a compromise, a truce between the two eternal adversaries. It was not a real organic unity. Very few unions covering the same trade merged. The reunification agreement stipulated that each International would have the same 'jurisdiction' it had had in the AFL or the CIO, which was in effect to multiply by two the 'jurisdictional' conflicts which had handicapped the American labor movement so heavily in the past.

Contrary to the hopes of some, trade-union unity did not by a long stretch enable a bold industrial unionism to galvanize a timorous craft unionism. Exactly the opposite occurred. The militant tradition of the CIO was now little more than a memory and its presence in the reunified federation did not permit the leap forward by Labor which the most optimistic had anticipated. On the whole it was the old craft unionism which set the tone in the new federation.

Next, unity was not total. It covered neither the engineers' International nor the miners' nor the railroad Brotherhoods; and, through the expulsions carried out, in particular that of the teamsters' International, it involved yet more divisive convulsions.

Furthermore, unity consolidated the dictatorship of the leadership within the trade-union movement, as well as anti-Communism (not to speak of the racist attitude towards the black workers, a subject which is dealt with (briefly) in chapter four of this book). It was the final step in the integration of the trade-union movement into the Government apparatus and the world leadership of the American Empire.

But, on the other hand, this unity was beneficial inasmuch as it added to Labor's power to a certain extent. It was, moreover, thought of that way by the mass of workers, whose instinct banked on a dynamic of unity. Walter Reuther was later to recall the atmosphere of 'electricity' and 'excitement' in which the news of the December 1955 fusion had been received. With a united labor movement, Reuther then felt, 'we were going to do marvellous things'. Right across the country the workers were saying to themselves: 'It's the beginning of a great crusade. It's the beginning of the biggest effort ever undertaken.'

In order to celebrate reunification a mass rally was organized in a Miami park at night on the occasion of the first meeting of the reunified federation's Executive Council. Although it was not exactly a working-class town, 19,000 workers gathered there enthusiastically. Eleven years later,[7] 'with a deep feeling of sadness', Reuther was to consider it 'most tragic' that 'the great promise of the merger [had gone] unfulfilled'.

Under the leadership of Federal President George Meany the AFL-CIO was to turn its back on the fundamental objectives which had inspired the fusion. It proved totally lacking in the 'crusading spirit' which it should have shown. It turned out to be incapable of keeping its promises. It confined itself to 'living in the past', becoming 'the comfortable and complacent guardian of the *status quo*' and, in Walter Reuther's stinging words, presenting 'an acute case of hardening of the arteries'.

But what Reuther failed to point out was that the trade-union federation was riveted to the established order as a result of its subordination to the two bourgeois political parties, especially the Democratic Party. What is more, since 1951, Reuther had thrown overboard the plan for a Labor

Party, which he had toyed with a short while before, and had tied himself to the Government Administration, in Detroit as well as Washington.

The Fiasco of the Opposition to the Taft-Hartley Act

The new federation was to fail lamentably in its steps to obtain the reform of the Taft-Hartley Act. The fusion convention of the AFL-CIO in December 1955 had carried a resolution which committed the federation to apply pressure on Congress to eliminate the Act's defects and to pass, instead, a liberal law inspired by the principles of the Wagner Act. But the re-unified labor movement revealed itself to be absolutely powerless to shift the rock-like Taft-Hartley Act.

In particular, Section 14b) of the Act, which the Labor leaders offered up for public execration and which, as we saw earlier, not only permitted, but encouraged, the various States to introduce their own anti-Labor legislation, was left untouched. Under this section of the Act about twenty States had brought in laws abolishing union control of hiring, dubbed 'right-to-work laws'. These States were generally the most backward, but it was feared that the precedent they had set would be imitated by other, more industrial States. That is what happened in Indiana and almost happened in California.

Walter Reuther was later to ridicule the totally sham agitation organized by the union leaders to obtain the repeal of Section 14b). He relates that, while the Executive Council was meeting in a luxury hotel in Florida, he had to examine a resolution proposing that the AFL-CIO desist from holding its conventions in any State which had passed anti-Labor laws. There was just one minor oversight – the meeting in question was taking place in one of the most notoriously anti-Labor States in the United States.

Even during the 'thousand days' of John Kennedy's Presidency the Taft-Hartley Act, which the young President had roundly criticized many times, remained intact. The most Kennedy did was to overturn the Republican majority, which was devoted to the trusts, on the National Labor Relations Board, so making possible a less Draconian interpretation of the Act.

President Johnson, who had voted in favor of the Taft-Hartley Act in the Senate, was in even less of a hurry than his predecessor to meddle with this law. At the end of 1965, during a meeting granted to them by the President, the Federal leaders tried to obtain clear assurances that he would actively support their campaign for the repeal of Section 14b). After being pressed for two hours and twenty minutes by his interlocutors, Johnson merely expressed his regrets; he was proposing to submit six other matters to Congress which seemed to him to be more obvious priorities. Up to his neck in the Vietnam war, he had other bones to chew on.

Things Get Worse: The Landrum-Griffin Act

Not only was the Taft-Hartley Act never amended; it was made worse by the 1959 Landrum-Griffin Act.

Firstly, this new piece of legislation removed anyone with a police record from a responsible position in the labor movement, making it possible in this way to get rid of militants who had been convicted for class-struggle activities. The Government arrogated to itself the right to supervise the election of trade-union officials. (It must be said that, although this constituted a dangerous interference, it did enable electoral fraud by a President of the electricians' International to be unmasked and the victory of the rival candidate to be upheld.) Under the pretext of protecting the functioning of workers' democracy those workers opposed to the union were encouraged to take legal action against it and its officials. The Secretary of Labor had full powers to investigate the union's internal affairs, send his agents into union Locals and inspect the membership lists, the financial administration, the records, etc.

Union officials were authorized to impose monitorship on Locals to ensure that their members observed contracts signed with employers. While railing at the new Act, the trade-union bureaucrats turned this power to full account; when a wildcat strike broke out, they never failed to smash it by disowning the strikers and putting the screws on the disobedient union Local.

The Landrum-Griffin Act gave the Secretary of Labor the power to ask a court for an injunction if he suspected that a union 'has violated or is on the point of violating' the law. In other words the Government was entitled to put a political detective in every trade-union office.

Labor characterized the Landrum-Griffin Act as 'the most Draconian legislative measure adopted since the passage of the Taft-Hartley Act'. But the union leaders waged a sterile, purely verbal fight against the new law. These failures did not prevent them from pouring millions of dollars into John Kennedy's and Lyndon Johnson's Presidential campaigns.

Incapacity in the Trade-Union Struggle

Another deficiency of the AFL-CIO was its passivity in the defense of salary levels in both national and inter-industry terms. In April 1962 President Kennedy, playing on his prestige and his good relations with the Labor leaders, managed to talk the union leaders into signing an agreement with the bosses under his aegis which provided for no general increase in wages and restricted any eventual raises to ten cents an hour, or 2.5 per cent. This was very much lower than the figure of 17 cents advanced by the unions, and bore no relation to the increase in the cost of living.

Kennedy had pulled off this feat by invoking the specter of 'inflation'. The unions had hardly had time to express satisfaction at their sacrifice when the steel bosses rushed to announce a rise of six dollars in the price of a ton of steel; the US President boosted himself into the bargain by succeeding in getting this increase cancelled.

But it was above all in the field of recruitment that the AFL-CIO's failure was flagrant. It devoted only *two to three per cent* of its total income to recruitment campaigns, while nearly 25 per cent was wasted on 'international affairs', where Labor made itself the errand boy of the American Empire.

On the eve of fusion the CIO Internationals were preparing to invest four million dollars in a recruitment fund, particularly aimed at a second attempt at organizing the South, which was undergoing rapid industrialization. The CIO had placed one condition on this recruitment plan: that after reunification, the AFL should follow suit. This was not asking very much, since the membership of the older establishment was double that of its younger rival. And yet the AFL would not make the gesture expected of it. The recruitment campaign, which was such a pressing necessity, had to be buried.

The result of these grave shortcomings was an absolute and relative decline in trade-union membership. According to the Labor Department's statistics, there were 17.9 million trade-unionists in 1966, only 400,000 more than in 1956. During this period the number of industrial workers went up by 11.5 million, so the proportion of organized workers fell from 33.4 to 28 per cent. Moreover, automation was producing rapid changes in the composition of the labor force. In 1950 blue-collar workers constituted 41 per cent of wage-earners and white-collar workers 37 per cent. By 1966 the relationship was reversed: blue-collar workers accounted for no more than 36 per cent, while white-collar workers now made up 45 per cent of the total work force. The latter were not so easily won to trade-unionism as the blue-collar workers; without an intensive effort to organize them, the percentage of organized to unorganized workers could only decrease still further.

Still more serious was the absence, by and large, from Labor's ranks of the most deprived social strata: these included many Blacks, Chicanos, migrant farm workers, uprooted young people, etc. These groups were envious and resentful of the beneficiaries of trade-union protection. With the exception of Walter Reuther and the organizations he ran, Labor did nothing to increase its popularity with these strata overlooked by the 'great society'.

CHAPTER 7

The combative sectors of Labor

Automation

The incapacity of the leadership was partially made up for by the spunk of the rank and file, which pushed the officials of the different Internationals into action. The causes of this combativity were twofold: the essential need of the workers to defend their purchasing power, which was threatened by the rise in the cost of living (16 per cent from 1958 to 1967), and what has come to be known as the 'second phase of the industrial revolution', that is to say the lightning progress of automation and computers, upheavals which tended more and more to replace men by machines. The specter of automation loomed behind every important strike in the sixties. In many cases wages became a less essential issue than jobs.

The formidable character of this revolution was underscored by Walter Reuther when he estimated that, if the auto industry was wholly automated, no more than 200,000 people would be needed to ensure the running of factories then employing 1,200,000 people. While car production rose between 1947 and 1962 by 70.14 per cent, the number of workers engaged in their production fell by 10.8 per cent. The Bureau of Labor Statistics put the number of American workers eliminated each year by automation at a minimum of 200,000. Overall unemployment went up from 1,900,000 in 1953 to 3,800,000 in 1959 and 4,200,000 in 1963 (going down again to 3,500,000 in August 1967, solely as a result of the Vietnam war). The steelworkers' International saw its membership fall from 1,200,000 in 1955 to 778,000 in 1960 due to technological progress. (In 1966 the war-induced boom brought this figure up to 925,000 again.) The time required to produce a ton of steel was reduced from eleven hours in 1952 to a little over seven hours in 1963. The engineers' International went from 992,000 members in 1959 to 646,000 in 1964. In thirteen years, from 1953 to 1966, the number of railroad workers was reduced by almost half and the number of coal-miners by more than half.

Automation had all sorts of repercussions on the labor market. It ended the practice of payment by the hour. Since it was now impossible to measure the individual worker's output: more and more American workers were paid on a weekly or monthly basis. Automation likewise abolished productivity bonuses. It gave rise to large-scale movement of labor, with workers having to change towns and lodgings in search of a job. It led industrial Internationals to seek maintenance and construction jobs, which had till then been reserved for the construction unions, for their laid-off members. This resulted in fresh 'jurisdictional' disputes between rival unions.

Labor did not challenge the need for technical progress and did not want to oppose it in principle, an attitude which it considered would be 'anti-social'. On the other hand it tried to protect its members against a 'blind' acceleration of automation and demanded that its extension should be controlled. It called for an 'equitable' share by the workers in the profits gushing from the use of the new technology. (There was, as we shall see, one exception: the miners' International, which encouraged the bosses' inclination to automation.) It was estimated in 1963 that, without the restraining hand of the unions, a further million workers would have been without work.

Among the measures against unemployment called for by Labor were the introduction of a guaranteed annual salary, the extension of the minimum legal age for leaving school, the lowering of the age of retirement, a reduction in the number of hours worked, the organization of leisure time, longer holidays, etc.

Some unions advocated that the workers should have a share in the extra profits procured by the introduction of automation. Thus, for example, an agreement was made by Kaiser Steel with the steelworkers' International in December 1962. This agreement provided for the profits accruing from the savings made on the basic annual cost of a ton of steel to be shared inasmuch as the cost was reduced by the progress of automation. The sums released in this way were paid into a special fund and the firm's workers received 32.5 per cent of the total amount in the form of monthly distributions. The very fact that the union as well as the employer was having to work out the production costs per ton should have given it the right to begin to keep tabs on the running of the firm. However, the workers in Kaiser Steel's main factory in Fontana, California were disappointed by the way in which this agreement was applied and protested at its poor results.

The Kaiser agreement was exceptional; most often the unions stressed the need to reduce the work week as compensation for the man-power which had become superfluous as a result of automation. In July 1962 George Meany declared to a conference of construction unions:

> 'If we continue to produce more and more with fewer and fewer workers, we have to reduce the hours of work of the American workers without reducing their income. And if that implies a week of 35, 34, 33, 30 hours or even less, then let's adopt it.'

At the end of 1963 the same Meany dwelt on the fact that a reduction of the work week to 35 hours would remedy both the unemployment problem and the race problem (the incidence of unemployment was and remains much higher among blacks, most of whom were unskilled, than among whites).

An example of the new trade-union demands flowing from the impact of automation was the agreement reached in 1962 by an electricity workers' local at the end of a strike. It included a thirty hour work week as well as three months' paid vacation every five years for all workers with 15 years service or more. But, here again, the result was exceptional.

As for the AFL-CIO leadership, it did not by any means wage a thoroughgoing struggle for a reduction in the work week and against automation. As we shall see, Walter Reuther reproached President George Meany for this (p.220).*

Class Struggle

In the absence of an overall fight coordinated at the top, various Internationals went into struggle to defend both the conditions of existence and the right to work of their members. The integration of the labor movement into the apparatus of the American Empire has not, as in many totalitarian countries, resulted as yet in the systematic prohibition of all strikes and generalized recourse to compulsory arbitration. American capitalism remains attached, to a certain extent, to

---

*In fact, there has been no downward trend in hours worked since 1948. There was a decline from 58.4 hours a week in 1901 to 42 hours a week in 1948, 'and little or no change since'. Most manufacturing workers are still working approximately 45 hours a week and compulsory overtime is an outstanding rank and file complaint [Ed.].

the principles of economic liberalism. It is not very favorable to Government interference in labor conflicts and, for its part, the Government thinks twice before intervening. Such at least was the tradition, particularly among Republican politicians; but the Democratic Administrations of Kennedy, and then Johnson, subsequently departed further and further from it, above all in relation to the public services. It became a normal practice for President Johnson to break strikes by means of court orders, with the Vietnam war serving him as a pretext.

Furthermore, the damage caused to the nation's economy by labor conflicts, however huge the figure at which it is estimated, is none the less considered normal in a country where everything is colossal; the wealth of a society of plenty makes it quite possible to absorb such damage.

So there is an often intense class struggle in which the Government interferes only in the last resort and after a good deal of hesitation. The very size of American industry and the masses of workers it employs give these battles a gigantic character, with the tenacity of the bosses matching that of the workers.

American trade-unionism is certainly reformist, inasmuch as it limits its action to the framework of the established order; but, leaving aside the World War II period, it has not, save during Nixon's New Economic Policy wage agreements, become bogged down in class collaboration, like, for example, the West German labor movement. It has retained – and this is not known widely enough in Europe – a tradition of militancy and direct action.

In the auto industry. – Social peace had prevailed in this industry for several years due to the sliding scale clause which the United Automobile Workers was successful in getting inserted into their labor contracts. At the beginning of June 1955 these contracts with both General Motors and Ford expired. The union then began the fight for a guaranteed annual income, which in this case meant guaranteed annual payment for 52 weeks' work, at the rate of 80 per cent of the average weekly wage, for workers employed by the firm for at least two years and a guarantee of 26 weeks' pay for those employed for at least one year.

After a strike had been threatened, and partially carried out, a compromise was reached: 26 weeks were obtained instead of 52, and 65 per cent of the wage instead of 80.

During another trial of strength at the beginning of September 1961 General Motors agreed to raise the number of guaranteed weeks from 26 to 52. At the same time the UAW signed an agreement with the American Motors Company, giving the workers 15 per cent of the firm's profits. This agreement was viewed with anxiety by the big auto companies, who considered it a 'revolution' in American industry, that is to say a first step towards workers' control of the running of industry.

In September-October 1964, another strike broke out in General Motors' ancillary firms. It lasted for a month and was mainly concerned with an improvement in working conditions: safety, rest periods during production-line work, etc. Walter Reuther declared that the auto workers were not interested solely in an improvement of their material situation, but felt they had 'the right to work in decency and dignity'.

In September 1967 – we will return to this point later – the UAW declared a strike at Ford's which lasted nearly two months (see p.224).

The Kohler strike. – In connection with the activity of the auto International, one cannot pass over a strike by UAW Local 833 which beat all records for duration: it lasted almost *twelve years,* from 5 April 1954, to 17 December 1965. The Kohler company owned factories in Sheboygan, Wisconsin, and its various products (plumbing articles, etc.) had nothing to do with the auto industry. But the UAW had succeeded in 1952, not without difficulty, in organizing the firm's workers.

Sheboygan was a typical company town, a place where everything, including the forces of law and order, belonged to the capitalist employer. The Kohler family, of German origin, exercised paternalistic domination over its 3,300 workers. Prussian-type discipline prevailed in its plants. It had always opposed the intrusion of labor unionism. In 1934, following a strike, Kohler had engaged in savage repression, after which it had formed a company union. Under legal compulsion it was forced to acknowledge the National Labor Relations Board election in 1952, which was won by the new Local 833. But it did not take Kohler very long to renege on the agreement which it was compelled to sign in 1953. Hence the strike.

Protracted legal proceedings were begun. Jack and Bobby

Kennedy appeared before the McClellan Senate Commission and proved that the company had armed itself with tear-gas, guns and clubs for use against the strikers. On two occasions, in 1960 and 1964, the NLRB decided against the employer and declared[1] that it 'at no time intended to accept the Union as the collective bargaining representative to be dealt with in good faith'. The Supreme Court rejected the employers' appeal.

The UAW and, with them, the whole American labor movement, showed the Kohler strikers a solidarity unparalleled in the history of Labor. A national boycott of Kohler products was organized. For the sake of survival, the strikers had to scatter across the United States in search of new jobs, while the company took on strike-breakers. When victory was finally achieved the strikers were reinstated, with the exception of fifty-seven militants accused of 'violence', and the company had to pay out 3 million dollars in back pay plus a million and a half dollars owing to the pension fund. In conclusion Walter Reuther declared that the determination of the Kohler fighters, supported by Labor as a whole,[2] had 'prevented many other "Kohlers" from happening'.

In the steel industry. – The leaders of the International Union in this industry had a strong leaning toward concocting peaceful settlements. But peace was quite often broken by the aggressiveness of a combative set of employers as well as by the sporadic restiveness of the rank and file. In 1952 a nation-wide strike went on for fifty-nine days. In 1955 the conflict which had led to another work stoppage was settled after eleven hours. In July 1956 there was a further national strike which lasted almost a month. The bosses sought to bind the union by a long-term agreement (four or five years) in order to protect the industry against any 'threat of interruption'. In spite of the fact that it too was keen to avoid strikes, the trade-union leadership could not reasonably tie itself down for too long a period at a time when the progress of automation threatened to bring about critical upheavals in production methods and conditions of man-power utilization. Finally a compromise was reached: the International committed itself, somewhat rashly as it turned out, to a contract of three years' duration.

In July 1959, with the expiry of the agreement in question, the 500,000 steelworkers stopped work. It was the sixth national steel strike since the end of World War II. Behind the demand for an increase in the hourly wage and an extension of the insurance and pension schemes which were obtained as a result of the 1949 strike, loomed the specter of automation; the steelworkers were trying to prevent the bosses modernizing the means of production too radically and cutting down on labor.

Apart from the half-million strikers, another half a million workers in related industries had to stop work for lack of steel. The strike cost the employers a staggering 5 billion dollars and the workers a billion dollars. The AFL-CIO donated millions of dollars to the strikers by way of solidarity. The negotiations made no headway for several months because of the arrogant attitude of the employers. Roger Blough, the President of US Steel, was bent on dealing the union a severe blow.

After beating around the bush for a while, President Eisenhower made up his mind to apply the Taft-Hartley Act. On 29 October he obtained an order from a Federal court in Philadelphia suspending the strike until 26 January 1960. Walter Reuther accused him of wanting 'to break the strike to play the game of his millionaire friends' and capitulating to Wall Street.

The application of the Taft-Hartley Act may have stopped the strike for a time; but it in no way helped to bring a settlement. The workers declared their determination to stop work once more as soon as the suspension period had expired. The negotiators were stymied. The union then requested arbitration by the Supreme Court. Finally, in order to avoid having to submit to the compulsory verdict of a court of arbitration, the employers resigned themselves to taking the road of conciliation. Voluntary arbitration was given by Richard Nixon, then the United States Vice-President, and the Labor Secretary, James Mitchell.

On 5 January 1960 a new agreement was signed, limited to to two and a half years. It was relatively advantageous for the workers. Apart from an increase in wages and the extension of the free insurance system, a 'social payment' equal in value to thirteen weeks' wages (about $1,500) was made to every worker at the time of his retirement. It was the first time that an innovation of this type had been introduced in American industry.

The longshoremen. – Early in October 1959 all the ports on the East Coast and in the Gulf of Mexico were brought to a standstill by a longshoremen's strike. Once again President Eisenhower resorted to the weapon of the Taft-Hartley Act. In January 1965 there was another strike by the 60,000 longshoremen on the Atlantic Coast which lasted thirty-three days. By 8,354 votes to 7,792 the rank and file had rejected a contract, despite the view of the President of the International that 'it was the best agreement obtained by the union in 72 years'. The stumbling-block was a clause providing for the gradual reduction in the number of members of work crews on account of automation. On 11 February a Federal judge ordered the immediate resumption of work for a five-day period. But the dispute was not wound up on the first try, since some South Coast Locals in Miami and Galveston came up with new grievances.

The seamen. – On 15 June 1961, a strike of 82,000 seamen began upon the expiry of a contract which the ship owners had refused to renew. Thirty ports were brought to a standstill and more than 100 boats immobilized alongside the dock. The dispute arose from the fact that some ship owners used American ships flying flags of convenience so as to be able to pay lower wages to the crews: about 20,000 men were cheated in this way.

This sea battle was supported by the teamsters' International (who were briefly joined by the longshoremen). A mutual assistance pact had in fact been signed a month earlier between Joseph Curran for the seamen, James Hoffa for the teamsters and Captain Bradley for the longshoremen, for the purpose of 'promoting long-term stability and progress in the maritime branch of the transport industry'.

The striking unions called for the appointment of an impartial commission whose task would be to define the cargoes considered indispensable to the country's safety and well-being. This request was aimed at avoiding recourse, in the name of the 'general interest', to the Taft-Hartley Act.

But President Kennedy had a Federal court give the strikers strict injunctions to resume work for the statutory period of eighty days. During that time the seamen and the ship owners reached agreement.

The railroad workers. – The twin spurs of automation and reduction in railroad usage led the railroad companies to draw up a plan for staff reductions affecting more than 37,000 engineers. Following this, a railroad strike was postponed in August 1963, after the Senate had passed a bill introducing compulsory arbitration.

A five-member conciliation board was to be granted full power to fix wages and working conditions, which were to remain in force for a period of two years. The companies agreed in the meantime to defer their new arrangement. For their part, the railway workers' Brotherhoods put off their planned strike until the passage of the bill.

A number of Democrats, though supporters of President Kennedy's Administration, considered the legislation to be an attack on trade-union freedom; they argued that this was the first time in United States history that compulsory arbitration had been imposed in this way by the authorities.

In July 1967 the conflict flared up again: engineers stopped work throughout the United States, since the negotiations between their representatives and those of the companies were increasingly leading nowhere.

The bill had been held over and not yet passed by Congress, but President Johnson lost no time in getting it through and signing it, after declaring: 'Every minute lost increases the damage caused to the economy and to the American war effort in Vietnam'.

The law ordered the immediate cessation of strike action and laid down a cooling-off period of ninety days to be followed by a binding settlement if the negotiations, to be conducted with the help of mediators, had come to nothing at the end of this time.

The printers. – Early in December 1962 the 3,500 New York printers organized in Local 6 of the printers' International stopped work, demanding a large increase in wages on four big dailies. The five rival newspapers voluntarily decided to cease publication out of solidarity.

The struggle lasted 114 days. It was led by an energetic young trade-union leader who emerged into the limelight at this point, Bertram Anthony Powers. Powers boasted of having prepared his men 'for years' for this test of strength. 19,000 workers in related industries were laid off as a by-product of the strike. It cost the newspaper proprietors more than a million dollars a day in lost publicity and the labor unions nearly seven million dollars in strike payments. It did considerable damage to New York trade at the height of the end-of-year holiday season. The losses incurred by the economy of the metropolis were estimated at between 200 and 250 million dollars. It led to wage claims by other printing unions (stereotypists, photogravure workers, photoengravers). It brought some of the newspapers concerned to the verge of bankruptcy. It resulted in the amalgamation of several of them and the folding of the *Herald Tribune*. The financial situation of the *New York Post* became so critical owing to the strike that it had to withdraw support from its colleagues and resume publication.

President Kennedy had stepped in with a call for arbitration, but to no avail. When the negotiations between the two sides finally produced a compromise, the union rank and file turned down the agreement by 1,621 votes to 1,557. The photoengravers in their turn rejected that part of the deal relating to them. In the end the strikers settled for a compromise, the printers on 26 March 1963, the photoengravers on 31 March.

It should be noted that the printers' International is one of the few unions to have a keen sense of workers' democracy. It organizes its elections according to a 'bipartite' system in which the opposition to the union leadership can truly safeguard its rights.

The Aircraft Maintenance Workers. – In July 1966 35,000 aircraft maintenance staff for five airlines went on strike, grounding virtually all civil air traffic in the United States. The strike lasted about fifty days. It was very difficult for the Federal Government to intervene because the Taft-Hartley Act does not in fact apply to the railroad, road and air unions. President Johnson therefore offered to mediate personally. His proposal was accepted, but the results were disappointing, with the White House offering the strikers a wage raise of only 3.2 per cent. The latter repudiated the Presidential compromise, rejecting it by a three-to-one majority. Questioned on television, trade-union militants did not hesitate to declare: 'Johnson has betrayed us'. A special Federal law had to be prepared to deal with the maintenance men. The Senate at first refused to vote on it, but then finally gave its approval to the bill forcing them back to work for a certain period of time. Secretary of Labor, Wirtz, faithful to economic liberalism, did not conceal his disapproval of this procedure. Each time, he said in substance, that Congress intervened in the settlement of a social conflict, it dealt a blow to the virtues of the normal procedure: negotiation.

Just when the bill was about to become law, an agreement was reached between the strikers and the companies, under the terms of which the former gained an increase of around 8 per cent, which was not far off their original demands and was considerably larger than the increase proposed by President Johnson. Even then it proved necessary to quell last-minute resistance by the unions of two of the companies on strike who considered the concessions made inadequate.

The New York public transport system. – On 1 January 1966 the people of New York woke up to a city with no subway service and no buses. Under the dynamic leadership of Mike Quill the 36,000 public transport workers were demanding a 32-hour, four day week (instead of 40 hours), a 30 per cent wage raise, an extension of annual vacation to six weeks and the right to retire at half salary after 25 years' service.

The New York State Supreme Court put a temporary ban on the strike. Then Mike Quill tore the injunction he had just received into a thousand pieces in front of the television cameras. Together with eight other union officials he was charged by the New York State Supreme Court with contempt of court for not abiding by the injunction and expressing his disobedience in the form of a challenge.

At a press conference held in a big hotel the hot-headed leader exclaimed:[3] 'The judge can drop dead in his black robes. Personally, I don't care if I rot in jail. I will not call off this strike.' Several deputy sheriffs then burst in, arresting the diehard and his eight colleagues in front of the television cameras. In the office of the prison to which he had just been taken, sixty-year-old Mike Quill suffered a heart attack, from which he was to die shortly after his release. This release from prison was indeed one of the clauses in the agreement which put an end to the strike thirteen days after it had begun. It was only a half-victory: a wage increase of

15 per cent. The dispute had cost the city an estimated one billion dollars.

The attitude of the AFL-CIO leaders toward the strike was one of hostility. They sent messages only to protest the jailing of the union leaders, but not to back the strikers' demands. President George Meany publicly criticized the strike and praised the mayor of New York, the Republican Lindsay, for accusing the union of placing itself outside the law. As for Walter Reuther, who had not opened his mouth during the work stoppage, he waited for the struggle to end before speaking of public sector strikes as 'outdated': 'Society cannot tolerate work stoppages which endanger the very existence of society.'

But Mike Quill's gesture remained engraved on workers' memories: the following year, on 23 May 1967, a meeting of 25,000 workers took place at Madison Square Garden to protest a recent New York State law prompted by the 1966 subway strike, the Rockefeller-Travia Act, which introduced severe penalties for strikes by public service workers. The President of the New York State AFL-CIO, imitating the deceased Mike Quill, pulled a copy of the Act out of his pocket and tore it to shreds, to the applause of the crowd.

In this connection it is worth mentioning that during the sixties, public service workers, teachers included, became one of the most combative sectors of the American labor movement. In 1966 this sector registered three times as many strikes as in 1965. At the beginning of September 1967 various teachers' strikes broke out, particularly in Detroit and New York – an unusual occurrence in the United States.

The rubber industry. – In April 1967 the rubber-workers' International, with a membership of 180,000, embarked on the longest strike in its history. The 'Big Five' in the rubber industry – Goodrich, Firestone, General Tire and Rubber, Goodyear, Uniroyal – had concluded a pact pledging to assist each other against the union. They had to give in after a struggle which, for certain factories, lasted nearly three months. The strikers won an increase in the hourly wage, longer vacations, and pensions, all of which marked an important step toward their essential demand: a guaranteed annual income.

CHAPTER 8

A new militancy?

The Pressure of the Rank and File

The profitability and dynamism of the American economy during the sixties, stimulated by the Vietnam war, enabled trade-union action to make further gains, in the wage field as well as in job security. The pressure from below on the trade-union leaders was to a certain extent sporadic; it still lacked coherence and too often concerned individual or subjective matters.

Nevertheless, from the end of 1964, onwards, there was something of a renewed upsurge of militancy. This spirit of rebellion, directed against the union leaders almost as much as against the employers, showed that, in spite of its bureaucratization, Labor was much less of a hierarchical organization and a totalitarian 'machine' than might have been supposed. Most contracts are signed at the national level and consequently limit the freedom of action of area and factory locals. However, these contracts only lay down the wage minimum, and there is nothing to prevent a local from winning a better deal from the boss than the one set out in the national contract, provided, however, that it does not have to resort to strike action to secure it.

The locals do, nonetheless, have a relative margin of autonomy. They constitute democratic communities which elect and control their officers and can take – or do not hesitate to take – a good many initiatives, particularly around problems specific to them, such as local relations between workers and employers, working conditions, safety, sackings, speed-ups, increased mechanization, etc.

In the auto workers' International in particular, some work stoppages decided on locally were disowned by the national trade-union leadership and therefore became wildcat strikes; but others hardly aroused any opposition from the leaders. This happened when the latter felt bypassed by the pressure from the ranks and preferred to provide a safety valve for the all-or-nothing assertiveness of their members. In this way they had to tolerate – and sometimes even authorize – local strikes. They were constantly harassed by a rank and file becoming more and more exasperated by the yoke of national contracts which lasted too long and by the low ceiling of the sliding scale – where it existed. Indeed the union members sometimes demanded that notice should be given terminating contracts, even though they had not expired, through invoking the so-called *force majeure* clause.

The main cause of this agitation among the rank and file was the persistent dwindling of buying power due, for the most part, to the inflation resulting from the extension of the Vietnam war. While the nominal value of wages was rising, real wages were being eaten into. In the autumn of 1966 the Department of Labor revealed that an average factory worker had obtained an increase of 2.59 dollars in his weekly wage between August 1965 and August 1966, but that, because of price increases, his buying power had fallen by 63 cents per week during the same period. It was forecast in July 1966 that the cost of living could increase by between 5 and 9 per cent a year if the conflict in Indochina were to drag on. The enrichment of firms working for the war had as its counterpart the relative impoverishment of the workers.

Another cause of this militant revival was a lowering of the average age of trade-unionists. Almost half the population of the USA was twenty or under in the sixties. In July 1967 14 per cent of the labor force was made up of young people between 16 and 21. Forty per cent of the members of the auto International, traditionally one of the most youthful unions, were under 30. (We shall come back to this phenomenon of rejuvenation at the end of this book.)

The first six months of 1966 brought to the surface a growth of working class combativity which plainly contradicted the self-styled experts on labor problems who had forecast a quiet year on the labor front. In the month of May 1966 alone about 2,870,000 individual working days were lost as a result of strikes. It was the highest May figure for seven years. In the first four months of 1967 the number of strikes – 1,635 – and the number of workers on strike – 846,000 – was found by the statisticians to have been the highest since 1953. In the month of April alone work stoppages reached the figure of 440 and involved 409,000 workers.

This renewed militancy also found expression within various International Unions in challenges to leaderships which appeared really securely in the saddle. In the auto International the young officials of the UAW locals began to rebel against Walter Reuther's over-heavy grip and attack him for his inveterate habit of trampling internal democracy underfoot.

In the electrical workers' International, originating from the Communist-inspired United Electrical Workers of America, the workers, spurred on by a local official, Paul Jennings, harried the President, James Carey, criticizing him for his dictatorial methods of control and, on 7 April 1965, Jennings was proclaimed President of the International by a large majority, after his predecessor had been convicted of electoral fraud.

Within the United Mine Workers, where the tradition of autocratic leadership was very deep-rooted, an opposition emerged to Tony Boyle, who had succeeded John Lewis in 1960 (Lewis was pensioned off with the title of 'honorary President'). This International, which, in contrast to its past, had by now completely isolated itself from the bulk of the American Labor movement, had a rather peculiar trade-union policy: it systematically encouraged mechanization and automation in order to enable the mining bosses to pay high wages. In point of fact the miners' wages went up by 73 per cent between 1959 and 1964, putting them among the highest-paid workers in the United States. The other side of the coin was the constant reduction in employment in the mines – a reduction of 33 per cent in 1964 compared with 1950 and 28 per cent compared with 1958. A third of the International's membership, which had fallen to 200,000, had lost their jobs over the previous ten years. Whole areas, such as the Appalachian Mountains, were literally emptied of their mining population, and the pits were closed down.

Moreover, the acute economic crisis affecting the coal industry led to a considerable fall in the income of the pension fund; so much so that in February 1962 retired miners' pensions had to be reduced from $100 to $75.

Tony Boyle's administration aroused a lot of discontent within his International. The oppositionists held a number of meetings. They even threatened to start strikes in some mines on their own initiative. This rebel faction was active in seven States.

In the steelworkers' International a group led by an ex-worker, I W Abel, succeeded in February 1965 in ousting the President, Dave MacDonald, who had earlier been pitchforked into the leadership of the steelworkers without ever having been one of them (he had begun as Murray's stenographer). The rank and file had been dissatisfied for a long time with the authoritarian administration of its President, who had had himself re-elected for a further three year term and had signed contracts which lasted too long, thus preventing any wage adjustments for several years.

However, it was pretty much a palace revolution: the new President, Abel, and his direct associates belonged body and soul to the trade-union bureaucracy. As the president of a Local vividly pointed out,[1] 'Why they've both been sleeping in the same bed for twenty years'. Apart from an indication that the rank and file was becoming agitated, MacDonald's replacement by Abel was in no sense a sign of radicalization.

The leaderships were ousted in four other important Internationals: those of the teachers, the local civil servants (State, county and municipal), the East Coast longshoremen and finally, and above all, the rubber workers, who found themselves a new leader: Peter Bommarito. In three smaller unions there were attempts by local and area leaders to overturn the leadership. We shall come back later to the activities of opposition groups in certain unions from 1970 to the present day (pp.237-240, 243, 247).

But the most typical rebellion against the trade-union leaderships was the one which occurred in the West Coast paper industry in 1964. Locals belonging to the two Internationals covering the industry broke with their national organizations. They then formed a new trade union, which won an election giving it representation of 22,000 workers spread over 40 factories and enabling a strike to be called.

Delano

The new upsurge of militancy also manifested itself, on a very different plane, in the organization of the farm workers. In September 1965 the farm workers at the Delano vineyard in California, most of whom were Mexican, went on strike. They were exploited by a powerful capitalist group, Schenley Products. They were guided by a committee for the organization of farm workers which was under the thumb of the trade-union federation. A few days afterwards they were joined in their strike by an independent union, the National

Farm Workers Association, which was led by a remarkable militant: Cesar Chavez.

Towards the end of the year signs of lassitude appeared among the strikers. It was then that, at Walter Reuther's instigation, the December congress of the AFL-CIO, after hearing a delegation of strikers, assured them of its solidarity. Armed with this assurance, a delegation led by Reuther went to Delano immediately after the Federal congress and addressed the strikers at a stirring meeting. It contacted the local authorities and managed to prevail upon the United States Senate to hold an on the spot investigation in which Robert Kennedy took part, among others.

Thanks to the financial help of the auto International and the department of industrial unions, the strike hardened. The strikers organized a big march on Sacramento, the capital of the State of California, shouting 'Huelga!' (the Spanish for strike) all along the way. In August 1966 the National Farm Workers Association, which had been independent till then, affiliated to the AFL-CIO. Shortly afterwards the vineyard workers finally induced the employers to sign a contract and recognize the union.

This strike was the point of departure for recruitment campaigns and similar struggles by rural and migrant workers in Texas and Florida. They were supported, like the one in Delano, by the auto International and the department of industrial unions. On the other hand George Meany, the federation President, proved more than reluctant to become involved.

Reuther's Resignation

The Delano fight contributed, though it was not its main cause, to the break between Walter Reuther and George Meany. The ill-will of the AFL-CIO President during the struggle had made the leader of the department of industrial unions indignant. He had had to go to great lengths to persuade the President of the federation to form a committee of support for the strikers. However, once the committee was established, the auto International, which had given more backing to the strike than any other trade-union organization, was deliberately excluded from it.

Early in 1967 Walter Reuther quit his position as Vice-President of the reunified federation, while his closest associates in the United Automobile Workers, Emil Mazey and

Leonard Woodcock, withdrew from the federation's Executive Council with him. A little later his position in the leadership of the AFL-CIO was taken by William Pollock, the President of the textile workers' International (ex-CIO).

Walter Reuther exercised his patience for a long time before breaking with Meany. He had to swallow a lot of insults without daring to take the dispute into the public arena. But those in the know were well aware that relations between the President and Vice-President of the reunified federation had become steadily worse. The fragile equilibrium of dual power finally snapped.

As sly as a fox, the resigning Vice-President bowed to the new wave of rank-and-file militancy and tried to keep in touch with the grass roots by taking more combative action. Throughout his checkered career he gave proof of his congenital opportunism, executing, as required, astonishing swings to the right (when the wind was blowing in a reactionary direction) and to the left (when the trend was toward radicalization). If, inveterate reformist though he was, Reuther felt that there were indications of an imminent awakening of the working class, he made sure he was well placed to be able, when the time came, to have a hold over it – that is to say to prevent it from going too far. Perhaps he was also not displeased to leave his mark on history and to pose as Labor's 'conscience' and the 'champion of the underprivileged' as he approached his sixtieth birthday.

The Causes of the Split

The reason most often given by the Press for the Reuther-Meany split was US foreign policy. Thus Reuther agreed to meet Mikoyan in the United States, while Meany held the Soviet visitor up to public obloquy. Later, in June 1966, Reuther and his International condemned the withdrawal of the AFL-CIO delegation from the International Labor Organization (ILO), which had been ordered by Meany without consulting all his colleagues. The occasion for this intemperate gesture was the election of a Polish delegate as the temporary chairman of a session.

Finally, Meany and Reuther by no means shared the same views on the Vietnam war. At the auto International's congress in May 1966 a resolution was carried which, while making the mistake of relying on President Johnson to sit down at the negotiating table, attacked the supporters of 'escalation' in Vietnam and declared that the war should not be won, but should be ended by a peaceful settlement. However, shortly afterwards, in August, the Executive Council of the AFL-CIO congratulated the President of the United States[2] 'for having demonstrated to the world' that his country was 'neither irresolute politically nor weak militarily' and stigmatized 'the reckless bombings against civilians'. Which bombings? Those perpetrated . . . by the communists. At the December 1967 Federal convention there was again much lauding of the Vietnam war. Reuther at first avoided openly confronting the two Presidents, Meany of the trade-union Federation and Johnson of the United States, on this question – perhaps because he was aware that the war had for a long time been far from unpopular in his own fief, the auto industry, especially in the aircraft industry, which falls within the province of the UAW and which was thriving as a result of war orders. Between a quarter and a third of the auto International's members were involved in production for 'national defense'. But the growth of a relatively important movement of opposition to the war led Reuther to take his distance from the official position. So, on 25 March 1967, he let his close associate Emil Mazey, the secretary-treasurer of the UAW, deliver a blistering attack on President Johnson at a pacifist meeting, predicting his defeat in the Presidential elections if he became further embroiled in the war.

To gain a better understanding of Walter Reuther's reasons, we went through the 'administrative letters' periodically addressed by the UAW to their Locals for the period December 1966-April 1967. In these letters, from which we have already quoted, the auto leader finally revealed his differences with George Meany to his members.

On the subject of foreign policy the disagreement was merely one of emphasis. Reuther was as faithful a servant of the American Empire as Meany. And he made no bones about it:[3]

> 'There is no basic difference between the UAW and the AFL-CIO in the commitment to resist Communist aggression and to struggle against all forms of tyranny that would destroy human freedom and enslave the human spirit. We in the UAW can be proud of our record of continuous and successful struggle against Communism and all other forms of totalitarianism.'

Reuther's criticism of Meany was rather that he had ill-served the cause of American world leadership:[4]

> '. . . the attitude of the AFL-CIO on most foreign policy questions has been narrow and negative and has not strengthened but rather weakened the free world's efforts to resist communism and all forms of tyranny.'

For Reuther[5] 'anti-communism in and of itself is not enough'. It was necessary[6] 'to eliminate social and economic injustice, which are the ingredients that communism exploits and attempts to forge into political power'.

But the disagreements between the two leaders went well beyond foreign policy. They related first of all to the Black problem. In the struggle against racial prejudice there was always a gulf between the thinly disguised racism of Meany and the old AFL unions, and the unity of action with the civil rights movement practised persistently, at the top, if not always at rank-and-file level, by Walter Reuther. This clash of views had come out into the open at the time of the 28 August 1963 march on Washington with which Meany refused to associate the AFL-CIO, while Reuther took part in it on behalf of the auto workers, going it alone. Reuther had 'argued', 'urged' and 'begged' in meetings of the Federal Executive Council, but to no avail. A majority of Council members confided to him in private that they were in favor of the march. But what was the use? 'A single man imposed his will.'

Yet these were relatively minor disagreements. The main bone of contention between Reuther and Meany concerned the principles and tactics of democratic trade-unionism.

Here Reuther seemed to forget the authoritarian and bureaucratic way in which he ran his own International and then the CIO. For the sake of his cause, he suddenly became the champion of workers' democracy:[7]

> 'Labor unity built upon a monolithic relationship can only be unity in form, not unity in substance. Unity in substance is possible only when the programs and policies of a free labor movement are the end product of a free and open debate, out of which diversity can be harmonized into a meaningful common denominator for joint action.'

With a virulence which was an attempt to compensate for his long years of forced silence, Reuther put the case against his President, George Meany:[8] the AFL-CIO 'suffers from a sense of complacency and adherence to the status quo and is not fulfilling the basic aims and purposes which prompted the merger of the AFL and the CIO. The AFL-CIO lacks the social vision, the dynamic thrust, the crusading spirit that should characterize the progressive, modern, labor movement which it can and must be if it is to be equal to the new challenges and the new opportunities of our 20th century technological society.'

The AFL-CIO under George Meany's leadership most certainly did not live up to these requirements:[9]

'. . . there is a fundamental difference between undemocratic, heavy-handed leadership and strong democratic leadership which encourages the democratic process and which demonstrates both the will and the ability to respect dissent and to forge labor unity out of the diversity essential to a free labor movement'.

And the attack was directed against Meany in person:[10]

'The chief officer of the AFL-CIO has used a heavy hand in discouraging in-depth discussions of basic policy issues and the objective evaluation of new ideas and new concepts . . . A democratic labor movement cannot be used as if it were the private and personal property of one person.'

Reuther went on to admit that for a long time he had felt compelled to submit to 'captivity': 'We were the prisoners of that exclusive little club known as the Executive Council of the AFL-CIO.' Those officials who had participated in the deliberations of the Federal leadership[11]

'have seen the great promise of the merger go unfulfilled and have become increasingly disturbed by the inaction, the indifference, by policies reflecting narrow negativism and by the lack of dynamic and inspired leadership in the AFL-CIO'.

He also acknowledged how much time had had to elapse before he ventured to challenge Meany:[12]

'Heretofore, we have refrained from a public airing of these disagreements hoping that somehow the merged labor movement would mature from unity in form into a unity in substance. Unfortunately this has not occurred.'

However, Reuther was worried lest his readers should think that his indictment was motivated by considerations of vanity or personal ambition. So he recalled that, when the fusion had taken place in December 1955, he had not solicited any office in the unified labor movement. He had unwisely allowed the Presidency and the post of secretary-treasurer to be given to representatives of the AFL. He had only been concerned – he was only ever concerned – with 'questions of principle'.

An Indictment of the AFL-CIO

The fight over 'principles' which Reuther began against Meany turned firstly on the AFL-CIO's internal regime. He accused the President of the federation of violating Federal statutes:[13]

> 'On occasion even the almost unanimous mandate of the AFL-CIO's Convention itself has been thwarted, if the constitutional provision or the Convention mandate did not meet with the personal pleasure of the President of the AFL-CIO.'

An example: the 1959 federal congress had created a mechanism which at last enabled 'jurisdictional' disputes between the various rival Internationals to be settled. But this decision was blocked by President Meany; and, at the following congress, it required the insistence of those Internationals belonging to the department of industrial unions to stop Meany from violating the mandate with which he had been entrusted by the previous congress. Even then he agreed[14] only 'after long, arduous and at times bitter wrangling'.

One of Reuther's main charges against Meany was the decline in Labor's numerical strength and the fall in the relative percentage of the organized to the unorganized. For the resigning Vice-President, Meany's lack of enthusiasm for recruitment campaigns had a precise cause: the 'narrow and restrictive', 'negative and unhealthy' policy of the AFL-CIO President, who allowed any International to use its veto to block a recruitment campaign by claiming exclusive 'jurisdiction' over a whole unorganized sector for itself alone. That is what happened in 1961, when 26 Internationals reached agreement on a recruitment campaign among the wholesale and retail trade workers, who numbered more than 4 million, and the President of a twenty-seventh opposed it.

The other cause of the movement's lack of success was the stinginess of the International Unions and the federation:[15]

> '. . . only as a comprehensive, co-operative, coordinated organizing crusade is undertaken within the whole labor movement, only as the whole labor movement commits its resources in money and manpower, can the total organizing job be done. The labor movement has the resources.'

In contrast to the general egotism, the department of industrial unions had proved its solidarity by not hesitating, for example, to throw its resources and organizers into various recruitment campaigns to build the teachers', Government employees' and farm workers' unions. But there were still a million teachers and three million Government employees to recruit – a handicap which has since been largely overcome – and Reuther demanded that five million dollars should be set aside for the recruitment of farm workers as well as for the organization of underprivileged workers.

Overall, the President of the auto workers was proposing that, for a six-year period, a quarter of the federation's income should be earmarked for recruitment, and that each affiliated International should contribute a dollar per year per member. The target to be reached was the doubling of the federation's membership, which was to be increased from 13½ million to 27 million – a figure which, as will be seen, never came anywhere near to being attained later on.

Another of Reuther's grievances was the deficiency of the AFL-CIO in the face of the technical revolution of the 20th century,[16] which,

> 'with automation, computerization and its fantastic new tools of science and technology, confronts the labor movement and the nation with new and urgent problems, compelling challenges and exciting opportunities.'

In particular it seemed to him that Labor could only safeguard its future in those industries most severely affected by automation (which were usually those largely won to trade-unionism) if it extended trade-union recruitment to the weaker sectors toward which the labor force was being displaced by technical progress.

According to Reuther, the AFL-CIO was not up to its task, even in the routine of everyday trade-union activity, that is to say in collective bargaining and the defense of the workers' immediate demands. Here again what was lacking was workers' solidarity. Labor was paralysed by the stinginess and the particularism of the craft unions. Reuther therefore called for the establishment of a national strike fund, to which each International was to contribute a dollar per year per member and which was to[17] 'insure that workers faltering under the attack of an employer bent on destruction of their union may rely upon the financial support of the total labor movement to win their battle'. These recalcitrant bosses would thus be made to understand that the struggle was no longer simply between their firm and their workers, but between their firm and the entire labor movement.

In order to inform the different Internationals better about the working conditions won in other sectors of industry, and so to prepare them for collective bargaining, Reuther set up in his department of industrial unions a data-processing center which analyzed every contract and fed all the information it contained through the computer. Within a minute the machine was able to supply more information than a research department could have done in three weeks. And a trade-union official could get information on any subject over the telephone in five minutes. 'This', Reuther concluded, 'is the way a modern Labor movement has to function.'

No less a sign that the AFL-CIO had failed in its task was its proven inability to secure the abolition, or at the very least the revision, of the anti-Labor Taft-Hartley Act. Its incompetence was just as obvious in yet another field, that of social welfare. (It flowed, in part, from the myopic outlook of a trade-unionism set in its corporatist ways and confining itself to the defense of working-class interests through collective bargaining with the bosses, without exerting sufficient pressure on the authorities to wring more substantial social benefits from them: this resulted in an imbalance from which those who suffered were the workers in the least important and the least unionized industries.) According to Reuther's account, the federation even lagged behind the Johnson Administration's projects in this field. And, citing the example of Sweden, Reuther was furious at the inability of the richest country in the world to do what had been done by a small European country for its elderly workers.

Reuther was concerned, as a practical man, to follow industrial development step by step, and he noted that the big corporations were increasingly diversifying their activities. Thus the Armour Packing Company, dealing theoretically in slaughtering and meat packing, had just taken over the engine-building firm of Baldwin. Ford bought out Philco, the electrical appliances firm. Wilson Packing Company, another slaughter-house firm, had just merged with the biggest sports equipment company. Reuther concluded that, since the big corporations were more and more intertwined, no labor organization could face them in isolation. Co-ordination was essential. Just as the craft union had had to give way to the industrial union, so now the industrial union had to give way to a type of trade-unionism capable of dealing with the power of a diversified corporation.

The social program worked out by Walter Reuther in opposition to the narrow routine of the craft unions naturally had reformist aspects to it. Reuther was not a revolutionary but a follower of European social democracy. His vision was warped by the illusion of the 'general interest', which was contradicted by the reality of the class struggle.

He imagined that the labor movement could tackle the problems of society 'as a whole' without abolishing the capitalist system. He showed himself ready to co-operate with citizens' associations to preserve and develop the nation's natural resources. He wanted to take a hand in reconstructing America's cities (which he rightly acknowledged to be 'the ugliest in the world'). He wanted Labor to take an interest in leisure, education, cultural problems, pollution of the sea and the environment, etc. He cherished the chimerical hope that the labor movement, which, according to the opinion polls, came a long way behind other social groups in the public's list of preferences, could make itself more attractive in the eyes of philistines. For example, he argued for a readjustment of the wage structure of public service employees on the grounds that they would no longer be able to resort to 'unpopular' strikes which were 'harmful to the community'.

Through so-called community action, which was nothing more than a sort of social assistance to the underprivileged, Reuther felt sure that he would attract the student youth, the academics and the liberal intellectuals to Labor.

What divided Reuther from Meany on this point was nothing but the classical conflict between on the one hand, old-fashioned trade-unionism, which deliberately restricted itself to strictly economic concerns, not only because it was aging and hidebound, but also because it was aware of the limits imposed on it by its capitalist partner, and, on the other hand, so-called 'constructive' trade-unionism, which wanted to extend its activity to the point of seeking to make all men happy. Reuther was without doubt right in attacking Meany for giving bad leadership to the day-to-day struggle, but he was on much weaker ground in flattering himself, in a super-capitalist country like the United States, that he was serving the 'general interest'.

A New and Short-Lived Federation

After setting out his complaints about the running of the trade-union federation and outlining his own program, Walter Reuther came right out and stated, by way of conclusion, that he would have to regain his freedom:[18] 'Under these circumstances, continuation of membership in these bodies [the AFL-CIO Executive Council, General Board and Standing Committees, Ed.] is merely an exercise in futility and we cannot, in good conscience, continue to serve.' And the UAW spokesman announced that he no longer intended to conduct the fight within the narrow, private and exclusive confines of the AFL-CIO, but would take it into the broader arena of the labor movement as a whole.

What about the accusation that, by doing this, he was 'dividing the labor movement'? He had a ready reply: 'What is called labor unity is not a museum piece. Labor unity must have a meaning. We are not seeking to destroy it. We are seeking to give it content.'

Were Reuther and the UAW going to find themselves alone in this new opposition? He thought that he could count on many devoted and sincere trade-unionists in the labor movement who shared his discontent and his concern but who still hesitated to express themselves publicly. He considered them worthy of respect:[19]

> 'We have chosen not to involve them in our present effort because, to have done so would have opened us to the charge that we were building a power caucus within the AFL-CIO and that this is not a principled fight but a political power drive.'

As a matter of fact, Walter Reuther and the millions of trade-unionists who followed him equivocated for a long time before breaking with the trade-union federation. The revolts of the Blacks, particularly the one in Detroit, the capital of the auto industry, justified Reuther's accusation that the AFL-CIO had become the guardian of the established order. They accentuated, at the very least, the dividing line between an anti-racist trade-unionism whose prototype was the leadership, if not always the rank and file, of the UAW, and the racism of George Meany's Federal clique. The revolts also had a contagious radicalizing effect on the vanguard of the labor movement, while strengthening the racial prejudices of the most backward sections. However, Reuther did not make a move during the Detroit uprising, and he waited for it to be crushed before proposing that the streets should be cleared of the rubbish which littered them. On the other hand, on 7 September, he called out the 160,000 Ford workers, spread over twenty-five states, on an unlimited strike; and doubtless the thought that George Meany's prestige would bear the cost of a victory in the auto industry crossed his mind. Significantly, the auto International declined to attend the AFL-CIO congress in December 1967.

The man was too intelligent not to think twice before initiating a split in which he would not be certain to carry with him at least the five million trade-unionists he had brought to the reunified federation in 1955. It was in fact unlikely that the leaders of the ex-CIO Internationals, who had become complacent old men, would feel like plunging into a quixotic adventure: no important International had shown any intention of so doing. Furthermore, President Johnson had given a cold reception to Reuther's vituperations against the AFL-CIO leadership and had not hidden his preferences for the conservative administration of George Meany. The UAW leader, riveted to the White House by very old chains, was obliged to humor the Democratic Administration.

Reuther nevertheless did burn his bridges in the end. He had already boycotted the AFL-CIO congress in December 1967; but it was not until 26 May 1969 that the split became final. On that date the two most important industrial Internationals, the United Automobile Workers and the teamsters' Brotherhood, met to found a new trade-union federation – the Alliance for Labor Action (ALA).

Frank Fitzsimmons, who had been in charge of the teamsters since Jimmy Hoffa's imprisonment, had for a long time been looking for an alternative federation to replace the AFL-CIO, from which his Brotherhood had been expelled. As for Reuther, he had finally made up his mind to get out of a conservative federation which he had given up any hope of ever fitting in with. At its foundation the new federation had about three and a half million members, consisting of two million teamsters and one and a half million auto workers. It kidded itself that it would attract Internationals which were not affiliated to the AFL-CIO, like the West Coast longshoremen, the electricians, the miners, etc. But none of these organizations allowed itself to be tempted by the adventure. Only the chemical workers' International joined the ALA with its 104,000 members, but the marriage lasted no more than three years: as early as May 1971 the chemical workers were back in the AFL-CIO.

The fiery Reuther drew the cynical, down-to-earth Fitzsimmons along with him in his fantastic projects only for a short while. He had already been dreaming about these projects while he was in the process of indicting George Meany from within the AFL-CIO and calling him a 'guardian of the status quo'. According to Reuther, the ALA was going to declare 'total' war on poverty and hunger , throttle inflation, raise workers' living standards, improve their working conditions, attack pollution, accomplish ecological miracles, and promote housing programs in underprivileged areas and urban ghettos, while lavishing medical care and better education on their occupants, all the time ensuring community control. Better still, the ALA was going to organize the unorganized by the armful. A recruitment campaign aimed at Southern workers was launched amid great publicity in Atlanta, Georgia. The new federation spent more than a million dollars on it, but the results were rather unspectacular. In fact these fine schemes were largely hot air.

The ALA did not survive for long. Within a short time a split took place between its two founders. The official reason given was that the auto International did not abide by its pledge to contribute $65,000 a month to the federation, whereupon the teamsters stopped their monthly payments of $100,000. But the real cause of the quarrel was quite different: a relatively progressive International like the UAW could not cohabit any longer with an organization of evil repute whose leadership was hopelessly corrupt and which, moreover, was discredited by its practice of raiding other trade-union organizations. We have already pointed out (cf.p.213) that the auto International had made itself the protector of the valiant little farm workers' International composed of California Chicanos. The teamsters indulged in odious assaults on the latter, to which we shall return later, and so created a gulf between their organization and that of the auto workers. The ALA wound up its affairs in January 1972.

Meanwhile, a tragedy had played a part in splitting the federation: on the night of 9-10 May 1970 Walter Reuther's private plane vanished in the fog and all its passengers died. Fate thus rid George Meany of an annoying rival. The UAW President's successor, Leonard Woodcock, was far from having inherited the deceased's strong personality and, with other factors intervening, his International had a tendency to sink further into class collaboration and integration into the system. In the nature of things, regular contact was established between George Meany and Leonard Woodcock, blurring, though not actually wiping out, the memory of the earlier schism. The auto International has for a long time been engaged in talks concerning an eventual return to the AFL-CIO. But it has not yet resigned itself to 'eating humble pie'; according to the latest information, there is no question of this, at least as long as George Meany hangs on to his post.

The other Internationals which had broken away from the old federation, or had not joined it, considered from time to time abandoning their isolation. Thus the West Coast longshoremen wavered more than once between a return to Meany's federation and a fusion with Fitzsimmons' teamsters. But these unitary impulses have not brought any results so far. As for the teamsters, Jimmy Hoffa's 'departure' looked like facilitating a reconciliation between them and Meany, but the latter, while treating them as considerately as possible, did not dare to take them back, in view of their persistently outrageous behaviour.

Nevertheless, in the absence of total unification at the highest level, the tendency towards fusion showed itself in some Internationals. They had become convinced that dispersion and division were obstacles to effectiveness, keeping 'jurisdictional' disputes alive and allowing the employers to play off one trade union against another. So in 1972 three Internationals covering the paper industry merged into one, while the brewery workers joined the teamsters, and the telephone workers negotiated their fusion with the postal workers. Besides, this tightening up of trade-union structures was paralleled, on the employers' side, by reorganization and a more intensive concentration of industry.

CHAPTER 9

Is Labor integrated?

Between Inflation, Unemployment and War

Recent years (1970-1975) have been marked by a number of factors which have placed the trade-union movement in difficult situations and which, as a result, have played a part in increasing its integration into the system. But to regard this integration as total would be to generalize to excess. The same factors which, for some organizations and in some cases, have operated in favor of integration have sometimes generated violent social conflicts in other parts of the labor movement, although the returns have often been limited.

What have been the factors involved? Inflation, the recession and unemployment, and the Vietnam war. Ex-President Nixon's barbaric pursuit of the Indochinese genocide had economic, financial and socio-political effects. True, it brought prosperity to the death-dealing industries and stimulated the expansion of production, but on the other hand it increased the budget and trade balance deficits, thereby accelerating the inflationary process. At the political and social level, it divided labor unionism, causing many a clash between the supporters and opponents of an imperialist venture doomed to eventual inglorious defeat.

Inflation. – In this area the AFL-CIO leaders acted as their own whipping-boy. In the name of the 'general interest', they had continually harassed the White House, proclaiming that its anti-inflation program was 'a complete and absolute failure'. On 11 July 1971, speaking on the radio, George Meany had urged Nixon to introduce price and wage controls, saying that that was what he would do if he were in the President's position; he did not really see any other means of curbing inflation. He said he was ready to accept any controls, provided of course that the plan was 'just' and 'equitable', and involved equal sacrifice for everybody. It is always dangerous for a Labor representative to put himself in the Executive's position and offer it advice. President Meany ought to have known that in a 'free enterprise' system it is always the poor who get the rawest deal.

The then current tenant of the White House, Nixon, hastened to pick up the ball thrown to his side of the court; he was careful to consult Meany in several discreet meetings and get him to underwrite his plans. The result was that, on 15 August 1971, Nixon put a 'New Economic Policy' into effect, in four stages. He swore to high heaven that wages and prices would be controlled with equal fairness. And, to inaugurate the first 'phase', he put a freeze on wages and prices for an initial period of ninety days. Meany made a song and dance about it, just for the record. The Presidential measures were too favorable to the bosses, on whose profits no freeze was imposed. The economic program was 'a form of socialism for the big firms'. And to the Press the immovable Labor leader threatened nothing less than a 'revolt'. But these growls, like the grudging welcome reserved for Nixon at the AFL-CIO congress in Miami, were just for show. Meany in no way tried to torpedo the new 'NEP'. He declared his readiness to co-operate with the Government on the stabilization plan. On 12 October the AFL-CIO agreed to an allocation of three union places on a Pay Board set up to control wages. The other trade union members on the Board came from the auto International and the Teamsters.

But Meany's about-face, not very much appreciated by the rank and file, was accompanied all the same by a few restrictions: the unions would sit on the Pay Board only as 'extras, without taking part in the voting'. And, so as not to merge with the Administration, they decided to create their own price monitoring committee. There was, in fact, every reason to be skeptical: the Pay Board was made up of fifteen members, and the five Labor delegates faced a majority of ten members, five of whom represented the employers and five the so-called 'general interest', in actual fact the Government.

From the moment the trade-unionists joined the Pay Board, Leonard Woodcock of the UAW showed particular reserve. Under the terms of the contract previously signed with the manufacturers, a wage hike and a bonus calculated on the cost of living index were shortly to be given to 750,000 of his members, and the wage controls now threatened to jeopardize this. On 22 March 1972 the three Federal delegates, followed the next day by Woodcock, withdrew from the Pay Board. They had already had enough. The departing members accused the Board of being dominated by the Administration and the bosses – something they might have noticed earlier. They found out that the mass of wage-earners was bearing the cost of the struggle against inflation. They admitted that they had been taken for a ride. Only Fitzsimmons of the teamsters remained on the Board, so confirming that he was even more integrated than the others into the system and more tied than they were, if that was possible, to 'Tricky Dick'.

During a further 'phase' of the Presidential NEP, it was dictatorially prescribed that wages could not rise by more than 5.5 per cent annually. Once again George Meany rushed to endorse this new form of wage freeze, while snivelling that the percentage was too low, by no means compensating for the rise in prices. But Labor's rank and file let their position be known when, still in May 1973, on the initiative of Harry Bridges of the West Coast longshoremen a big united demonstration was organized in San Francisco in order to protest inflation and the one-sided control of wages. Among others, the rubber workers felt the consequences of the freeze severely: the tire producers' new contract contained a rise of only 5.3 per cent. The same was true for the auto workers, whose sliding-scale clause was limited to just under 7 per cent for three years. The teamsters were tied down to a similar contract. On the other hand, prices in 1973 had risen by something like 8 per cent, and this percentage increased in 1974.

The steelworkers' leadership, for its part, did not beat about the bush. On the initiative of I W Abel, former activist and now a dyed-in-the-wood bureaucrat, a 'no-strike' pledge until the end of 1980 was signed with the magnates of heavy industry on 29 March 1973. Work stoppages were to be replaced by compulsory arbitration with decisions being given by an arbitration board of five, who were supposedly impartial and whose decisions were final. This procedure, which was binding on half a million workers, was elegantly dubbed the Experimental Negotiating Agreement (ENA). And, on 26 April 1974, a contract signed with US Steel was limited to a derisory annual wage increase of 3.3 per cent. There was great discontent among the rank and file, and an organized opposition – a caucus – came into being. But it was not yet capable of ousting the existing leadership, as President Abel had done not so very long before.

Elsewhere, the wage freeze had aroused the anger of the

longshoremen in 1971: first that of the 15,000 on the West Coast, then that of the 45,000 on the East Coast and in the Gulf of Mexico. Harry Bridges' men had walked out on 1 July. They were joined three months later by their colleagues in the East and the South. Nixon threatened to resort to the Taft-Hartley Act to force the strikers to suspend their action for a period of eighty days. However, he hesitated to make use of this procedure, since it would have obliged the unfortunate employers to continue to honor the old contract and to pay the guaranteed wage. After 134 days on strike, which caused international trade to decline by a billion and a half dollars, the West Coast longshoremen finally obtained a wage raise of over 20 per cent in March 1972. But the Pay Board whittled the increase down to 15 per cent, while reducing the wage hikes won by the East Coast longshoremen from 12 to 9.8 per cent.

In conclusion, the inflation provoked by the Vietnam war, combined with Nixon's NEP, hit the workers. Their purchasing power was 7.4 per cent lower in 1973 than it had been in 1972 and 5.2 per cent lower in 1974 than in 1973. The trade-union bureaucracies, integrated into the system as they were and led astray by the myth of the 'national interest', proved incapable of sparing the working masses these dismal cuts in their standard of living. While technological progress was increasing the profitability of production, the workers' share in the national wealth created by them was diminishing.

Unemployment. – By August 1971, more than 5 million Americans were out of work. The memory of the Great Depression haunted people. A month earlier, George Meany had strongly criticized, but to no avail, Nixon's refusal to ratify a program of public works which would have reduced the number of unemployed, even though it had been passed by Congress. The war had priority in the distribution of the budgetary manna.

The Indochinese War. – On 1 May 1970, George Meany had publicly declared that the aberrant military intervention in Cambodia had the full support of the American people as well as of his federation. A week later, on 8 May, a group of workers confirmed this in their own way: they attacked and injured a dozen students who were protesting the escalation of the war in Cambodia by demonstrating in Wall Street. Then they broke into a college and New York City Hall. These 'hardhats', from what they said, could not stomach those long-haired hippies who spit on the Stars and Stripes and burnt their draft cards in public. A little later, on 20 May, growing bolder, about 50,000 construction workers marched through the streets yelling patriotic slogans, waving flags, and cheering Nixon and the Vietnam war. In fact the nucleus of this parade was made up of a small detachment of workers employed on construction projects in that part of Manhattan and a handful of professional hoodlums from the port of New York. But they had received their orders from Peter Brennan, the leader of the New York construction unions and a personal friend of Nixon's. A delegation of these same people, led by the same Brennan, went to Washington on 26 May to offer the warmongering US Head of State a hard hat, the traditional emblem of their trade, bearing the inscription: 'Commander in Chief'. Brennan was subsequently rewarded for this deed of valor when, on 22 December 1972, Nixon appointed him Labor Secretary, not without having first of all talked it over with Meany and Fitzsimmons.

The chauvinistic outbursts of May 1970 were not at all to the liking of the leaders of the auto International, who, as is known, were hostile to the Vietnam war. So, shortly after the incidents, a representative of the UAW attended an anti-war demonstration which brought together a huge crowd of young people a stone's throw from the White House. He apologized on behalf of American Labor.

The Integration of the Labor Leadership

The umbilical cord which tied the central trade-union leadership to the United States President revealed itself in various ways. For instance, the 31 December *New York Times* headed an article thus: 'Key posts offered to Labor by Nixon'. The article reported that, according to a well-informed White House official, the President had offered to appoint a representative of the trade unions to a high post in each department of the Federal Government. The proposal had been made to those trade-union leaders who belonged to the National Productivity Commission. Labor's representatives had shown themselves ready to accept the role of trade-union emissaries as Assistant Secretaries in the most important

Government agencies. The journalist described this initiative as 'without precedent in the history of the labor movement' and as 'an exemplary and decisive turn in the traditional relationships between the working class and the Government'. But his memory was short, for under Roosevelt the union leaders had been brought into various war offices and one of them, Sidney Hillman, 'the trade-union statesman', had become a trusted adviser to the United States President (cf. pp.93-94). Later on, the Marshall Plan administration had recruited its salesmen from the ranks of Labor (cf.pp.177-78).

Integration could work in both directions. Meany considered paying Nixon in his own coin. He offered the management of an important new department of the AFL-CIO to a close associate of the President, W J Usery, Jr. However, the latter preferred to remain in Richard Nixon's dubious but more lucrative entourage. If he had accepted, this leading Government official would probably have become the no.3 man in the federation hierarchy and would therefore have eventually been in line to succeed Meany. It would have been a significant example of integration between the two bureaucracies, that of the Administration and that of the trade unions. (We should also keep in mind the very long-standing involvement of Jay Lovestone, the head of the federation's Department of International Affairs, with the CIA [cf.p.186].)

At a conference in New York on 19 May 1972, Meany declared that Labor and Business had a common interest in promoting 'national well-being'. In his eyes the strike weapon was outmoded. Besides, he had never really gone along with it. On 22 June 1973, a revolutionary newspaper, *The Militant,* pointed out that 'the union bureaucrats are anxious not to do anything . . . that might be interpreted as contributing to inflation. They are more worried about the value of the dollar, high interest rates and all the other workings of the capitalist system than they are about the living standard of the workers.' On 27 July the same newspaper spoke of the 'immense pressure of the Government and the union bureaucrats to contain wage increases within the fixed limits'.

The 5 November 1974 issue of *Le Monde* emphasized that in the American trade-union movement, 'proposals for a socialist economy are rare and almost always emanate from minority currents stifled by the vast administrative machine of the labor organizations'. A few days later, on 24 November, a correspondent of the same newspaper who had attended the auto International's convention in Los Angeles wrote that it had struck him as 'the expression of a complete integration into the economic system'. This harsh judgment, it will be recalled, concerned one of the least reactionary organizations in the labor movement.

Integration can also be seen in the trade-union leaders' personal wealth. Thus the 15 May 1973 *Wall Street Journal* revealed that George Meany and Lane Kirkland, the President and Secretary-Treasurer of the AFL-CIO respectively, were among the main shareholders in a prosperous health resort in the Dominican Republic. Further examples of union bureaucrats becoming capitalists will be given later on.

The Teamsters

The reader is already acquainted with the intensely corrupt past of the teamsters' Brotherhood (cf.pp.189-190). This sprawling organization did not only contain truck drivers. In 1961 it had undertaken a large-scale unionization campaign, as if it was itself a federation. Among others, it had signed up airline employees, notably air hostesses, chain store employees, telephone operators, bakers and even policemen. The means used for this recruiting drive were often brutal. Thus, in order to annex the New York telephone workers' union, the teamsters' gangsters had resorted to dynamiting, acts of sabotage, and physical threats or pressure. In 1969 the teamsters had appealed to the Mafia hoodlums to help them gain recognition by the National Labor Relations Board as the official union negotiating with the airline companies.

The President of the Brotherhood, Jimmy Hoffa, as we have already mentioned, had been serving a jail sentence since 1967 for various financial intrigues. Leadership of the organization had been assumed by the Vice-President, Frank Fitzsimmons. In June 1971 Hoffa gave notice from jail that he would not be seeking re-election and he urged the teamsters' congress, which began in Miami on 5 July, to elect Fitzsimmons, his stooge, as his successor. The new President had himself awarded \$125,000 a year, \$25,000 more than his predecessor, beating all records for trade-union salaries. This amount was further increased later to \$150,000 plus unlimited 'expenses'. Hoffa's gesture was not altogether disinterested:

by retiring he was to receive a lump-sum pension of a million dollars. His wife, who was in charge of the women's section, was to continue to collect $45,000 a year and their son, the Brotherhood's lawyer, $30,000 a year.

On Christmas Eve 1971 Nixon ordered the release on parole of this victim of the 'blind crusade' which the Kennedy brothers had begun against corruption (cf.p.187). Behind the scenes Hoffa, who, paradoxically, had retained his popularity among the rank and file, continued to pull the strings. His committed supporters organized a cocktail party in Washington in May 1973, followed by a banquet in his honor. On that occasion he could not conceal his intention of stepping once more into the Presidential shoes. But the crook had a tragic end awaiting him: he disappeared on 30 July 1975. As the 12 September *Le Monde* conjectured, he was 'probably removed by his former associates, who were not eager to reinstall him in his lucrative and privileged position'. Later the FBI made a statement that Hoffa had been killed by gangsters. The big question was: would the thread of the judicial enquiry lead to Frank Fitzsimmons?

Now the undisputed master of the field, Fitzsimmons continued with renewed vigor the malpractices and speculation which had cost Hoffa his freedom. With the assiduous help of the Mafia, he set about pillaging the teamsters' pension fund, a colossal hoard, through all sorts of underhand dealings which were exposed by the *Los Angeles Times* of 29 July 1973: huge real estate deals amounting to over 40 million dollars and the acquisition of numerous businesses in Southern California had been financed by 'loans' drawn from the pension fund. In the same way millions of dollars had been lent to the Mafia for the building of casinos in Las Vegas and the opening of private clubs for a gangster clientele. Moreover, money embezzled from the pension fund played a role in the Watergate Affair. Fitzsimmons, assured of immunity, took out $175,000 on behalf of a certain Murray Chotiner, who was one of Nixon's buddies. Following a series of investigations regarding irregularities in the administration of the pension fund, the experts discovered considerable discrepancies in the accounts.

The Teamsters and the Farm Workers

We referred earlier on (cf.p.213) to the militant activity carried out in California by the United Farm Workers, a trade union composed of Chicano farm laborers and led by the strong personality of César Chavez. The UFW was confronted by big capitalist agricultural interests – *Agribusiness*, as it had been nicknamed – entrenched in the American Farm Bureau Federation, the stronghold of the farming bosses. The struggle was certainly unequal, but the workers had benefited from the active support of the most progressive sections of the labor movement, and especially of the auto International. But, from 1970 onwards, the teamsters started to lay claim to the California farm workers. In fact, as a result of the dues check-off system, the venture looked as if it would turn out to be extremely profitable. As trade-union dues were deducted by the farm owners from their employees' wages and then transferred to the union, the Brotherhood would in this way pocket eight dollars a month for every farm worker it recruited.

In order to establish themselves in what was a new field for them, the teamsters offered their services to the big California farmers. Since the Brotherhood controlled the entire transport system and all the trucks, the employers, for their part, saw only advantages in favoring these benevolent allies. They subsidized their recruitment campaigns, signed fake contracts with their recruits and, above all, used them to break the strikes of Chavez's Chicanos. On 29 December 1972, Fitzsimmons spoke at a convention of the Farm Bureau and proposed an alliance against the 'revolutionaries' of the United Farm Workers. Assured of a go-ahead from the employers, he did not hesitate to use violence to achieve his goals. He had the headquarters of Chavez's union blown up five times from the date of its opening in December 1972. In June 1973 the union's office in Denver, Colorado, was likewise ransacked. On the night of 27 June shots were fired at the home of one of the union leaders where Chavez just happened to be staying. Fitzsimmons hired bullies, who were paid fifty dollars a day plus seventeen and a half dollars' expenses to intimidate and attack the farm workers' pickets with chains, knives, belts, pipes and other improvised weapons. Chavez's members were threatened by their employers with the loss of their jobs if they did not join the scab union set up by the teamsters. It was David against Goliath: the members of the militant organization, numbering some 70,000, had to put up with attacks by a Brotherhood two million strong and as rich as the Rockefellers.

The AFL-CIO could not stand idly by. It eventually decided in favor of massive intervention. It gave the farm workers 1.6 million dollars for their strike fund. The strikers were thus able to collect seventy-five, then ninety dollars' relief money a week. This gesture of solidarity could surprise only those who fail to see the contradictions and ambivalence of American Labor. For the action taken by Chavez's farm workers against the multi-millionaire California farmers took on all the characteristics of a class struggle. Yet the trade-union bureaucracy, with George Meany at its head, could not avoid rushing to the assistance of the weaker party. But it had been pushed into it by the auto workers, the steelworkers, the coal-miners, the telephone workers and others besides. The California strikes had furthermore aroused the sympathy of fairly broad sectors of public opinion. And besides, it was in Meany's interest to restrain Fitzsimmons' expansionist greed.

However, the hand extended to the farm workers was soon withdrawn. In June 1973 the AFL-CIO bigwigs had declared themselves ready to renew their financial assistance. But, a few months later, they renounced their promise and refused to give any more backing to Chavez's union. In reality Meany had all the time been running with the hare and hunting with the hounds. He had not lost contact with Fitzsimmons, in the hope of fixing a secret deal with him. This bargaining went through its ups and downs. Sometimes the teamsters agreed to withdraw their strike-breakers from the California vineyards and lettuce fields; sometimes they violated the confidential pledges they had made to Meany. And the Tsar of Labor could only denounce them for going back on their word, swearing to take 'appropriate' action against them. In the end the Federal mountain brought forth a mouse.

There were at least two reasons for Meany's duplicity: firstly, he was anxious to deal tactfully with one of the most powerful unions, with which, in spite of its expulsion from the federation, he shared common bureaucratic interests and the same desire for integration into the system, and he did not despair of bringing it back in to the fold; secondly, Chavez's union had caused quite a stir by adopting an audacious and relatively effective form of action against the big California landowners – a boycott. By doing so, he was sailing close to the wind, legally speaking, to Meany's great displeasure. The boycott in question had become a national affair. Throughout the United States, and particularly in the important cities such as Cleveland, Chicago, Boston, etc., consumers were persuaded not to buy the grapes and lettuce of farmers who were breaking the Chicanos' strikes. The boycott was planned American-style, that is to say with vast resources. Chavez dispatched 500 organizers to some sixty cities to get the operation into shape; they were joined by 40 employees of the AFL-CIO, which initially supported the boycott. Arnold Miller, the new President of the miners' International, went to La Paz, California, to announce his organization's support for the boycott. Boycott committees and picket lines were set up. They made sure that restaurants, school cafetarias, grocery stores and supermarkets did not handle foodstuffs produced by the scabs.

The firm which dealt with Chavez (and there were not many of them) marketed their produce in crates bearing the union label – a black Aztec eagle – and so escaped the boycott. On the other hand the two main companies which were channelling the California grapes picked by the strikebreakers to the consumer, Safeway and A & P, were subjected to a boycott as rigorous as it was vigilant. As a result, the producers suffered heavy losses, due both to consumer/union solidarity and to the poor quality or deterioration of the produce. But it was not long before the police intervened and proceeded to arrest boycott pickets, especially in Chicago. The myth of 'free enterprise' took a knock and Meany, concerned to placate the legalist prejudices of the middle class, backed down. The AFL-CIO national congress, which was held in Florida, at Bal Harbor, in October 1973, simply refrained from supporting the farm workers' boycott. Business-as-usual trade-unionism had quickly regained the upper hand over class struggle.

With the Miners: From Boyle to Miller

We saw earlier (cf.p.212) how a rebel tendency had arisen in opposition to the autocratic running of the United Mine Workers by Tony Boyle, John Lewis's successor. Tony, whom his mentor honored in 1960 by naming him as his successor, had learnt from the old man how to run the International with an iron hand. After showing perfect servility for long, patient years under the previous regime, he got his revenge by dominating in his turn. The only thing which he had not inherited from Big John was his genius. He made up for it by a total lack of scruple which was finally to lead him to crime.

The union leadership cheerfully trampled internal democracy underfoot. Boyle himself appointed most of the organization's district and local officials. This omnipotence was achieved through various forms of manipulation; at conventions those delegates whose 'loyalty' could be relied upon had their travelling expenses paid while representatives of other sections of the union could not attend for lack of money. But it was above all by manipulating the retired miners that for over ten years Boyle ensured his periodic re-election. In fact a good third of the International's members were in this category. If they did not bow to the wishes of their President, they ran the risk of no longer receiving their pension checks. Six hundred out of 1,200 locals were empty shells, since they were composed almost solely of retired miners. In addition, nineteen of the International's twenty-three districts had been placed under receivership, which meant not only that Boyle could legally appoint their officials himself but also that the rank-and-file members had no say in the way their district was administered and the union's money – which came from their dues – spent. This arbitrary procedure was based on a tendentious interpretation of the 1959 Landrum-Griffin Act (cf.p.195), which provided for receivership of locals only in extreme cases of maladministration and financial irregularity. So the Labor Secretary accused Boyle of breaking the law.

In 1969 the rank and file opposition, led by Joseph Yablonski, had called for the democratic election, without pressure from the leadership, of all union officials. It charged Boyle's dictatorial 'machine' with giving the vote to between two and three times as many union members as there actually were. It also accused him of setting up a pension fund on which he was the only one to be registered. Boyle saw to it that the opposition was defeated at the congress in late 1969. On New Year's Eve of the same year, the bodies of Yablonski, his wife and his daughter were found riddled with bullets at their home in Clarksville, Pennsylvania. It was not until 1973 that, following certain confessions, a Grand Jury decided to charge Boyle with having inspired this triple murder; one of his closest friends had hired the assassins. But, meanwhile, Boyle had already been sentenced, on 27 June 1972, to five years in jail for embezzling the International's funds. Nevertheless, he had only been locked up for six hours when he got out on bail.

The mine-owners regretted Tony Boyle's elimination. He had strangled, or tried to break, numerous wildcat strikes, from Illinois to western Ohio. To try and insure that Boyle hung onto his job, the bosses had given him a helping hand. When, shortly after 1 October 1971, 80,000 miners had gone on strike, their contract having expired without a new one being signed, the employers agreed to practically all the union's demands and the Pay Board, departing from its habitual rigor, ratified a wage increase of 15 per cent for the miners.

But when Boyle was charged with murder he had already lost the leadership of the miners. At their December 1972 congress they had ousted him and replaced him by the leader of the rank and file opposition, 'honest' Arnold Miller, who had taken over from the unfortunate Yablonski. This fact, which is comparatively rare in the annals of American trade-unionism, should be underlined. It shows that all is not as rotten as one might think in this State of Denmark that is Labor. To be sure, rank and file oppositions had already, albeit with difficulty, defeated previous union leaderships in the past (p.212). But, to take the example of the steelworkers' union, the new leadership around I W Abel had shown itself before very long to be just as arbitrary as its predecessor. The new President of the miners' International, on the other hand, seemed to keep his promise to restore internal democracy, reduce the number of union bureaucrats and lower officials' salaries.

The UMW convention which was held in Pittsburgh, not far from the coal fields, from 3 to 14 December 1973, demonstrated the American workers' capacity, when the need arises, to break with their misleaders. The new structure which the International adopted introduced an advanced form of trade-union democracy. Decisions were no longer made by the leaders alone; they were submitted to the rank-and-file members, who were in the future to get all the explanations they wanted in their locals. The convention met under a banner bearing the inscription 'For a rank and file union'. Arnold

Miller announced that contracts would henceforth be written in the language of the miners, who would no longer need to call in 'a Philadelphia lawyer' to understand what they said. He undertook to redraft the union's statutes so as to guarantee members' rights. This time most of the delegates were no longer retired, but young people between twenty and thirty who had never participated in trade-union affairs. They could express themselves freely, put forward conflicting views, turn down proposals made by the Executive and reject reports which did not have their assent. In this spirit, before the discussion was closed, the delegates voted against a new procedure for relations between workers and employers, even though it had been the result of negotiations, since it threatened, in their eyes, to restrict the initiatives of the rank and file and curb wildcat strikes. The convention broke up on an enthusiastic note, and it was decided that the International's head office would be moved away from the politicians and transferred from Washington to the coal fields. César Chavez, who had been invited as a guest of honor, told the delegates: 'You are celebrating your rebirth'.

As he had promised, Miller instituted a radical clean-up. Twenty of the twenty-four members of the Executive Bureau were dismissed. The same thing happened to Boyle's daughter, who was earning $40,000 a year as an 'assistant', and his brother, who was getting paid $27,000. The son of the late Joseph Yablonski was appointed the union's new lawyer. Tony Boyle had retired with a pension of $50,000 a year, which was reduced to $30,000. The union's fleet of luxury Cadillacs was sold. Thus purged and rejuvenated, stimulated by this new wave of militancy at the grass roots, the International declared a strike of 120,000 miners in November 1974. After losing its throne, coal had once again become king as a result of the energy crisis and the increase in oil prices. This reversal of the situation put the miners in a militant mood. The extension of the strike led to the laying off of 17,000 steelworkers and railroad workers. In the end the mining bosses had to give in.

The East Coast Seamen after Curran

We saw earlier (p.171) how Joseph Curran ran the National Maritime Union (the union which in the days of the CIO organized the East Coast seamen) for three decades first in collaboration with the Communists, then against them. This International had lost its former dynamism and like so many others had long since become bureaucratized. Curran, too, had become a capitalist. He had bought a farm in New York State where he made a profit breeding choice cattle. He owned an estate in sunny Florida. He travelled in a Cadillac and pocketed an annual salary of some $85,000 plus expenses. When the time came for his 'golden handshake', on 1 March 1973, he had to choose between a life pension of around $50,000 a year and a lump sum of a million dollars. His successor, Shannon Jerome Wall, elected for four years, was voted an annual salary of $49,000 plus expenses. Younger than Curran, and less well-paid, Wall was totally free of the militant tradition of the NMU-CIO. He publicly stated his intention of co-operating with the shipowners, since, as he himself put it so well: 'We cannot afford to kill the goose that lays the golden egg.'

The UAW from Reuther to Woodcock

The auto International, which had for a long time been the spearhead of the American labor movement, did not resist the degeneration and bureaucratization of Labor much better. Leonard Woodcock, Reuther's successor, had made a career for himself by specializing in relations with the gigantic General Motors. He had gained a reputation as a cunning negotiator. He was far from possessing the relative broadness of outlook or, more exactly, the liberal political pretensions of his defunct predecessor. In the evening of his life Reuther had held the Vietnam war up to public obloquy and had taken steps towards the radical students, whom Meany's clique detested. Woodcock, at the beginning of his reign, thought he had to strike up the same tune, but he did so with less conviction. At the UAW convention in April 1970 a resolution was carried accusing the loathsome Spiro Agnew, the United States Vice President, and John Mitchell, who had not yet had to resign as Attorney General, of launching a repressive campaign against pacifist draft resisters. As one delegate to the convention declared, Nixon's acolytes had sought 'to make protest unpopular' and had called the young people who were opposed to the Vietnam war 'impudent snobs'. In July, Woodcock, meeting his old General Motors opponents, attributed the responsibility for runaway inflation to the war rather than to the pressure of wages, not without reason.

At the end of the year the auto International staged a sixty-seven day strike against General Motors. The bone of contention was the thorny problem of the escalator clause which, as noted earlier (p.20), the UAW had secured in 1948 and which was one of the most effective ever won by American trade unions. But in 1967 General Motors had imposed a partial restriction altering the mechanism of wage increases resulting from rises in the cost of living. The 1970 strike was successful and the sliding scale was fully re-established. In the future, re-adjustments were to be quarterly in order to avoid excessive delays in relation to the upward rate of inflation. The calculations were based on the official cost of living index. For every price rise of 0.35 of a point on the index, a cent was added to the workers' hourly earnings.

The next UAW convention was held in Atlantic City from 23 to 28 April 1972 and was marked by a complete change in the composition and a drop in age of the approximately 3,000 delegates. Sixty per cent of them had not taken part in the 1970 convention. Woodcock affirmed that he had never fostered illusions in the Pay Board which, to the great relief of his members, he had recently pulled out of. However, there was a pause in the militant action of the International. The overall economic situation and that of the auto industry in particular had deteriorated. The competition from cars imported from Europe, which were more compact and consumed less fuel, was placing it in a difficult position. Unemployment was getting worse and the International no longer enjoyed the same freedom of action it had had in the good old days of the auto boom.

At the following convention held in Los Angeles early in November 1973, in the presence of nearly 4,000 delegates (a figure considerably higher than the one for the previous convention), the ambivalent character of the International was demonstrated in a particularly obvious way: on the one hand, in the field of politics, the organization remained relatively progressive. It was the first to call for the removal of Nixon, who was bogged down in the Watergate Affair. Thus the delegates gave a warm welcome to the two brave journalists from the *Washington Post* who had brought the scandal out into the open. But as far as the International's internal life was concerned, the convention developed quite differently. The outgoing Executive proposed that the frequency of national conventions should be extended from two to three years. The delegates, whom this symptom of growing bureaucratization did not escape (for it implied a corresponding lengthening in the unelected term of office of union leaders), were shown by several votes to be very closely divided. In the end the chairman of the session, turning this wavering to account, declared the resolution carried. Few delegates dared to protest such an undemocratic procedure. Open oppositionists could be counted on the fingers of one hand. The opposition group, the United National Caucus, had succeeded in grouping only about forty delegates. The leadership of the International was becoming more and more authoritarian with the years.

Yet at rank and file level a change was taking shape which was not yet perceptible in the deliberations of the national convention. We noted earlier (cf.p.211) that by 1967 40 per cent of the union's members were under thirty years of age. In the plants newly built by General Motors the average age in February 1972 was twenty-four. Among these young workers the militant tradition of the thirties and forties was being reborn. They made clear their wish to democratize their organization to the highest degree and to develop struggles, if need be against their national leadership, by resorting to wildcat strikes.

A first strike of this type broke out at the General Motors factory in Norwood, Ohio. It lasted 174 days, from April to the end of September 1971, and ended in defeat. Leonard Woodcock took advantage of this to argue that in future they must not 'let any local be almost mortally wounded, as General Motors tried to do in Norwood'. And he concluded that it was preferable to organize short, harrying strikes launched by strong plant Locals, with the aim of dislocating production in the assembly factories. But this tactical argument concealed the bureaucracy's preference for strikes which it could control.

However, the combativity of a youthful rank and file prevailed again over the national leadership's reluctance to allow itself to be outflanked. At the beginning of March 1972 Local 1112 in Lordstown, Ohio, near Cleveland, where General Motors assembled the Vega with a labor force of 7,800 young workers, went on strike against a speed-up. This work stoppage had been preceded, for several months, by repeated sabotage of the production machinery. An innovation: the strike pickets were made up of men wearing masks so as not to be identified and then laid off. The dispute lasted three weeks, but its initiators did not succeed in slowing the rhythm of work. It may also be that the trade-union bureaucracy gave only half-hearted support to this test of strength, since it was not pleased at having allowed itself, once again, to be bypassed. Without doubt it also disapproved of the means of direct action – sabotage and others – which went beyond the sacrosanct limits of capitalist legality.

As a concession, Woodcock created a diversion by stressing the necessity of trade-union control over health and safety standards in the plants. These demands were characterized as 'revolutionary', since they were said to grapple with 'areas in which the employers' authority had never been challenged'. But the rank and file took this talk at face value. In the course of one month, September 1973, three wildcat strikes broke out at Chrysler over the very issues of on the job safety and health hazards. The shops were occupied by the strikers, as they had been in the far-off days of the sit-downs in early 1937 (cf.pp.108-113). The police intervened to clean out the demonstrators.

A few weeks later, in November, the skilled workers at Ford's voted against the new contract which was submitted to them by the negotiators. It was the first time in the International's history that the ranks had refused to approve a contract. In short, in spite of the leadership's integration and growing bureaucratization, the rank and file in the auto industry has perhaps not spoken its last word.

A Spate of Strikes

We have already seen, in relation to the longshoremen, the miners, the farm workers, the auto workers, etc., how strike action has not by any means disappeared in the USA. We shall now look at some of the other labor disputes, chosen from among the most important which occurred between 1970 and 1976. This list is bound to be incomplete. In the most diverse branches of the trade-union movement, in the least spectacular work situations and in the most remote parts of this immense country, the rank and file are constantly taking up the strike weapon, the last resort of the exploited. But whether they are wildcat strikes or not, public and even trade-union opinion is often unaware of them. They are absent from the written or spoken media and are swept under the carpet by bureaucracies afraid of their contagiousness and the force of their example. In March-April 1970, in an explosion of anger, the 600,000 post-office employees stopped work right across the country, defying the Government, their employer. Post offices in more than 200 cities were forced to close. The movement got off the ground among the New York postmen led by Gus Johnson, the President of the local postal workers union. So as not to inconvenience private users, it was decided to restrict the boycott to business mail. Business was hard hit. The dispute became a State matter. The Governors again and again fell back on the intervention of their National Guardsmen. The Federal executive issued injunction after injunction and had its troops transport the mail. Many strikers were threatened with dismissal. Finally Nixon and the Postmaster General engaged in some horse trading with George Meany and reached a temporary compromise: the postal workers' wages were increased by 6 per cent. It was not until 18 June that the House of Representatives, haunted by a possible renewal of the strike, added a further 8 per cent.

In the spring of the same year, from March to May, 100,000 teamsters in sixteen cities struck to demand the review of a national contract which the teamsters' national bureaucracy had signed on 23 March and which they considered inadequate. In Cleveland the strikers blocked the main traffic arteries for a good month. In November it was the turn of the New York Equity workers to go on strike. On 30 June 1971, 20,000 copper miners walked off the job. The rail unions decided to take strike action on three lines from 16 July.

In the same month, July 1971, the communications workers called a national strike against their employer, the private monopoly, Bell Systems. The dispute lasted nearly a week and involved half a million telephone workers. Guided by a leader not tainted by bureaucratism, Joseph Beirne, it culminated in an agreement that wages were to be increased by a substantial percentage every three years.

In August, statistics revealed that at that point over 100 unions were involved in strikes. In February-March 1972 there was a forty-five-day strike at Kaiser Steel's ultra-modern factory in Fontana, California, which ended, on 16 March, in victory.

We should also draw attention to the ending, in July 1972, of a strike unlike the others, since, after the one at the Kohler company, which lasted twelve years (cf.pp.202-203), it beat all the bitter records for length, lasting nine years, one week and a day: the strike by the 2,000 railroad workers on the Florida East Coast Railway. However, unlike the UAW in the Kohler strike, the United Transportation Union's members endured a humiliating defeat: a company spokesman said that the only way strikers could resume work would be 'to bid for jobs, take a physical, and re-read the rules on how to operate a railroad'.

In February 1973 the teachers in Philadelphia took industrial action and a call was put out for a general strike to support them. The strikers, who were State employees, had to face severe repression. It would take too long to recapitulate here all the episodes of the disputes which, over the last few years, have mobilized American teachers, who have become particularly militant. We should, however, mention the entry into the trade-union movement of a very large number of public sector workers, at least in those States which have not opposed unionization. Trade-union membership among these workers went from a million in 1958 to 2,400,000 in 1972.

In July 1973 there was a national strike by the independent truckers, that is to say those not affiliated to the teamsters' Brotherhood. The Federal and State authorities issued threats in vain, while in the State of Michigan, the National Guard was placed on the alert. Frank Fitzsimmons did not miss the chance to discredit a dissident movement which, according to him, involved a 'very small percentage of teamsters'.

In San Francisco a retail clerks' strike had been going for six months by July 1973.

In 1972-73 a strike brought the Farah factories – which make men's slacks in the States of Texas and New Mexico, with the main factory being in El Paso, Texas – to a standstill for a year and a half. The workers, almost all Chicanos, were affiliated to the men's garment International, which supported their struggle. As in the case of the California farm workers, the trade-union movement organized a national boycott of Farah products. The company suffered substantial losses in this way. In an attempt to get round this consumers' strike, the firm tried to sell its slacks under all sorts of fancy labels. Here again the response was solidarity and direct action.

On 1 June 1974 the entire male garment industry – organized into the Amalgamated Clothing Workers – stopped work. The International, which had been Sidney Hillman's and which was now led by Jacob Potofsky, had always placed its faith in mutual understanding between employers and workers. It had not taken national strike action since 1921.

In the spring of 1975 the social outlook was fairly unsettled. The postal workers and the East Coast longshoremen threatened to go on strike again. And the Federal Government resorted to the Taft-Hartley Act to suspend a strike warning given on 18 April by one of the most important railroad Brotherhoods.

The year 1976 was marked by several conflicts which ended with differing degrees of success for the labor movement and which marked the hardening of positions on either side as unemployment gained ground. A nation-wide strike by the workers in the rubber industry halted tire production between April and August, when it ended with a wage raise which was, nevertheless, limited to 6 per cent. Ford was brought to a standstill when its entire work force, 176,000 of them, came out on strike for a month. A strike by packing-shed workers in the California fruit and vegetable industry was quickly settled in July-August by the intervention of a Federal mediator. The economy of the country was seriously disrupted by a three-month strike of 17,000 United Parcel Service workers (UPS is the major transporter of packages and 'quick' freight). In San Francisco, however, 2,000 municipal workers – primarily skilled craftsmen – suffered a crushing defeat after a prolonged, city-wide strike, which left them with their wages drastically slashed. This was an ominous precedent for other public sector workers.

Finally, and above all, wildcat strikes swept through the coal mines in West Virginia in July. They spread to Kentucky, Maryland and Ohio. This development was all the more remarkable in that the miners did not hesitate to challenge the authority of their new union President, Arnold Miller. As pointed out earlier, the latter had initiated a process of democratization and renovation of the union. The rebellious rank and file, expressing itself through the locals, accused their national leader of not having defended them with sufficient energy by agreeing that current disputes should be settled by the courts and not by arbitration on the spot. The result was that the Federal courts fined the International $25,000 for each working day lost through unofficial strike action. It was this penalty which led to a resumption of the action, since it aroused an impulse of solidarity among the miners. The losses in coal were evaluated at 400,000 tons a day. Yet another example of a trade-unionism which, at rank-and-file level, has not allowed itself to become 'integrated'.

Some Final Facts about Labor

To conclude this brief overview of the recent past of the American Labor movement, here are some figures.

The AFL-CIO's membership from 1972 to 73 varied between 13 and 14 million. By the end of 1974 it had risen to 16 million. To this should be added the two million teamsters and the 1½ million auto workers still outside the federation, which, roughly speaking, makes a total of 20 million organized workers.

That is a lot and not very much. One worker out of four is a trade-unionist in the United States today. The relative stagnation of the labor movement led to a fall in the rate of unionization from 31 per cent in 1960 to 27.4 per cent in 1970. Walter Reuther had put his finger on one of the causes of this failure in his indictment of George Meany. It was not the only cause. Integration, ideologically and practically, through all kinds of para-State bodies did the rest. The workers no longer always recognized the union as theirs.

The proportion of union members is, however, higher in industry than in other wage-earning activities. The rate of unionization is more satisfactory among the black workers, where it reaches around 40 per cent. Half the 20 million trade-unionists are thirty or under. Some five million of them are barely over twenty. Militant youth is coming forward, more on the shop floor, in so-called wildcat form and in the locals, than in national union conventions, where the choice of delegates is screened somewhat and young delegates are perhaps intimidated by the size of the gathering or the authoritarianism of the chairman. Neither in the auto nor in the steel industry, for example, have opposition caucuses so far made any real progress or succeeded in getting through the bureaucratic barriers which keep them in check. There is only one precarious exception: the triumph of the democratic rank and file opposition in the miners' International.*

Yet this muffled underground pressure from its young members looks like Labor's last hope. To be sure, they are far from having acquired a socialist consciousness, but they alone are in a position, in the future, to shake the power of a strongly entrenched leadership. It is not out of the question that, as a result of a worsening of 'economic tensions', as Marcuse says, they will discover for themselves new forms and vehicles of struggle bypassing the often decrepit structures of the traditional trade-union movement and bringing organized and unorganized workers together in rank-and-file committees.

---

*See the introduction by John Amsden for a brief description of some of the more recent developments in the labor movement, in the steel-workers' union and the UMW as well as elsewhere [Ed.].

Notes

INTRODUCTION BY JOHN AMSDEN

1 David Montgomery, 'Working Class Unrest', *Journal of Social History*, Summer 1974.
2 Phillip Foner, *History of the Labor Movement in the United States*, International Publishers, New York 1947-1965, six vols.
3 Robert W E Michels, *Political Parties: a Sociological Study of the Oligarchical Tendencies of Modern Democracy*, London 1915.
4 On the 'stretchout' see Irving Bernstein, *The Lean Years*; on 'audacious robbery' see Amsden and Brier, 'Coal Miners on Strike', *Journal Interdisciplinary History*, Spring 1977.
5 John Amsden, 'Taylorism and Working Class Insurgency in the United States, 1909-1922', read at the annual conference of the Mid Atlantic Radical Historians Organization (MARHO), New York, April 1977. Unpublished.
6 David Brady, *Steelworkers in America: the Non-Union Era*, Cambridge, Mass. 1960.
7 See amongst others, Gabriel Kolko, *The Triumph of Conservatism. A Reinterpretation of American History, 1900-1916*, London & New York 1964, and James Weinstein, *The Corporate Ideal in the Liberal State, 1900-1918*, Boston, Mass. 1968.
8 H M Douty, 'The Slowdown in Wages, a Postwar Perspective', *Monthly Labor Review*, Aug. 1977.
9 US census data; see also Alice H Amsden (Ed.) *The Economics of Women and Work*, Penguin Books, forthcoming. (Winter 1979-80.)
10 Edward Kelly, *Industrial Exodus*. This is a pamphlet published by a group called Conference/Alternative State and Local Public Policies, Washington D.C. 1977.
11 Constance Bogh Di Cesare, 'Changes in the Occupational Structure of US Jobs', *Monthly Labor Review*, March 1975.
12 US Census Office, *Statistical Abstract of the United States*, 1977.
13 An excellent account of the strike is given by Jim Green in *Radical America*, May-June 1978.
14 William Kornblum, 'A Crisis in Basic Steel', *Dissent*, Spring 1978.

CHAPTER ONE: FROM THE KNIGHTS OF LABOR TO THE IWW

1 Philip S Foner, *The Great Labor Uprisings of 1878*, Pathfinder, New York 1977, back cover.
2 Samuel Gompers, *Seventy Years of Life and Labor*, New York 1925, p.83.
3 Ray Ginger, *The Bending Cross, a biography of Eugene V Debs*, Rutgers 1949, p.46.
4 Emma Goldman, *Living My Life*, New York 1931, p.84.
5 *Writings and Speeches of Eugene V Debs*, New York 1948, p.198.
6 *Ibid.*, pp.285-286.
7 André Philip, *Le problème ouvrier aux Etats-Unis*, 1927, p.519.
8 Daniel De Leon, *Socialist Reconstruction of Society*, reissued by Socialist Labor Party, New York 1919, p.46.
9 *Founding Convention of the Industrial Workers of the World*, Manifesto, pp.5-6.

CHAPTER TWO: FROM THE IWW TO THE CIO

1 Eugene Debs, 'A Plea for Solidarity', *op.cit.*, pp.366-372.
2 William Z Foster, *The Great Steel Strike and its Lessons*, New York 1920, p.2. and *passim*.
3 See V I Lenin, *Selected Works*, Moscow 1971, Vol.III, pp.345-418 and especially p.377.
4 William Z Foster, *From Bryan to Stalin*, 1937, pp.171-173.
5 James A Wechsler, *Labor Baron, a portrait of John L Lewis*, 1944, p.35; also MacAlister Coleman, *Men and Coal*, New York 1943, p.113 and pp.139-141.
6 'Conversations with Trotsky on the transitional program', 1938, in *Trotskyism in the United States, 1940-1947, Balance Sheet*, published by Johnson-Forrest tendency, Aug.1947, p.29.
7 James P Cannon, *The History of American Trotskyism*, New York 1944, p.159.
8 Edward Levinson, *Labor on the March*, New York and London 1938, pp.158-159.

CHAPTER THREE: THE WAR AND ITS AFTERMATH

1 MacAlister Coleman, *op.cit.*, p.221.
2 William Z Foster, *American Trade Unionism*, p.307, quoted in Sidney Lens, *Left Right and Center, conflicting forces in American Labor*, Illinois 1949, p.344.
3 *Daily Worker*, 2 April 1945 (quotation translated from French).
4 James A Wechsler, *op.cit.*, pp.98-100.
5 *Ibid.*, p.107.
6 *The Militant*, 1 June 1946, p.2.
7 W J Cash, *The Mind of the South*, New York 1941, p.395.
8 W E Burghardt Du Bois, *Black Reconstruction*, London and New York 1935, p.704.
9 CIO Proceedings, 25 November 1948.
10 Quotation translated; original in *Labor and Religion, an address by Van A Bittner delivered at the Cathedral Church of St Paul in Boston, Massachusetts*, leaflet.
11 'Organizing the Unorganized', CIO Proceedings, 23 November 1948, p.217.

CHAPTER FOUR: THE BLACKS AND LABOR

1 Philip S Foner, *History of the Labor Movement*, 1942, p.270.
2 *Ibid.*, p.271.
3 Du Bois, *op.cit.*, pp.21 and 25.
5 James S Allen, *Reconstruction*, 1937, pp.108-109 and 153-174.
6 Ray Giner, *op.cit.*, pp.259-260.
7 See also H Cayton and G Mitchell, *Black Workers and the New Unions*, 1939, p.81.
8 Brailsford R Brazeal, *The Brotherhood of Sleeping Car Porters*, New York 1946, p.166.
9 Cayton and Mitchell, *op.cit.*, p.199.
10 Herbert Northrup, *Organized Labor and the Negro*, 1944, p.163.
11 *The C.I.O. and the Negro Worker*, p.4.
12 Howe and Widick, *The U.A.W. and Walter Reuther*, New York 1949, pp.210-211.
13 *Ibid.*, p.232.
14 *UAW-CIO Outlaws Discrimination*, 1945.
15 Reuther, speech reported in *Detroit News*, April 12 1943, quoted in Howe and Widick, *op.cit.*, p.221.

CHAPTER FIVE: TAFT-HARTLEY

1 AFL Proceedings, 14 October 1947, p.488.
2 *Ibid.*, pp.489 and 492.
3 *Ibid.*, p.493.
4 *The Militant*, 1 and 8 Nov.1948.

5 AFL Proceedings, 16 Nov.1948, p.288.

CHAPTER SIX: TRADE UNION REUNIFICATION

1 Reuther, UAW Administrative Letter.
2 'Principles', in *Report of A.F. of L.*, 1881, p.3.
3 *CIO Constitutional Convention*, 'Constitution', 1938, p.126.
4 *Proceedings of the First Constitutional Convention of the A.F. of L. and CIO*, 1955, p.20.
5 Arthur Goldberg, *Labor United*, 1956, p.210.
6 Report to the CIO by President Walter Reuther, 17th Constitutional Convention, Dec.1955, p.24.
7 Reuther, UAW Administrative Letter, No.1, 8 Feb.1967, p.4.

CHAPTER SEVEN: COMBATIVE SECTORS

1 NLRB decision, quoted by Emil Mazey, *Judgement at Kohler, UAW Solidarity*, Feb.1966, p.7.
2 Speech at San Francisco, Dec. 1965, quoted in *Judgement at Kohler*, p.7.
3 *The Militant*, 10 Jan.1966, p.1.

CHAPTER EIGHT: A NEW MILITANCY

1 The President of Local 2659, quoted in *The Militant*, 8 Feb. 1965, p.4.
2 Statement of the AFL-CIO Executive Council, in *Free Trade Union News*, vol.21, no.9, Sept. 1966, p.1.
3 Reuther, UAW Administrative Letter, no.16, 28 Dec.1966, p.1.
4 *Ibid.*
5 *Ibid.*
6 *Ibid.*
7 *Ibid.*, 8 Feb.1967, p.9.
8 *Ibid.*, 28 Dec.1966, p.1.
9 *Ibid.*, 8 Feb. 1967, p.4.
10 *Ibid.*, same page.
11 *Ibid.*, 28 Dec. 1966, p.4.
12 *Ibid.*, 28 Dec. 1966, p.4.
13 *Ibid.*, 8 Feb. 1967, p.5.
14 *Ibid.*
15 *Ibid.*, 5 April 1967, p.2.
16 *Ibid.*, 8 Feb. 1967, p.4.
17 *Ibid.*, 20 April 1967, p.7.
18 *Ibid.*, 8 Feb. 1967, p.5.
19 *Ibid.*, p.10.